Critical praise for this book

"*Realizing Hope* extends to just about every major domain of human concern and mode of human interaction, and investigates with care and insight how, in these domains, parecon-like principles could lead to a far more desirable society than anything that exists, and also how these goals can be constructively approached. It is another very valuable and provocative contribution to the quest for a world of much greater freedom and justice." – Noam Chomsky, USA

"*Realizing Hope* opens many doors for social vision and strategy. At a moment when Africa needs an alternative to nationalist politics, *Realizing Hope* is amazingly timely. Pan-Africanists and Black Marxists alike will find much in this book to enrich and expand our politics." – Mandisi Majavu, South Africa

"A better world is indeed possible and not just a Utopia. Michael Albert points the way towards a society based on participation and justice. Utopia is somewhere that does not exist yet. This book can help turn a dream into reality." – Vittorio Agnoletto, Italy

"Albert captures the best of the spirit of the new global social movements. He combines close empirical insights with a magisterial conceptual grasp. We will be arguing about this work for years." – Andrej Grubacic, Serbia

"*Realizing Hope* mulls over the better society that we may create after capitalism, provoking much thought and offering a generous, hopeful vision of the future. Albert's prescriptions for action in the present are modest and wise; his suggestions for building the future are ambitious and humane." – Milan Rai, Britain

"Millions across the world are coming together in hitherto unprecedented networks of solidarity to struggle against poverty, inequality, discrimination, and war. These fighters proclaim that a better world is possible. *Realizing Hope* challenges us to imagine how." – Sudhanva Deshpande, India

"*Realizing Hope* goes beyond the primarily economic framework of participatory economics to open the crucial but too rarely posed questions of how to coordinate economic change with the changes we need in other spheres of life." – Jeremy Brecher, USA

"Michael Albert passionately argues for a different future where equity, diversity, justice, and self-management are more than just distant dreams. *Realizing Hope* does not shy away from the awesome complexity of human issues, nor does it reek of the stultifying dogmatism of so many left-wing tracts. One can disagree at places, but it forces the reader to think and be conscious of choices." – Pervez Hoodbhoy, Pakistan

"Anyone disgusted with existing society – which is to say, just about everyone – who wants to know if there are any alternatives will find *Realizing Hope* informative, provocative, creative, engaging, and, yes, full of hope." – Stephen R. Shalom, USA

About this book

Something is profoundly wrong with capitalism. Vast inequalities of wealth and power will not take the world to a better future. 'What is the alternative?' is a question echoing all around the globe. Michael Albert has wrestled with this question for many years, and his answer regarding economics has captured the imagination of many. 'Participatory Economics' – 'Parecon' for short – Albert's proposed economic system to replace capitalism, rejects competitive anti-sociality, individualist greed, commercial homogenization, and corporate hierarchy, and in their place elevates solidarity, equity, diversity, and self-management.

In *Realizing Hope*, Albert goes further to offer insights about how whole areas of life might be desirably transformed in a new society. Whether exploring the way we work, our relationship to the earth, the transformation of global financial institutions, science, technology, the family, culture, sport, art, or education, people rather than profit always take centre stage.

About the author

Michael Albert was radicalized in college at MIT in Cambridge, MA, in the sixties and active in campus, national, and community efforts then and later. He co-founded South End Press, *Z Magazine*, the Z Media Institute, and ZNet where he continues to work. He has been involved in diverse movements and written widely about contemporary relations, history, and especially social change strategy and vision. *Realizing Hope* is his seventeenth book.

Other books by Michael Albert

What is to be Undone (Porter Sargent Press)
Unorthodox Marxism (co-authored by Robin Hahnel; South End Press)
Socialism Today and Tomorrow (with Robin Hahnel South End Press)
Marxism and Socialist Theory (co-authored by Robin Hahnel; South End Press)
Beyond Survival (editor along with David Dellinger; South End Press)
Liberating Theory (co-authored by Lydia Sargent, Robin Hahnel, Mel King, Noam
     Chomsky, Leslie Cagan, Holly Sklar; South End Press)
Looking Forward (co-authored by Robin Hahnel; South End Press)
The Political Economy of Participatory Economics (co-authored by Robin Hahnel; Princeton
     University Press)
A Quiet Revolution in Welfare Economics (co-authored by Robin Hahnel; Princeton
     University Press)
Previews and Premises (with Alvin Toffler; South End Press)
Stop the Killing Train (South End Press)
Thinking Forward (Arbeiter Ring Press)
Trajectory of Change (South End Press)
Moving Forward (A K Press)
Parecon: Life After Capitalism (Verso Books)
Thought Dreams (Arbeiter Ring Press)

Realizing
HOPE
Life Beyond
CAPITALISM

Michael Albert

Zed Books
LONDON & NEW YORK

Fernwood Publishing
NOVA SCOTIA

Realizing Hope: Life Beyond Capitalism
was first published in 2006
in Canada by Fernwood Publishing Ltd,
8422 St Margaret's Bay Road (Hwy 3) Site 2A, Box 5, Black Point, Nova Scotia BOJ IBO
and in the rest of the world by Zed Books Ltd, 7 Cynthia Street, London N1 9JF, UK and
Room 400, 175 Fifth Avenue, New York, NY 10010, USA.

www.zedbooks.co.uk

The right of Michael Albert to be identified as the author
of this work has been asserted by him in accordance with
the Copyright, Designs and Patents Act, 1988

Cover designed by Andrew Corbett
Set in 10/13 pt Melior by Long House, Cumbria, UK
Printed and bound in Manitoba, Canada
by Hignell Book Printing

Distributed in the USA exclusively by Palgrave Macmillan, a division of
St Martin's Press, LLC, 175 Fifth Avenue, New York, NY 10010.

A catalogue record for this book
is available from the British Library

US Cataloging-in-Publication Data
is available from the Library of Congress

Library and Archives Canada Cataloguing in Publication
Albert, Michael, 1947-
   Realizing hope : life beyond capitalism / Michael Albert.
Includes bibliographical references and index.
ISBN 1-55266-181-4
   1. Distributive justice. 2. Economics--Sociological aspects. 3. Social
structure--Economic aspects. 4. Cooperation. 5. Social change. 6. Quality
of life. I. Title.

HB523.A42 2005   330.1   C2005-906759-4

Canada ISBN 1 55266 181 4 pb

Zed Books ISBN 1 84277 720 3 hb
Zed Books ISBN 1 84277 721 1 pb

Zed Books ISBN 978 1 84277 720 6 hb
Zed Books ISBN 978 1 84277 721 3 pb

Contents

Acknowledgements

I thank a number of friends who read through and commented on one or more chapters of this book, providing essential critique and new insights. These include Ezequiel Adamovsky, Alex Callinicos, Brian Dominick, Jerry Fresia, Andrej Grubacic, John Hepburn, Robert Jensen, Stan Karp, Mandisi Majavu, Adele Oliveri, Cynthia Peters, Justin Podur, Vijay Prashad, Nikos Raptis, Stephen Shalom, Norman Solomon, and Chris Spannos.

Major thanks go to four other collaborators.

Anna Hardman of Zed Books sought this work based on some internet gossip and ushered it through publication painlessly, providing useful editorial advice as well.

Lydia Sargent read and commented on the whole book, greatly improving its focus and range.

Andrea Sargent edited the whole book, providing coherence, succinctness, and style to my clunky manuscript.

Robin Hahnel was my partner in developing the participatory economic model.

Introduction

THE STUPENDOUSLY INFLUENTIAL and celebrated British economist John Maynard Keynes wrote, "[Capitalism] is not a success. It is not intelligent, it is not beautiful, it is not just, it is not virtuous – and it doesn't deliver the goods. In short, we dislike it, and we are beginning to despise it. But when we wonder what to put in its place, we are extremely perplexed".

Suppose we escaped Keynes' perplexity and attained a desirable post-capitalist economy. What changes would need to occur alongside this new economy? What features would the new economy have to incorporate to mesh successfully with extra-economic innovations? How would broad future prospects affect current strategies for change?

Societies must resolve disputes, deal with criminality, establish shared norms and rules, and implement collective pursuits. What impact would a new participatory economy have on political functions? How might new political structures effect a desirable economy?

Societies involve women and men being born, maturing, aging, and dying. What impact would a participatory economy (or parecon for short) have on relations between the sexes, living arrangements, methods of procreation, styles of nurturance, and the content and practice of socializing new generations? What would kinship improvements require of participatory economics?

People live extended lives and pass through different age groups. What implications would a participatory economy have for intergenerational relations, and what would healthy intergenerational relations require of a parecon?

People develop diverse cultures and form racial, ethnic, and religious communities. What implications would parecon have for cultural communities? How might innovative cultural community relations affect economic structures?

Societies exist in the context of other societies. Will a participatory economy foster war or peace, strife or cooperation, international equity or widening inequality? In turn, how might new international relations affect economic structures?

Economies exist in nature. Would a parecon lead to environmental disasters? Would it produce wise environmentalism? What about other species, from the smallest one-celled creatures to great elephants and whales, from bugs that kill to bugs that sustain, plants that overrun to plants that nourish, and pets we love to predators we fear? What implications would a parecon have for species other than humans, and what implications would prioritizing sound ecological and species policies have for a parecon?

Scientists have long investigated our world from its most minuscule subatomic byways to its most gargantuan extragalactic vistas. How would participatory economics affect the knowledge and activities of scientists? What would healthy scientific practice imply for a parecon?

Humanity utilizes scientific knowledge plus experiential skills to create technologies for production, shelter, locomotion, health, entertainment, etc. Would pareconish technological developments be accelerated or obstructed? What would happen to technology's direction, content, and use? What would desirable technological innovation require from a participatory economy?

Health matters. Economies directly and secondarily influence our bodies and minds. How would a parecon affect medicine and medical care and what would having a healthy society require from a parecon?

People need education. Would a participatory economy call forth the best pedagogy we can imagine or would it limit our pedagogical imaginations? What would having desirable pedagogy require from a parecon? Would a parecon meet education's admission and graduation requirements?

What about information? What implications would a parecon have for journalism's content and process? What would desirable journalism require of a parecon?

Humans engage in visual, auditory, textual, and tactile arts. Would parecon facilitate artistic creation or reduce artistic quality? What would a parecon demand from artists? What would artistic creativity demand from a parecon?

Would sports be diminished or enhanced by parecon? What will become of competition in non-economic realms when we have a cooperative rather than competitive economy? What would desirable play require of a parecon?

Finally, what does participatory economics tell us about who are the agents of social change and who are likely to oppose social change? What does it tell us about the demands, arguments, evidence, and inspiration necessary to create lasting opposition to capitalism? What does it tell us about the features our organizations ought to embody to win desired aims rather than results we must later disavow? What is the connection between participatory economics and Marxist, anarchist, and other approaches to economy and social change?

How does participatory economics view its own fallibility? How will parecon interact with its own advocates and critics? Will parecon welcome critique and innovation, including renovation? Or will parecon tend toward defensiveness, inflexibility, and even sectarianism?

One goal of *Realizing Hope* is to indicate the broader social merits of participatory economics and encourage readers to explore further the interconnections of economic vision and strategy with other spheres of social life. A second goal is to provoke and even modestly help inform proposals of worthy vision and strategy for each other area addressed here.

1 Parecon

ECONOMIES INCORPORATE AN almost infinite array of components. Even if they have the same type of economic system, two different societies, whether France and Mexico, or the U.S. and South Africa, will have a myriad of economic differences ranging from population numbers and skills to resources and infrastructure, different industries, organizational approaches, patterns of ownership, secondary economic institutions, class histories and relations, and details of organization.

The same will hold for other economic types than capitalism. Different societies with new participatory economies, say a future Italy, Mexico, the U.S., Malaysia, Venezuela, Poland, Turkey, and South Africa, will have different features beyond the few shared ones that define the economic type. Participatory economics is a proposal for the defining features of a post-capitalist economy.

Capitalism

Capitalism's first defining feature is private ownership of the means of production. A few per cent of the population own almost all industry, machinery, resources, and farmland. They control the disposal and use of this property. They accrue profits from their property's productivity.

Capitalism is also defined by corporate divisions of labor and authoritative decision making. About 20 per cent of the employees of capitalist workplaces do mostly conceptual and empowering tasks, while the other 80 per cent do mostly rote and obedient tasks. The 20 per cent make many decisions and affect social choices. The 80 per cent make few decisions and mainly obey orders.

People's income in capitalist economies comes mostly from their bargaining power. We get from economic output what we can take. Ownership of property conveys rights to profit. The control one has over needed assets or skills, the value of the output one generates, one's social attributes like gender and race, and one's organizational affiliations such as union membership, also convey greater or lesser ability to accrue income.

Another defining feature of capitalism is markets. Markets mediate the amount of any particular good or service produced, the relative valuations of different products, and their distribution to different actors. Buyers and sellers benefit themselves, oblivious to impact on others. I sell at the highest price I can get the least costly items I can deliver. You buy at the lowest price you can offer the most valuable items you can amass. We fleece each other.

Competition drives growth and determines relative valuations. The preferences and bargaining power of buyers and sellers determine prices. The preferences of people who are affected by but aren't directly involved in specific transactions go unaccounted. Your desire for a car you seek to buy influences its price. My dislike for the pollution that it will spew doesn't influence its price. In market exchanges those with more power make out like bandits and "nice guys finish last".

Beyond private ownership of means of production, corporate workplace organization, authoritative decision-making, remuneration for bargaining power, property, and output, and market allocation, myriad variations in secondary institutions, population, local history, and impositions from other parts of society distinguish different instances of capitalism from one another. South Africa is different from the United States. England circa 1900 is different from England circa 2000. India is different from Mexico.

Referring to capitalism, John Stuart Mill, one of the foremost philosophers of the nineteenth century wrote, "I confess that I am not charmed with the ideal of life held out by those who think that the normal state of human beings is that of struggling to get on; that the trampling, crushing, elbowing, and treading on each other's heels, which form the existing type of social life, are the most desirable lot of human beings".

More recently, the great Latin American writer Eduardo Galeano explained how capitalism has nearly all its valuations upside down: "From the point of view of the economy, the sale of weapons is indistinguishable from the sale of food. When a building collapses or a plane crashes, it's rather inconvenient from the point of view of those inside, but it's altogether convenient for the growth of the gross national product, which sometimes ought to be called the 'gross criminal product'."

In my own view, only briefly evidenced here, capitalism is a thug's economy, a heartless economy, a base and vile and largely boring economy. It is the antithesis of human fulfillment and development. It mocks equity and justice. It enshrines greed. It does not serve humanity.

I doubt that many who are reading this book will contest these claims. Similar characterizations of capitalism, for example, are rampant in contemporary literature and other media. In fact, I think that while many people might talk about a humane capitalism, or might not publicly decry capitalism, deep down this isn't due to denying capitalism's ills or to feeling capitalism is liberatory. It is due to feeling there is nothing possible but capitalism, so that operating within its jurisdiction is unavoidable and decrying capitalism is whining about the inevitable. In any event, given my distaste for capitalism, I feel the need to proceed to a better economy.

Parecon's values

Participatory economics has completely different defining features than capitalism. Extensive explorations of its economic logic are available online at the parecon web site (www.parecon.org). I don't want to repeat all that here, but preparatory to discussing participatory economics and the rest of society I do want to summarize parecon's main features. Parecon seeks to fulfill four key values: solidarity, diversity, equity, and self-management.

Solidarity

The first value a good economy ought to have bears upon how its workers and consumers relate to one another. In capitalism, to get ahead, one must trample others. To increase your income and power you must ignore the horrible pain suffered by those left below or even help to push them farther down. In capitalism, not only do nice guys finish last, but in my own somewhat more aggressive formulation of the same sentiment, "garbage rises".

In contrast to the capitalist rat race, a good economy should be a solidarity economy, generating sociality rather than social irresponsibility. Its institutions for production, consumption, and allocation should propel even antisocial people into addressing other people's well being to advance their own. To get ahead in a good economy, in other words, you should have to act on the basis of considering and respecting the conditions of others.

Interestingly, this first parecon value, so contrary to the capitalist logic of "me first and everyone else be damned", is entirely uncontroversial. Only a psychopath would argue that if we could have the same output, the same conditions, and the same distribution of income, an economy would be better if it produced more hostility and anti-sociality in its participants than if it produced more mutual concern. Other than psychopaths, we all value solidarity and would prefer not to trample others. Solidarity is thus parecon's first value.

Diversity

The second value a good economy ought to advance has to do with the options an economy generates. Capitalist market rhetoric trumpets opportunity but capitalist market discipline curtails satisfaction and development by replacing what is human and caring with what is commercial, profitable, and in accord with existing hierarchies of power and wealth. The tremendous variety of tastes, preferences, and choices that humans naturally display are truncated by capitalism into conformist patterns imposed by advertising, by narrow class-delimited role offerings, and by coercive marketing environments that produce commercial attitudes and habits.

As a result, within capitalism we seek best sellers regardless of their impact on society, instead of seeking a wide range of sellers with as desirable an impact as possible. We seek the one most profitable method of doing each task instead of many parallel methods suiting a range of priorities, and we seek the biggest of almost everything, virtually always crowding out more diverse choices that could engender greater and more widespread fulfillment.

In contrast, responsible institutions for production, consumption, and allocation not only wouldn't reduce variety but would emphasize finding and respecting diverse solutions to problems. A good economy would recognize that we are finite beings who can benefit from enjoying what others do that we ourselves have no time to do, and also that we are fallible beings who should not vest all our hopes in single routes of advance but should instead insure against damage by exploring diverse parallel avenues and options.

Interestingly, this value of diversity, like solidarity, is entirely uncontroversial. Only a perverse individual would argue that, all other things being equal, an economy is better if it homogenizes and narrows options than if it diversifies and expands them. So we value diversity, not homogeneity. Diversity is parecon's second value.

Equity

The third value we want a good economy to advance has to do with distribution of outputs. Capitalism overwhelmingly rewards property and bargaining power. It says that those who own productive property, by virtue of their ownership, deserve profits. It says that those who have great bargaining power based on anything from monopolizing knowledge or skills, to using better tools or organization, being born with special talents, or being able to command brute force, should get whatever they can take.

A good economy would instead be an equity economy whose institutions for production, consumption, and allocation not only wouldn't destroy or obstruct equity, but would propel it. But what is equity?

People seeking equity, of course, reject rewarding property ownership. It can't be equitable that due to having a deed in your pocket you earn 100, 1000, or even a million or ten million times the income some other person earns who works harder and longer than you. To be born and inherit ownership and by virtue of that ownership, despite having done nothing of merit, to vastly exceed other's circumstances and influence, cannot possibly be equitable.

We also reject rewarding power with income. The logic of Al Capone, Genghis Khan, and the Harvard Business School is that each actor should earn as remuneration for their economic activity whatever they can take. This norm worships not equitable outcomes, but being a thug. Since we are civilized, we of course reject it.

What about output? Should people get back from the social product an amount equal to what they themselves produce as part of that social product? After all, what reason can justify that we should get less than what we ourselves contribute, or for that matter that we should get more than our own contribution? Surely we should get an amount equivalent to what we produce, shouldn't we?

It may seem so, but suppose Bill and Jill do the same work for the same length of time at the same intensity. If Jill has better tools with which to generate more output, should she get more income than Bill, who has worse tools and as a result generates less output even though working as hard or harder?

Similarly, why should someone who happens to produce something highly valued be rewarded more than someone who happens to produce something less valued though still socially desired – again, even if the less productive person works equally hard and long and endures similar conditions as the more productive person?

Extending the same logic, why should someone who was lucky in the genetic lottery, perhaps inheriting genes for big size, musical talent, tremendous reflexes, peripheral vision, or conceptual competency, get rewarded more than someone who was genetically less lucky?

You are born with a wonderful attribute. You didn't do anything to get it. Why, on top of the luck of your inheritance, are you rewarded with greater income as well? There is no earning happening. No high morality is evidenced. You were just lucky.

In light of the implicit logic of these examples, it seems that to be equitable, remuneration should be for effort and sacrifice in producing socially desired items.

If I work longer, I should get more reward. If I work harder, I should get more reward. If I work in worse conditions and at more onerous tasks, I should get more reward. But I should not get more for having better tools, or for producing something that happens to be valued more, or even for having innate highly productive talents, nor should I get more even for the output of learned skills (though I should be rewarded for the effort and sacrifice of learning those skills), nor, of course, should I get rewarded for work that isn't socially warranted.

Unlike our first two values, solidarity and diversity, our third value of rewarding only the effort and sacrifice expended in socially valued work, is quite controversial.

Some anti-capitalists think that people should be rewarded for the overall volume of their output, so that a great athlete should earn a fortune, and a good doctor should earn way more than a hard working farmer or short order cook. An equitable economy, however – or at any rate a participatory economy – rejects that norm.

Pareconish equity requires that assuming comparable intensity and duration of work, a person who has a nice, comfortable, pleasant, and highly productive job should earn less than a person who has an onerous, debilitating, and less productive but still socially valuable and warranted job, due to the sacrifice endured. Parecon rewards effort and sacrifice expended at socially valued labor; it does not reward property, power, or output. You have to produce socially valued output commensurate to the productivity of your tools and conditions, yes, but you are remunerated not in accord with the value of the output, but with the effort and sacrifice you expend.

There are two other anti-capitalist stances regarding remuneration. They have in common that they take a wise insight to a counterproductive extreme.

The first approach says work itself is intrinsically negative. This stance wonders why anyone thinking about a better economy would worry about organizing or apportioning work. Why not eliminate it?

This stance correctly notices that our efforts to innovate should seek to diminish onerous features of work in favor of more fulfilling features. But it moves from that worthy advisory to advocating entirely eliminating work, which is nonsense.

First and most obviously, work yields results we do not want to do without. The bounty that work generates justifies the costs of undertaking it. In a good economy, people would desist from excess work before suffering insufficient returns for it. In parecon, we expend our effort and make associated sacrifices only up to the point where the value of the income we receive outweighs the costs of the exertions we undertake. At that point, we opt for leisure, not for more work.

Second, as the famed geographer and anarchist Peter Kropotkin expressed the point, "Overwork is repulsive to human nature – not work. Overwork for supplying the few with luxury – not work for the well-being of all. Work, labor, is a physiological necessity, a necessity of spending accumulated bodily energy, a necessity which is health and life itself".

In other words, the merits of work are not solely in its outputs, but also in the process and the act itself. We want to eliminate work that is onerous and debilitating, yes, as well as eliminating unjust remuneration for it, but we do not want to eliminate work per se. We need to keep work, but to figure out how to do it differently than now.

A second and related anti-capitalist stance claims that the only criterion for remuneration ought to be human need. "From each according to ability, to each according to need" defines this perspective.

What this stance rightly highlights is that people deserve respect and support by virtue of their very existence. If a person can't work, surely we don't starve them or deny them income at the level others enjoy. Their needs, modulated in accord with social averages, are met. If, likewise, someone has special medical needs, these too are met even beyond the volume, intensity, or type of work the person is able to do.

The problem with rewarding need arises not when we are dealing with people who are physically or mentally unable to work, for which it makes perfect sense, but when we try to apply the norm to people who have no special medical needs interfering with their working.

For example, can I do no work and still benefit from society's output? Can I do no work and consume as much as I choose, with no external limits? This is obviously not viable. We could have no one at all working and at the same time have everyone expecting to consume more than now.

Usually what those who advocate payment for need and people working to capacity have in mind is that each actor will responsibly opt for an appropriate share of consumption from the social total and will responsibly contribute an appropriate amount of work to its production.

But how do I know what is appropriate to consume or to produce? And, for that matter, how does the economy determine what is appropriate?

It turns out, in other words, that in real practice the norm "work to ability and consume to need" assumes working and consuming in accord with social averages. It assumes people responsibly going over and under social averages only when warranted.

But when is it warranted? More, how does anyone know what the social averages are? How does anyone know the relative values of outputs if we have no measure of the value of the labor involved in their production or the extent to which anyone wants them? How do we know if labor is apportioned sensibly and if we need innovations to increase output of some items or diminish output for others? How do we know where to invest to improve work conditions? How does the economy decide how much of anything to produce?

Whether one believes that remuneration for need and working to one's ability is a higher moral norm than remuneration for effort and sacrifice – and this too is an open question – the former is not practical unless there is an external measure of need and ability, a way to value different labor types, a way for people to determine what is warranted behavior, and an expectation that we will all do so. But all that is precisely what rewarding effort and sacrifice instead of rewarding need provides, even as it also enables people to work and consume more or less as they choose, and permits everyone to judge relative values in tune with true social costs and benefits. In other words, the values lurking behind the desire to remunerate need are, it turns out, fulfilled more desirably and fully by rewarding effort and sacrifice.

So, we have our third value, a controversial one even among anti-capitalists. We want a good economy to remunerate effort and sacrifice, and, when people can't work, to provide income and health care based on need.

Self-management

The fourth and final value on which a good economy ought to be built has to do with decisions.

In capitalism owners have tremendous say. Likewise, managers and high-level lawyers, engineers, financial officers, and doctors, each of whom monopolize empowering work and daily decision-making positions, have substantial say. On the other hand, people doing rote and obedient labor rarely even know what decisions are being made, much less influence them.

In contrast, a good economy will be a richly democratic economy. People will control their own lives consistent with others doing likewise. Each person will have a level of influence that won't impinge on other people's rights to have the same level of influence. We will all affect decisions in proportion to how we are affected by them. This is self-management.

Imagine that a worker wants to place a picture of his daughter on his workstation. Who should make that decision? Should an owner decide? Should a manager decide? Should all the workers decide? Obviously none of that makes sense. The worker whose child it is should decide, alone, with full authority. He should be a dictator in this particular case. Sometimes making decisions unilaterally makes sense.

Now suppose instead that the same worker wants to put a radio on her desk to play loud, raucous, rock and roll. Who should decide? We all intuitively know that the answer is that those who will hear the radio should have a say, and that those who will be more bothered or more benefited should have more say. The worker no longer gets to be a dictator, nor does anyone else.

At this point, we have implicitly arrived at a decision-making value. We easily realize that we don't want a majority to decide everything all the time. Nor do we always want one-person one-vote with some lower or higher percentage than a majority deciding. Nor do we always want one person to decide authoritatively, as a dictator. Nor do we always want consensus, or any other single approach to discussing issues, expressing preferences, and tallying votes. All the possible methods of making decisions make sense in some cases but are horribly unfair, intrusive, or authoritarian in other cases. Different decisions require different approaches.

What we hope to accomplish when we choose from among all possible means of decision-making and discussing issues, setting agendas, and sharing information, is that each person influence decisions in proportion to the degree he or she is affected by them. And that is our fourth parecon value, called self-management.

Parecon's institutions

When people ask, what do you want?, we can reasonably say we want solidarity, diversity, equity, and self-management, but that is not alone sufficient to answer their question. If we advocate institutions whose logic leads to other values or has damning flaws in other respects, as markets, corporate organization, and private ownership do, what good is our rhetorical attachment to fine values? We need to advocate fine values, yes, but we also need to advocate a set of institutions that can make our values real without compromising economic success.

Worker and consumer councils

Workers and consumers need a place to express and pursue their preferences. Historically, when workers and consumers have attempted to seize control of their own lives, they have invariably created worker and consumer councils as the means to do so.

In a parecon, while worker and consumer councils are essentially like those that have historically emerged in past struggles, there is an additional commitment to self-management. Parecon's councils use decision-making procedures and modes of communication that apportion to each member a degree of say in each decision proportionate to the degree he or she is affected.

Council decisions could be made by majority rule, three-quarters, two-thirds, consensus, or other possibilities. Different procedures could be used for different decisions – fewer or more participants could be involved, information dispersal and discussion procedures might vary, and different voting and tallying methods could be employed.

Consider, as an example, a publishing house. It could have teams addressing different functions, such as promotion, book production, editing, etc. Each team might make its own workday decisions in the context of broader policies decided by the whole workers' council. Decisions to publish a book might involve teams in related areas, and might require, for example, a two-thirds or three-quarters affirmative vote, including considerable time for appraisals and re-appraisals. Many other decisions in the workplace could be one-person one-vote by the workers affected, or could require slightly different majorities or methods of accounting and challenging outcomes. Hiring might require consensus in the workgroup that the new person would join, because a new worker can have a tremendous effect on a group that he or she is constantly working with.

The point is, workers decide in groups of nested councils and teams both the broad and the narrower workplace decisions, both the norms and the methods for decision-making, and then also the day to day and more policy-oriented choices.

Longer presentations of parecon assess ease of operations, efficiency and quality of outcomes, etc. But for here, the reader may note that for full self-management the decisions of a workplace regarding what to produce must also be influenced by the people affected by its production. Those who consume the workplace's books, bicycles, or band-aids must affect their production. Even those who don't get some other product because energy, time, and assets went to the books, bicycles, or band-aids and not to producing what they wanted, have to affect the choice. And even those tangentially affected, such as by pollution, have to have influence. Accommodating the will of the workers with the will of other actors in appropriate balance is a matter of allocation, not of workplace organization, and it enters our discussion shortly.

Remuneration for effort and sacrifice

Parecon's next institutional commitment is to remunerate effort and sacrifice, not property, power, or even output. But who decides how hard we have worked? Clearly our workers' councils must decide within the context of the broad economic setting established by all the economy's institutions.

If you work longer, and you do it effectively, you are entitled to more of the social product. If you work more intensely, to socially useful ends, again you are entitled to more social product. If you work at more onerous or dangerous or boring but still socially warranted tasks, again, you are entitled to more social product.

But you aren't entitled to more social product by virtue of owning productive property because no one will own productive property in a parecon – it is all socially owned. And you won't be entitled to more because you work with better tools, or produce something more valued, or have personal traits that make you more productive, because these attributes don't involve effort or sacrifice but instead luck and endowment. Your work has to be socially useful to be rewarded. Effort, duration, and sacrifice producing outputs that aren't desired is not remunerable labor.

Greater output is appreciated, of course, and it is important that means of eliciting it are utilized, but there is no extra pay for greater output. Yes, my working longer or harder yields more output, and greater output can even be a revealing indicator of greater effort. But while output is often relevant as an indicator, the absolute level of output is irrelevant to the level of remuneration.

Rewarding output is not only morally unwarranted, it is far from the best way of eliciting increased output, since output depends on tools, genetic endowment, colleagues, and other factors we have no individual control over. If one seeks to increase output by offering incentives, one should remunerate effort expended in socially valued labor. Effort is the variable the worker controls that impacts output. It's as simple as that.

Both morally and in terms of incentives, parecon does what makes sense. We get extra pay when we deserve it for our greater sacrifice at work. As to how the economy elicits appropriate use of productive capacities by properly utilizing technology, organization, resources, energy, and skills, that is a matter of allocation, still to come. As for how in each workplace the duration of our work, its intensity, and its onerousness are determined by the workers' council, that too, while having many possible locally determined forms, becomes clearer as we proceed.

Balanced job complexes

Suppose that as proposed we have worker and consumer councils. Suppose we also believe in participation and even in self-management. But suppose as well that our workplace has a typical corporate division of labor. What will happen?

The roughly 20 per cent at the top of the corporate division of labor will monopolize daily decision-making positions and the knowledge essential to comprehending what is going on and what options exist. They will set agendas. The decisions of these managers, engineers, lawyers, doctors, and other empowered actors will be authoritative. Even if workers lower in the hierarchy have formal voting rights in workers' councils committed to self-management, their participation will only be voting on plans and options put forth by the more empowered workers I call the coordinator class.

The will of this coordinator class will decide outcomes, and in time this empowered group will also decide that it deserves more pay to nurture its great wisdom. It will separate itself not only in power but in income and status. In other words, it isn't enough to have worker and consumer councils that try to implement self-management and remuneration on the basis of effort and sacrifice. If, on top of those features, we have a division of labor which sabotages our efforts and imposes class divisions, our greatest hopes will be dashed against the structural implications of our job design.

As Adam Smith harshly argued, since "the understandings of the greater part of men are necessarily formed by their ordinary employments, the man whose life is spent in performing a few simple operations, of which the effects too are, perhaps, always the same, or very nearly the same, has no occasion to exert his understanding … and generally becomes as stupid and ignorant as it is possible for a human creature to be". Even if the effects are less disastrous, surely the person doing "a few simple operations" will not be an equal master of economic outcomes with those whose daily work inspires, informs, enlightens, and empowers them.

So what is parecon's alternative to familiar corporate divisions of labor? We seek to extend the insights of William Morris, the noted nineteenth-century artist and wordsmith, who noted that in a better future we would not be able to have the same division of labor as now. We would have to get rid of servanting and sewer emptying, butchering and letter carrying, boot-blacking and hair dressing, as jobs unto themselves. Morris felt we would apply ourselves to production not to sell things, but to make things prettier and to amuse ourselves and others.

Morris was right, not only about changing the motives of work to meeting needs and developing the potentials of those enjoying the products and doing the labor, but also about the need to alter the division of labor en route to that achievement.

Parecon concurs, therefore, with Smith's perception of the debilitating effect of corporate divisions of labor and with Morris's aspirations for future work. That is why participatory economics utilizes what it calls balanced job complexes.

Instead of combining tasks so that some jobs are highly empowering and other jobs are horribly stultifying, some jobs convey knowledge and authority while other jobs convey only stultification and obedience, and those doing some jobs rule as a coordinator class accruing to themselves more income and influence while those doing more menial work obey as a traditional working class subordinate in influence and income – parecon says let's make each job comparable to all others in its quality of life and even more importantly in its empowerment effects.

From a corporate division of labor that enshrines a coordinator class above workers, we move to a classless division of labor that elevates all workers to their fullest potentials.

Each person has a job. Each job involves many tasks. Of course each job should be suited to the talents, capacities, and energies of the person doing it. But in a parecon each job must also contain a mix of tasks and responsibilities such that the overall quality of life and especially the overall empowerment effects of work are comparable for all.

In a parecon there won't be someone doing only surgery and someone else only cleaning bed pans. Instead people who do surgery will also help clean the hospital and perform other tasks so that the sum of all that they do incorporates a fair mix of conditions and responsibilities.

A parecon doesn't have some people in a factory who only manage operations and others who only do rote tasks. Instead people throughout factories do a balanced mix of empowering and rote tasks.

A parecon doesn't have lawyers and short order cooks or engineers and assembly line workers as we now know them. All the tasks associated with these jobs must get done, of course, but in a parecon they are mixed and matched very differently than they are in capitalist workplaces. Parecon has a new division of labor.

Each parecon worker does a mix of tasks that accords with his or her abilities and also conveys a fair share of rote, tedious, interesting, and empowering conditions and responsibilities.

Our work doesn't prepare a few of us to rule and the rest of us to obey. Instead, our work equally prepares all of us to participate in self-managing production, consumption, and allocation. Our work equally readies all of us to engage sensibly in self-managing our lives and institutions.

But what happens if we have a new economy that has worker and consumer councils, self-managing decision-making rules, remuneration in accord with effort and sacrifice, and also balanced job complexes – if we combine all this with markets or with central planning for allocation? Would that constitute a good economy?

Allocation: markets and central planning

Even without capitalists owning workplaces, markets would immediately destroy the remuneration scheme. They would reward output and bargaining power instead of effort and sacrifice.

Markets would also force buyers and sellers to try to buy cheap and sell dear, each fleecing the other as much as possible in the name of private advance and market survival. Markets, in other words, would generate anti-sociality.

Markets would explicitly produce dissatisfaction because it is only the dissatisfied who will buy and then buy again, and again. As the general director of General Motors' Research Labs, Charles Kettering introduced annual model changes for GM cars. He put the point: business needs to create a "dissatisfied consumer"; its mission is "the organized creation of dissatisfaction". The idea was that planned obsolescence would make the consumer dissatisfied with the car he or she already had.

Prices in a market system wouldn't reflect all social costs and benefits. Market prices take into account only the impact of work and consumption on the immediate buyers and sellers, but not on those peripherally affected, including those affected by pollution or, for that matter, by positive side effects. This means markets routinely violate ecological balance and sustainability. Markets subject all but the wealthiest communities to a collective debit in water, air, sound, and other public goods.

Markets also produce a decision-making hierarchy and not self-management. This occurs not only due to disparities in wealth translating into disparate power, but because market competition compels even council based workplaces to cut costs and seek market share regardless of the ensuing implications. To compete, even workplaces with self-managing councils, equitable remuneration, and balanced job complexes, must insulate from the discomfort that cost-cutting imposes precisely those people whom they earmark to figure out what costs to cut and how to generate more output at the expense of worker (and even consumer) fulfillment.

In other words, to cut costs and otherwise impose market discipline there would emerge due to market logic a coordinator class located above workers and violating our preferred norms of remuneration as well as accruing power to themselves and obliterating the self-management and equity we desire.

That is, under the pressure of market competition, the firm I work for must try to maximize its revenues to keep up with or outstrip competing firms. If my firm doesn't do that, we lose our jobs and have only equitable poverty. So we must try to dump our costs on others. We must seek as much revenue as possible, even via inducing excessive consumption. We must cut our costs of production, including reducing comforts for workers and unduly intensifying labor to win market share, regardless of benefits and costs to others.

To relentlessly conceive and pursue all these paths to market success, however, would require both a managerial surplus-seeking mindset and also freedom for the managers from suffering the pains that their choices induce. So we hire folks with appropriately callous and calculating minds such as business schools produce. We give these new employees air conditioned offices and comfortable surroundings. We say to them, okay, cut our costs to ensure our livelihood in the marketplace.

In other words, we impose on ourselves a coordinator class, not due to natural law, and not due to some internal psychological drive, but because markets force us to subordinate ourselves to a coordinator elite lest we lose market share and revenues, and eventually go out of business.

There are those who will claim that all these market failings are not a product of markets per se, but of imperfect markets that haven't attained a condition of perfect competition. This is a bit like saying that the ills associated with ingesting arsenic occur because we never get pure arsenic, but only arsenic tainted with other ingredients.

On the one hand, calling for perfect markets ignores that in a real society there is literally no such thing as frictionless competition, so of course we will always get imperfect markets. But even more importantly, it also ignores that the oppressive features of markets we have highlighted do not diminish when competition is enlarged. This is not just true in our thought experiment, but also in past practice. Historically, the closer economies have come to a pure market system without state intervention and with as few sectors as possible dominated by single firms or groups of firms, or with as few unions as possible, the worse the social implications of the sort we describe above have been. For example, there have rarely if ever been markets as competitive as those of Britain in the early nineteenth century, yet, under the sway of those nearly perfect markets young children routinely suffered early death in the pits and mills of the Black Country. The point is, well-functioning markets get various economic tasks done but do not promote excellence in any form. Indeed, they do not resist, and even facilitate, cultural and moral depravity.

And the same broad result of market allocation destroying the benefits sought via councils, equitable remuneration, and balanced job complexes has historically held for central planning as well, though for different reasons. Central planning elevates central planners and their managerial agents in each workplace, and then, for legitimacy and consistency, also elevates all additional actors in the economy who share the same type of credentials.

In other words, the central planners need local agents who will hold workers to norms the central planners set. These local agents must be authoritative. Their credentials must legitimate them and reduce other actors to relative obedience. Central planning thus, like markets, imposes a coordinator class to rule over workers who are in turn made subordinate not only nationally but also in each workplace.

The allocation problem that we face in trying to conceive a good economy is therefore that (as evidenced by the old Yugoslavia and Soviet Union) even without private ownership of means of production, markets and central planning each subvert the values and structures we have deemed worthy. They obliterate equitable remuneration, annihilate self-management, horribly mis-value products, impose narrow and antisocial motivations, and impose class division and class rule – which is to say, they trample and destroy the values we wish to elevate and advance.

Allocation is the nervous system of economic life. It is both intricate and essential. To round out a new economic vision we must conceive a mechanism that can properly and efficiently determine and communicate accurate information about the true social costs and benefits of economic options, and that can then apportion to workers and consumers influence over choices proportional to the degree they are affected. Desirable means of allocation must allocate resources, labor, and the products of labor in a flexible manner able to reapportion appropriately in the case of unexpected crises or shocks. And it must not homogenize tastes but instead abide diverse preferences, preserve privacy and individuality, engender sociality and solidarity, and meet the needs and capacities of all workers and consumers rather than aggrandizing a few. It must operate without class division and class rule but with equity and classlessness, and without authoritarianism and disproportionate influence for a few people but with self-management.

Self-management of allocation is no little ambition given that virtually everyone is at least to some degree affected by each decision made in an economy. In any institution – factory, university, health center, or whatever – many interests will have to be represented in decision-making. There is the work force itself, the community in which it is located, users of its products or services, and institutions that compete for the same resources. To have democracy, much less self-management, entails that there are structures that displace and eliminate private ownership of the means of production, and that also involve all affected parties appropriately in determining outcomes.

While private ownership is problematic, as critics of capitalism have always indicated, the deeper and arguably even deadlier villains, as we have all too briefly indicated above, are corporate divisions of labor and also markets and central planning. We not only need "directly democratic" worker and consumer councils with balanced job complexes, but also connections among councils that preserve and enhance equitable participation and facilitate democratic decisions being as well informed and insightful as possible.

Participatory planning

Suppose in place of top-down allocation via centrally planned choices, and in place of competitive market allocation by atomized buyers and sellers, we opt for informed, self-managed, cooperative negotiation of inputs and outputs by socially entwined actors who each have a say in proportion as choices affect them, who each access accurate information, and who each have appropriate training, confidence, conditions, and motivation to develop, communicate, and express their preferences.

Those allocation attributes, if we could conceive institutions able to make them real, would, as we desire, compatibly advance council-centered participatory self-management, remuneration for effort and sacrifice, and balanced job complexes. They would also provide proper valuations of personal, social, and ecological impacts and promote classlessness.

Participatory planning is conceived to accomplish all this. In participatory planning, worker and consumer councils propose their work activities and consumption preferences in light of best available and constantly updated knowledge of the full social benefits and costs, locally and nationally, of their choices.

Workers and consumers cooperatively negotiate workplace and consumer inputs and outputs. They employ a back and forth communication of mutually informed preferences using indicative prices, facilitation boards, rounds of accommodation to new information, and other participatory planning features which permit people to express, mediate, and refine their desires in light of feedback about other people's desires.

Workers and consumers indicate via their councils their personal and group preferences. They learn what preferences others have indicated. At each new step they alter their preferences, keeping in mind the need to balance a personally fulfilling pattern of work and consumption with the requirements of a viable overall plan. Each actor seeks personal and collective group well being and development. Each can improve his or her situation only by acting in accord with more general social benefit.

As in any economy, consumers take into account their income and the relative costs of available products and then choose what they desire. This occurs for individual consumption, groups, neighborhoods, and regions, through consumer councils. Workers in their workers' councils similarly indicate how much work they wish to do in light of requests for their product and their own labor/leisure preferences.

In a participatory economy no one has any interest in selling products at inflated prices or in selling more than consumers actually need – because imposing high prices and inducing sales beyond what will fulfill people are not how income is earned. Nor is there any need to compete for market share. Rather, motives are simply to meet needs and to develop potentials without wasting assets, which is to say, to produce what is socially acceptable and useful while compatibly and cooperatively fulfilling one's own as well as the rest of society's preferences. This is true not because people are suddenly saints, but because cooperation is lucrative. Merciless mutual fleecing is personally counter-productive in a parecon.

Preferences for desired production and consumption are communicated by means of special mechanisms developed for the purpose. Negotiations occur in a series of planning rounds. Every participant has an interest in most effectively utilizing productive potentials to meet needs, because everyone gets an equitable share of output that grows as overall social output grows.

Each person also favors making investments that reduce drudge work and improve the quality of the average balanced job complex, because this is the job quality that everyone on average enjoys.

Plans are of course continually updated and refined. It isn't that there are no errors or imperfections in the day to day and year to year operations of a participatory economy. It is that deviations from ideal choices arise from ignorance or mistakes and in no way systematically benefit one sector above others. Mistaken choices and deviations don't snowball or multiply.

To choose what role and position to occupy in a parecon, one consults one's own personal tastes and talents. Of course each person will be better suited and more likely to be happy at some pursuits than at others and will naturally prefer the former. However, there is no choice that one can individually make or that a group can collectively make that would accrue what other members of society would deem unjust power, wealth, or circumstance.

Participatory economics creates a context of classlessness and social solidarity. In a parecon I can get better work conditions if the average job complex improves. I can get higher income if I work harder or longer with my workmates' consent, or if the average income throughout society increases. I not only advance in solidarity with others. I influence all economic decisions in my workplace and even throughout the rest of the economy at a level proportionate to the effects of those decisions on me.

Parecon not only eliminates inequitable disparities in wealth and income, it attains just distribution. Parecon doesn't force people to undervalue or violate other people's lives, but produces solidarity. Parecon doesn't homogenize outcomes, but generates diversity. Parecon doesn't give a small ruling class tremendous power while burdening the bulk of the population with power-lessness, but produces appropriate self-managing influence for all.

Parecon's economic viability and worthiness are argued in great detail in the book *Parecon: Life After Capitalism* (Verso Press), as well as on the parecon web site at www.parecon.org, including addressing detailed concerns about produc-tivity, efficiency, incentives, social relations, etc. Readers who aren't familiar with parecon's features and who haven't yet thought through their logic may wish to consult either of those sources for a far more in depth treatment than this one chapter could deliver.

But suppose you have decided at this point that yes, it seems that parecon can produce goods and services to meet needs and that it can allocate them justly while also supporting worthy values. Should you become a strong advocate of parecon, while also trying to improve its features with your own insights? An argument against your doing that as yet is that it could still be that while parecon works in the abstract, it would fail in reality due to incompatibilities with other parts of society. Another doubt could be that while parecon is nice in theory, in practice it is unattainable due to strategic obstacles.

In other words, are the implications of a parecon for the rest of society desirable or are there broader social problems that undercut the worth and viability of parecon? And if it is worthy, can we get from where we are to parecon? Assuming, at least for now, economic desirability, those are the broader questions we address in coming chapters.

2 Polity

MY OWN COUNTRY, the U.S., arguably has one of the most democratic political systems now operating. Yet even if there weren't huge concentrations of corporate wealth and power dominating political outcomes, even if media didn't constrain and manipulate information to distort political preferences, even if the two parties weren't two wings of a single corporate party, even if there weren't diverse idiotic and at best anachronistic structures like the electoral college, even if elections weren't winner take all affairs in which upwards of half the voting population have their desires ignored, even if elections weren't easily hijacked by outright fraud, clearly modern electoral and parliamentary democracy would still diverge greatly from a system that provokes desirable participation, elicits informed opinion, and resolves disputes justly.

So, what do we want instead of current political systems and, even more centrally for this book, how will what we politically desire relate to a participatory economy?

To fully address the practical symbiosis between a desirable economy and a desirable polity one would ideally like first to describe a compelling new political vision and then examine its interface with economics. Luckily for us, though positive political vision has not yet been spelled out as fully as participatory economics has, the U.S.-based activist and political scientist Stephen Shalom, among others, has at least begun the process in his preliminary presentation of Parpolity, available on the internet via the Participatory Society subsite of ZNet at www.zmag.org/pps.htm.

Parpolity is a political vision that seeks to further the same values as parecon. Since parpolity describes many characteristics a good political system would have, we can usefully take it as a touchstone in this chapter.

Anarchist roots

The French anarchist Proudhon wrote, "To be governed is to be watched over, inspected, spied on, directed, legislated, regimented, closed in, indoctrinated, preached at, controlled, assessed, evaluated, censored, commanded, all by creatures that have neither the right nor wisdom nor virtue... To be governed means that at every move, operation, or transaction, one is noted, registered, entered in a census, taxed, stamped, authorized, recommended, admonished, prevented, reformed, set right, corrected. Government means to be subject to tribute, trained, ransomed, exploited, monopolized, extorted, pressured, mystified, robbed; all in the name of public utility and the general good. Then at first sign of resistance or word of complaint, one is repressed, fined, despised, vexed, pursued, hustled, beaten up, garroted, imprisoned, shot, machine gunned, judged, sentenced, deported, sacrificed, sold, betrayed, and to cap it all, ridiculed, mocked, outraged, and dishonored. That is Government. That is its justice and morality!"

The problem that arises for serious people responding to Proudhon's and many other inspiring anarchist formulations is that they do not specify how to transcend the regimentation typical of state and government. They don't explain how each citizen and community can freely determine its own actions organizationally. How do we legislate shared norms, implement collective programs, and adjudicate disputes, including dealing with violations of sociality? How do we prevent humans from being reduced to atomistic units clashing and jangling, and instead compose a society where the actions of each person collectively benefit all other people?

The need for political vision

One thug with a club can disrupt even the most humane gathering. Thugs with clubs, in all variants, whether aroused by liquor, jealousy, arrogance, greed, pathology, or some other antisocial attribute, won't disappear from a good society.

Likewise, a dispute that has no means of resolution will often escalate, even in the best of environments, into a struggle that vastly transcends the scope of its causes, whether the escalating dispute occurs between the Hatfields and McCoys, northern and southern states, rural and urban areas, France and Germany, or Pakistan and India.

What prevents social degradation due to thugs? What prevents escalating disputes? More generally, if we lack agreed social norms, people will repeatedly have to start social projects from scratch. We won't be able to benefit from a set of previously agreed responsibilities and practices. We will suffer endless negotiation, which will curtail the implementation of the norms and practices we desire.

In a good polity will we have known responsibilities we cannot violate, or will everything we do be up for grabs with each new day? In the former case, we might attain civilized existence. In the latter case, we would only have chaos. To have social success, we need political structures.

Put differently, while it is true that even the most desirable mutually agreed roles and responsibilities will, to some degree, limit our range of options, desirable mutually agreed roles will also make the range of all options available to us vastly larger than were these roles absent. Having red and green lights at intersections constrains our driving options but it also keeps us alive. Having diverse rules that we all abide by can permit, as with traffic signals, each of us to operate far more effectively and diversely, even as it also narrows our choices in some contexts. If institutional norms limit options agreeably, the coherence they can bring can more than outweigh the limitations they impose.

If I violate my previously agreed upon roles and responsibilities, it likely throws into question and perhaps completely disrupts other people's expectations, actions, and options. We don't want freedom to kill. We don't want freedom to drive through red lights. We want freedom that facilitates further freedom and expands people's means to enjoy it. We want to escape needless restrictions, but we want to do this only consistent with others having the same freedoms we have while also preserving previously agreed responsibilities.

So we need to establish institutions that let us accomplish political functions in accord with our values, just as we needed to establish economic institutions that let us accomplish economic functions in accord with our values. The question for political vision is: what are desirable new political institutions?

Failed political visions

One failed answer comes from the perspective called Marxism Leninism. As history has verified, the "dictatorship of the proletariat" translates virtually seamlessly into the dictatorship of the party, the politburo, and, in the worst case, even the megalomaniacal dictator. That this trajectory could ever have been equated with a desirable form of political life will always blemish horribly the political history of "the Left".

Outlawing all but a single "vanguard" party ruled by "democratic centralism" subverts democracy. Democratic centralism systematically impedes participatory impulses, promotes popular passivity, nurtures fear, and breeds authoritarianism even against the far better aspirations of many Leninists. To routinely outlaw external opposition and suppress or manipulate internal dissent by transferring members between branches does not engender democracy. However anti-authoritarian specific Leninists' motivations may be, Leninist practice does not lead to anti-authoritarian polity.

Western-style electoral "democracy" is another answer to the political vision question, and while it is arguably better than the Leninist one-party state and dictatorship, it is nonetheless a far cry from participatory democracy. Highly unequal distributions of wealth stack the deck before the political game begins. Citizens choose from pre-selected candidates screened for compatibility by society's corporate elites. Even if removing private ownership of productive assets overcame money-related problems within a Western-style democracy, participatory democracy requires more than voting infrequently for a representative to carry out political activity largely alienated from popular will and often contrary to popular interests.

The question arises, what mechanisms can permit and promote engagement, deliberation, and decision-making that gives all citizens appropriate say, whether directly or through representatives, and that preserves essential rights while serving justice?

Parpolity

Having admittedly quickly rejected Leninism and parliamentary democracy, the first important thing to realize is that political life will not disappear in a desirable society. The structure of political life will transform, yes, but its relevance to citizens will intensify rather than diminish.

Politics will no longer be privileged groups perpetuating their domination. Nor will oppressed constituencies battle an unjust status quo. But having a desirable polity doesn't mean having universal agreement. While the goal of social diversity dictates that competing ideas should be implemented whenever possible, many times one program will have to be implemented at the expense of others. The problem of public choice will therefore not disappear. Even more, since a desirable society will kindle our participatory impulses, in a good society debate will sometimes heat up rather than cool down.

Stephen Shalom succinctly outlines issues that will still inspire debate and dispute: "Here are just a few issues that will continue to vex us: animal rights (should meat-eating be outlawed?), pornography (is it inherently oppressive to women or an expression of individual autonomy?), prostitution (in a society without economic exploitation is it possible for someone to 'choose' to be a sexual worker?), deep ecology (to what extent should we treat the environment not just as something to be saved so that it can continue to sustain us in the future, but as something of value independent of all human benefit?), drug legalization, multilingualism, children's rights, allocation of expensive or scarce medical resources, like heart transplants, cloning, surrogate motherhood, euthanasia, single-sex schools, and religious freedom when the religions violate other important societal values, like gender equity."

If that list doesn't make the point, Shalom continues: "On top of this, there are issues that are generally supported by the Left, but not universally so, and about which I can imagine continuing debates in a good society: for example, the extent to which we should recognize abortion rights or preferential policies for members of previously oppressed groups. And then there are issues that would arise from the fact that the whole world may not become 'a good society' all at once ... how will we deal with questions of foreign policy, trade, or immigration?"

After which Shalom summarizes, "In short, even in a society that had solved the problem of economic exploitation and eliminated hierarchies of race, class, and gender, many controversies—many deep controversies—would still remain. Hence, any good society will have to address issues of politics and will need some sort of political system, a polity".

The broadest goals, if not the structural means of embodying a new polity, are already pretty well understood and enunciated. A truly democratic community insures that the general public has the opportunity for meaningful and constructive participation in the formation of social policy. A society that excludes large areas of crucial decision-making from public control, or a system of governance that merely grants the general public the opportunity to ratify decisions taken by the elite groups, hardly merits the term democracy. A central question is, however, what institutional vehicles will best afford and even guarantee the public truly democratic opportunities?

Ultimately, political controversies must be settled by tallying people's preferences. Obviously voting will be better informed the greater access voters have to relevant information. One condition of real democracy, therefore, is that groups with competing opinions can effectively communicate their views. Democratization of political life must include democratization of the flow of information and commentary via a new media of the sort discussed in Chapter Ten of this book.

Participatory democracy requires not only democratic access to a transformed media and the possibility for people to form and utilize single-issue political organizations to make their views known, but also a pluralism of political parties with different social agendas. There is no reason to think, in other words, that having a good economy or society means that people won't disagree about major matters in ideological ways. An absence of class difference doesn't imply an absence of all difference.

If we reflect briefly on the history of political life within the left and on the consequences of attempting to ban parties, factions, or any form of political organization people desire to employ, it should be clear that bans are the stuff of repression and authoritarianism.

But can we offer more by way of political vision than these broad and very general intimations of possible features of a desirable polity? Well, we can at least reproduce some of Stephen Shalom's thoughts about political vision, which seem to me instructive and valuable.

Values

We might start with values, and, saving a lot of time, note that parecon's economic values not only make good economic sense, but with a little tweaking make good political sense as well.

Surely a polity should produce solidarity, not anti-sociality, and should value and generate diversity rather than homogenizing outcomes. So these two economic values transfer easily into politics.

For the economy, equity addresses the distribution of rewards. For polity, the analogue of equity is justice, which addresses the distribution of rights and responsibilities, including the redress of violations of social agreements. So with this minor tweak, equity transfers into justice.

Self-management is arguably even more a political value than an economic one, both in its origins and its logic, and is therefore certainly a worthy political aim. Politics should facilitate actors having influence on decisions in proportion as those decisions impact on their lives.

So borrowing and adapting from parecon, for politics we have as guiding values solidarity, diversity, justice, and self-management. Moreover, accomplishing these values implies accomplishing other more familiar political values, including liberty, participation, and tolerance.

Institutions

In Shalom's conception of a desirable polity there are matters of legislation, adjudication, and collective implementation. For legislation, Shalom advocates "nested councils" where "the primary-level councils will include every adult in the society" and where, Shalom suggests, "the number of members in these primary-level councils [might plausibly] be somewhere between 25–50".

Thus everyone in society is in one of these basic political units. Some folks are elected to higher level councils as well, since in Shalom's parpolity vision, "each primary-level council will choose a delegate to a second-level council", which would again be composed of 20–50 delegates. And this would proceed again, for another layer, and another, "until there is one single top-level council for the entire society". The delegates to each higher council "would be charged with trying to reflect the actual views of the council they came from". On the other hand, "they would not be told 'this is how you must vote,' for if they were, then the higher council they were attending would not be a deliberative body".

Shalom suggests that "the number of members on each council should be determined on the basis of a society-wide decision, and perhaps revised on the basis of experience, so as to meet the following criteria: small enough to guarantee that people can be involved in deliberative bodies, where all can participate in face-to-face discussions; but yet big enough so that (1) there is adequate diversity of opinion included; and (2) the number of layers of councils needed to accommodate the entire society is minimized".

Shalom clarifies, perhaps contrary to most people's intuitions, that "a council size of 25, with 5 layers, assuming half the population consists of adults, can accommodate a society of 19 million people; a council size of 40, again would need 5 layers to accommodate 200 million people; a 50-person council could accommodate 625 million people by the fifth level. With a sixth level, even a 25-person council could accommodate a society of about half a billion people", thus making a case that his layered councils are flexible and well within practical possibility.

What happens in these proposed political councils?

Legislation is enacted, which is to say voting on norms and collective agendas takes place. The councils are deliberative and public. The idea is to utilize them to approximate, as much as possible within a sensible time frame and in accord with the importance of particular issues, self-managed decision-making.

Sometimes higher level councils vote and decide. Sometimes they deliberate and report back and lower level councils vote and decide. The exact combination or range of combinations of voting at the base versus voting in higher level councils, and of procedures for presenting, debating, and tallying viewpoints, and of how precisely council members are chosen, are all, among many other features, degrees of political detail we don't have to address in a cursory chapter like this. Shalom has begun considering the issues, and no doubt more needs to be done, including, of course, learning from future experiences.

For purposes of discussing the relation between parecon and a desirable polity, however, it is enough to say that a worthy legislative branch will likely incorporate face to face nested councils using open methods of information transfer, debate, and voting aimed at providing all actors self-managing say over the decisions that affect them.

Shalom's discussions of the role not only of tallying votes but also of contributing time, energy, and funds to political struggles as part of the process of guaranteeing self-management, as well as of the dynamics of representation and deliberation, are all highly instructive. So are other people's explorations of voting procedures such as instant run off voting, and of decision mechanisms such as consensus, but again, they are beyond what we need to include here.

What about shared executive functions?

On the one hand, parecon takes care of a lot of what we typically know as executive functions in contemporary politics and, in doing so, helps pinpoint the remaining truly political element. Think of delivering the mail, of investigating and trying to limit outbreaks of disease, or of providing environmental protection. All of these pursuits involve a production and allocation aspect handled by the structures of participatory economics, including balanced job complexes, remuneration for effort and sacrifice, and participatory decision-making. The workers' council delivering mail would in these respects not be particularly different from the workers' council producing bicycles, nor would the Center for Disease Control (CDC) worker's council be very different in its economic aspects from a typical hospital, and likewise for the Environmental Protection Agency (EPA) and a typical research institute.

But in another sense the three examples are different from their parecon counterparts. The Post Office, CDC, and EPA operate with the sanction of the polity and carry out tasks the polity mandates. Particularly in the case of the CDC and EPA, executive agencies act with political authority that permits them to investigate and sanction others where typical economic units would have no such rights and responsibilities.

It follows that the executive branch is largely concerned with establishing politically mandated functions and responsibilities which are then typically carried out according to the norms of the participatory economy but with a political aspect defining their agendas and perhaps conveying special powers. If it aids understanding, this overlap between polity and economy is more or less analogous to the overlap between culture and economy visible when churches function in the economy for their inputs and perhaps some of their outputs too, but do so with a cultural/religious definition. The change in economics to having a parecon instead of capitalism is part of what makes a polity or culture or family or other aspect of society new in a new society, but the heart of their alteration is the change in their intrinsic logic.

Presumably the means for an executive branch to politically mandate its agendas and establish lasting mechanisms to oversee them would be largely the deliberation and votes of a legislative branch, on the one hand, and economic planning on the other, as well as the establishment of empowered entities with their own rules of operation, like the CDC and other politically empowered agencies.

But then what would be the role of a judiciary in a parpolity?

As Shalom asserts, "Judicial systems often address three kinds of concerns: judicial review (are the laws just?), criminal justice (have specific individuals violated the laws?), and civil adjudication (how are disputes between individuals resolved?)".

For the first, Shalom offers a court system that would operate more or less like the Supreme Court does now, with hierarchical levels adjudicating disputes arising over council choices. Is this the best approach we can imagine, and can it be refined or transformed to further enhance self-management? This certainly merits close consideration.

For criminal matters and civil adjudication, Shalom proposes a court system modestly different from what we have now, plus a police force that would of course have balanced job complexes and enjoy remuneration for effort and sacrifice.

Regarding having a police function and associated work force in a desirable society – which is actually for many people more controversial than having courts – I agree with Shalom and don't really see any alternative or any intractable problems. There will be crimes in a good society, sometimes violent and sometimes even horribly evil, and investigation and capture of criminals will be serious matters requiring special skills. It seems obvious that some people will do that kind of work, with special rules and features to ensure they do it well and also consistently with social values – just as some people will spend some of their work time flying airplanes or treating patients or doing other difficult and demanding jobs that require special skills and have special rules to ensure they are done well and consistently with social values.

The contrary idea – that policing would be unnecessary in a humane system – is not realistic. Sure, in a good society many reasons for crime would be eliminated and criminal acts would likely be far fewer, but that doesn't mean there will be no crime at all. And the idea that policing will be needed but can be done on an entirely voluntary basis makes no more sense than saying flying planes or doing brain surgery will be needed but can be done entirely on a voluntary basis. It fails to realize that policing, and especially desirable policing, like flying planes or doing surgery, involves special skills and knowledge. It fails to recognize the need for training and likely also special rules to avoid misuse of police (or transport or medical) prerogatives.

Beyond the implications of pareconish workplace structure and decision-making for police motivations, might there be a special limited duration for police work? Might there be empowered community review mechanisms to oversee specific rules of police operations and evaluation? Will the different approaches of a good society to determining guilt or innocence and to administering punishment and rehabilitation impact police functions very differently than old approaches they replace? The answers are all conceivably yes, perhaps even very likely yes, but again, the details are beyond our purview here.

It is not the police part of the judicial system, it seems to me, but the courts part, the legal advocacy part, and the jury part that may be most difficult to improve dramatically in a better society.

On the one hand, as Shalom argues, the advocate model, in which lawyers work on behalf of clients regardless of guilt or innocence, makes considerable sense. We don't want people having to defend themselves, so that those who are good at it have a tremendous advantage over those who are not good at it. We therefore need well-trained lawyers and prosecutors available to all disputants.

We also want these advocates to try hard, of course. But at the same time, the injunction that prosecutors and defense attorneys should seek to win favorable verdicts regardless of their knowledge of the true guilt or innocence of the accused and by any means that they can muster because that approach will yield the greatest probability of truthful results strikes me as about as believable, in certain respects, as the injunction that everyone in an economy should seek selfish private gain as the best means of benefiting society as a whole and engendering sociality. However, as to how to adapt or replace the combination of courts, judges, juries, and aggressive advocacy with different mechanisms, beyond new norms of remuneration and job definition that economic innovations indicate, I have no good ideas.

The shared political vision on the left, for locales, countries, or internationally, whether for legislative, executive, or adjudicative functions, is still in a modest state, in my view, and needs developing to justify future advocacy. Nonetheless, many broad guidelines exist, and it is certainly possible to think about the relation of both existing economies and parecon to political prospects.

Parpolity and economy

Milton Friedman, a far right-wing University of Chicago-based Nobel prize winning economist of immense repute, argues that "viewed as a means to the end of political freedom, economic arrangements are important because of their effect on the concentration or dispersion of power". This is true enough. And indeed economic institutions are also important for the way they train us either to participate in decisions as equals or to be docile as subordinates, and for the way they help us to attain the social skills and habits of involvement and participatory decision-making, or, instead, for the way they diminish those skills and habits.

Friedman goes on to add that "the kind of economic organization that provides economic freedom directly, namely, competitive capitalism, also promotes political freedom because it separates economic power from political power and in this way enables the one to offset the other".

This claim, however, unlike Friedman's prior more general observation, is one of the most absurd utterances to be found in the domain of political or economic thought. The truth is that capitalist economics produces gigantic centers of concentrated power in the form of its corporations and their ruling elements. It also produces atomized, weakened, de-centered and disconnected workers and consumers. Further, it provides diverse means to translate corporate economic might into political influence by corporations controlling com- munication, information, and the finances of electioneering, as well as coercing political officials. Finally, capitalist economy ensures that the isolation and disconnection of workers are further enforced by media manipulation and the alienation that comes from the population knowing that political outcomes are predetermined.

The result of all this is that corporate lobbies and other elites determine political agendas and ensure that elections choose between candidates who differ primarily in how best to maintain elite prerogatives and advantages. Most of the population doesn't even participate in the electoral charades, and among those who do participate, most have no other option than to repeatedly favor a lesser evil.

Parpolity, or any desirable political system that movements might advocate, will require an economy that doesn't elevate some people to positions of power over other people. It will need the economy to immerse the whole populace in an environment of participation, self-management, sociality, and solidarity so that all citizens might best fulfill parpolity's requirements and enjoy its possibilities.

Parpolity will need, and in turn help produce, citizens who have broadly the same power, who have a social inclination to participate, and who have habits of sociality and solidarity – and precisely the same can be said for a parecon.

Likewise a desirable polity will need and help produce citizens schooled to benefit from managing their own affairs in accord with collective well being while respecting diverse needs and outcomes – which is true for a parecon as well.

Parecon and parpolity are, by design, welcome partners in social organization. They share the same underlying logic of seeking to attain equitable outcomes in a solidaritous and diverse environment, under the self-managing auspices of those affected.

If we think of a parpolity and a parecon each as a kind of social system that takes in people and then sends them out after impacting on their consciousnesses, habits, degrees of fulfillment, talents, knowledge, skills, and inclinations, we see that each requires and produces what the other provides and needs.

And indeed, due to the similar requirements they each offer the other, it is more than plausible that a parpolity and a parecon could mutually combine to become a classless "political economy" that delivers solidarity, diversity, equity/justice, and self-management.

Addendum: Parpolity and political strategy today

Parpolity's main implications for political and social strategy have to do with two dimensions of activism – what we demand and how we organize ourselves.

Having a political vision will hopefully tell us a variety of things we might demand in the present. That is, we could try to win changes in government and political practices now that advance the logic of parpolity. These might include instant run-off voting procedures, vast extensions of public media and debate, new means of the public choosing executive programs, and as yet unclear judicial reforms.

When movements fight for such demands in the present, two very broad criteria that arise from political vision ought to inform their activity. First, of course, they should be trying to win improvements in people's lives. Second, they should be trying to make changes that empower people to win more gains and that educate and inspire people to want to do so.

On both counts, by examining the features of a proposed political vision, we ought to be able to discern present day changes that would benefit, empower, and inspire people, as well as increase desires to enjoy the political future we seek.

But an additional implication of political vision for present practice has to do with movement organization and structure. If we want the politics of the future to have certain features and properties, surely we should try as much as we can to incorporate those features and properties into current operations.

In other words, our movements should, in their internal political structure and practices, elevate solidarity, diversity, justice, and self-management. The conditions under which we operate today are constrained in ways unlike those of a future society, of course. We have to deal with repressive structures all around us. But nonetheless a central implication of political vision is that as soon, and as much, as we are able to do so, we should seek to build movements based on grassroots organization and participation and even on nested tiers of councils for organizational decision-making.

As a political vision becomes more compelling and is shared by more people, desirable ways to adjudicate movement disputes, enact shared movement agendas, legislate movement norms, and otherwise arrive at movement decisions should become clearer and, over time, easier to incorporate in our efforts.

Let me raise one possible lesson. Typically, contemporary movements have two forms. They either organize around a single issue and involve a focused fight for wages or health care or women's right to choose or some other single issue goal. Or they are composed of many organizations teaming up to promote a shared, usually quite narrowly defined, agenda. What our movements seeking to win specific gains are usually not, however, are very broad and diverse agglomerations of people who mutually respect divergent viewpoints and operate effectively together despite and even in celebration of their differences.

The fragmentation of our movements into single-issue efforts or into coalitions that bury differences and come and go with events bears only minimal resemblance to a good society or polity. It isn't that in the future there won't be people with single primary concerns or even organizations that are narrowly focused or coalitions that come in and out of fashion. It is that a good society itself-will not primarily isolate people and groups into narrow concerns. It will, instead, be overwhelmingly a community with diverse views and agendas in which we respect each other's concerns and incorporate them into our overall efforts to maintain social cohesion.

If a movement is to be the harbinger of, and a school for, a new society, it should not be primarily atomized and narrow. It should somehow incorporate differences and deal with them; in so doing, it will make itself-steadily stronger.

Suppose that instead of only creating coalitions organized around a narrow list of agreed demands, an encompassing movement of movements, say, or perhaps we might call it a revolutionary bloc, was also created. This would be an amalgam of all organizations, projects and movements, and their members, and maybe include individual members also, all of whom subscribed to some broad range of values, priorities, and organizational norms including and encompassing a wide range of differences.

This new movement structure would take its leadership regarding aspects of its focus from those of its members most directly dealing in the focused areas –

thus in the U.S., for example, from the women's movement about gender issues, from black and Latino movements about race, from the anti-war movement about peace issues, and from labor and consumer movements about economic matters. Instead of the whole structure being defined by a little part of the overall priority of each component group that all shared, the whole structure would be the sum total of all the key priorities of all its component groups, contradictions and all, just as a society is. This new movement structure would indeed be a new society in embryo. Its internal organization and operations would presumably reflect our aspirations for the new society we seek, including incorporating the modes of council organization, election processes, and means of communication characterizing our political vision, as well as the diversity of views our new society would contain.

Some further comments on these strategic matters will appear in future chapters. For now, however, the critical claim, in light of the agenda of this book, is that while the problem of envisioning improved political structures is still in process, and while we can't know for sure until we are further down that track what political features we should advocate, it nonetheless seems we can be reasonably confident that participatory economics produces people and conditions that will contribute to political justice and easily honor a desirable polity's requirements.

3 Kinship

HOW WOULD A participatory economy affect and be affected by a good society's procreation, nurturance, socialization, sexuality, and organization of daily home life? What would change about relations between women and men, homo and heterosexuals, and members of different generations?

Historically the organization of society to benefit men at the expense of women has been ubiquitous. The price has been incalculable in lost female lives, lost female freedom, and lost female creativity and initiative, and in derivative losses for children and men as well. Transcending all this injustice, in all its myriad forms, is obviously a central part of attaining a desirable future society.

Kinship vision

Movements currently have very little clarity about what revolutionized kinship relations will be like in a new society. What altered or new institutions will organize procreation, nurturance, and socialization? How will the structures and social roles associated with home life change? Will there be families as we now know them? What kinds of collective gatherings, of day care mechanisms, and of extended networks will there be? Will child-rearing diverge greatly from what we know now? What about courting and sexual coupling? How will the old and young interact?

Presumably, good kinship will liberate women and men — rather than causing the latter to dominate the former. We want to escape systematic sexism, homophobia, and ageism. We want to enjoy innovations whose structural character we can only guess at until we have experimented with more complete visionary proposals.

It isn't that a desirable new society will eliminate all problems associated with gender, meet all unmet gender desires, or fulfill all un-manifested gender capacities. Even in a wonderful society, we can confidently predict that there will be unrequited love. Sex will retain turmoil. Rape and other violent acts will sometimes occur. Social change won't eliminate people losing friends and relatives to premature death. A better world won't make all adults equally adept at relating with children or the elderly, or vice versa.

Though we won't enjoy a utopian elimination of all gender or sex related conflict, we can certainly reasonably demand an end to systematic violation of women, gays, children, and the elderly. But how? Not how will we get to this better future, but what will kinship institutions defining a vastly better future look like?

Sexism means men having dominant and wealthier conditions. It includes long standing habits of male dominated communication and behavior. It is produced and reproduced by patriarchal institutions that differentiate men and women coercively, as in rape and battering, and also more subtly by mutually accepted role differences, as in home life, work, and celebration, not to mention via the cumulative impact of past sexist experiences on what people think, desire, feel, and habitually or even self consciously do.

If we want to find the source of gender injustice it stands to reason we need to determine which social roles impose circumstances, motivations, consciousness, and preferences that elevate men above women.

One structure we find in all patriarchal societies is that men father but women mother. That is, men and women play quite dissimilar roles with regard to the next generation. One conceptually simple structural kinship change would be to minimize this mothering/fathering differentiation between men and women.

What if, instead of women mothering and men fathering, women and men each related to children with the same mix of responsibilities and behaviors (called parenting), rather than with one gender having almost all the nurturing, tending, cleaning, and other maintenance tasks (called mothering), and the other gender having many more decision-based tasks (called fathering)?

I doubt that replacing gender-defined mothering and fathering with gender-blind parenting would alone eliminate all the defining roots of sexism, but I think it might be one necessary component of doing so.

I first encountered this idea in the work of Nancy Chodorow in a book titled, *The Reproduction of Mothering*. Chodorow makes the case that mothering is a socially, not a biologically defined role, and that when acting as mothers, women produce daughters who in turn not only have mothering capacities but desire to mother. "These capacities and needs," Chodorow continues, "are built into and grow out of the mother-daughter relationship itself. By contrast, women as mothers (and men as not mothers) produce sons whose nurturant capacities and needs have been systematically curtailed and repressed."

For Chodorow, the implication is that "the sexual and familial division of labor in which women mother and are more involved in interpersonal affective relationships than men produces in daughters and sons a division of psychological capacities which leads them to reproduce this sexual and familial division of labor".

Chodorow summarizes by claiming that "all sex-gender systems organize sex, gender, and babies. A sexual division of labor in which women mother organizes babies and separates domestic and public spheres. Heterosexual marriage, which usually gives men rights in women's sexual and reproductive capacities, and formal rights in children, organizes sex. Both together organize and reproduce gender as an unequal social relation".

So perhaps gender relations in a vastly improved society will have men and women both parenting, with no division between mothering and fathering.

Another structure many feminists question when thinking about improved sex-gender relations is the nuclear family. This is difficult to define precisely, but certainly involves whether the locus of child care and familial involvement is very narrow – resting with the two biological parents – or instead includes an extended family or even friends and community members.

It seems highly unlikely that a good society would have for its gender relations rules that require only a few typical household organizations and family structures, disallowing all others. We wouldn't expect that adults would have to live alone, or in pairs, or in groups, or in any limited array of acceptable patterns. The key point is likely to be that multiple and diverse patterns of family life will exist, all promoting gender equity rather than imposing gender hierarchy.

While I don't feel equipped to describe such possible choices, I both hope and assume that the men and women that are born, brought up, and then themselves bear and bring up new generations in a new and much better society will be diverse, capable, and confident in their demeanor without systematic differentiations that limit their life trajectories to some narrow gender-defined mold.

The same can be said, broadly, about sexuality and intergenerational relations. I don't think we know, or arguably as yet even have a very loose picture of what fully liberated sexuality will be like in all its preferences and practices. Nor can we now know what diverse forms of intergenerational relations future adults, children, and elders will establish. What I think we can say, however, is that future desirable societies won't elevate a few patterns above all others and that widely chosen options will ensure that some people do not dominate others based on gender, sexuality, age, or any other social or biological characteristic.

We have very little idea what specific sex-gender patterns will emerge in a better future – for example, monogamous and not; heterosexual, homosexual, or bisexual; transformed care-giving institutions, families, and schools; and perhaps other political and social spaces for children, adults, and the elderly. But we can guess with confidence that people of all ages and genders engaging in non-oppressive consensual sexual relations will be free from stigma.

All the above is admittedly vague and modestly formulated. Will renovated kinship include even the structural features intimated above? I don't know. But even without knowing the inner attributes of new kinship institutions and while waiting for kinship vision to emerge more fully from feminist thought and practice, we can confidently say some useful things.

Kinship institutions are necessary for people to develop and fulfill their sexual and emotional needs, organize daily life, and nurture new generations of children. But current kinship relations elevate men above women and children and warp human sexual and emotional potentials.

In a desirable society we will eliminate oppressive, socially imposed definitions so that everyone can pursue their lives as they choose whatever their sex, sexual preference, and age. There will be no non-biologically imposed sexual division of labor, with men doing one kind of work and women doing another kind simply due to their being men and women, nor will there be any hierarchical role demarcation of individuals according to sexual preference. We will have gender relations that respect the social contributions of women as well as men, and that promote sexuality that is physically rich and emotionally fulfilling.

It is likely that new kinship forms will overcome the possessive narrowness of monogamy while also preserving the depth and continuity that comes from lasting relationships. New forms will likely destroy arbitrary divisions of roles between men and women so that both sexes are free to nurture and to take initiative. New forms will likely also give children room for self-management, even as they provide the support and structure children need. But what will make all this possible?

Obviously, women must have reproductive freedom – the freedom to have children without fear of sterilization or economic deprivation, and the freedom not to have children through unhindered access to birth control and abortion. But feminist kinship relations must also ensure that child-rearing roles do not segregate tasks by gender, and that there is support for traditional couples, single parents, lesbian and gay parenting, and more complex, multiple parenting arrangements. All parents must have easy access to high quality day-care, flexible work hours, and parental leave options. The point is not to absolve parents of child-rearing by turning over the next generation to uncaring agencies staffed mainly by women (or even women and men) who are accorded low social esteem. The idea is to elevate the status of child-rearing, encourage highly personalized interaction between children and adults, and distribute responsibilities for these interactions equitably between men and women and throughout society.

After all, what social task could be more important than caring for the coming generation of citizens? So what could be more irrational than patriarchal ideologies that deny those who fill this critical social role the status they merit? In a desirable society, kinship activity must not only be arranged more equitably, but the social evaluation of this activity must be corrected as well.

Feminism should also embrace a liberated vision of sexuality respecting each person's inclinations and choices, whether homosexual, bisexual, heterosexual, monogamous, or non-monogamous. Beyond respecting human rights, the exercise and exploration of different forms of sexuality by consenting partners provides a variety of experiences that can benefit all. In a humanist society without oppressive hierarchies, sex can be pursued solely for emotional, physical, and spiritual pleasure and development, or, of course, as part of loving relationships. Experimentation will likely not merely be tolerated, but appreciated.

We need a vision of gender relations in which women are no longer subordinate to men and are free at last to make full use of their talents and intelligence. We need a vision in which men are no longer superior to women and are free to nurture. We need a vision in which childhood is a time of play and increasing responsibility with opportunity for independent learning but not fear, and in which loneliness does not grip as a vice whose handle turns as each year passes.

A worthy kinship vision will reclaim living from the realm of habit to make it an art form we are all capable of practicing and refining. But I won't pretend that all this can be achieved overnight. Nor is there reason to think a single kind of parenting institution is best for all. While the contemporary nuclear family has proven all too compatible with patriarchal norms, a different kind of nuclear family will no doubt evolve, along with a host of other kinship forms, as people experiment with how to achieve the goals of feminism.

Economics and women and men

Capitalist economics is more subtle in relation to gender than some critical analysts think. There is nothing in the defining institutions of capitalism – private ownership of productive property, corporate divisions of labor, authoritative decision making, and markets – that even notices, much less differentiates and hierarchically arrays men and women according to a strictly economic dynamic and logic. On the other hand, if a society's sex–gender system hierarchically differentiates men and women, capitalist economy will not ignore that reality but will aggressively exploit it.

Thus, if men and women are arrayed by familial and other kinship relations so that the former have expectations of relative dominance, capitalist economy will operate in light of this situation.

Suppose an employer seeks to hire a manager. Imagine the workforce is male and a woman and a man apply, and the woman is more suited to the actual tasks involved. Nonetheless, in a sexist society the man is far more likely to get the job – and this is true even if the employer has no gender biases at all.

The reason is that the employer needs the workforce to feel obedient and subordinate to the manager, and needs the manager to feel authoritative and superior to the workforce. It is far less likely for a workforce to reject the preconceived sexual ordering of society than to accept it.

In other words, the corporate division of labor utilizes rather than challenges the gender hierarchy established by kinship. It places men above women and thereby obeys rather than violates the expectations emanating from kinship.

Similarly pay patterns will also reflect the differential bargaining power that sexism imposes on men and women. Men, all other things being equal, will extract more pay for the same work because owners can and will exploit the subordinate position and lesser bargaining power of women.

These are the minimal accommodations of capitalist economies to sexist kinship relations. Capitalism's hierarchies don't challenge and largely incorporate gender hierarchies. Women disproportionately occupy subordinate positions. Women earn less and partly as a result suffer female poverty, ill health, rape, and other violence.

It is important to realize, however, that gender hierarchies can have a still deeper impact on economic relations. The styles and patterns of male and female behavior produced by a patriarchal sex–gender system can impose on economic roles so strongly that the latter begin to incorporate the features of the former, rather than only accommodating or exploiting them.

In other words, women's economic jobs can take on attributes of nurturance, care giving, and maintenance which are in no sense required by, or even entirely logical in light of, economic dictates alone. Similarly, men's roles can take on patterns imposed by kinship definitions even when such patterns run contrary to purely economic logic.

Because of this we may see economic workplace jobs – initially imposed by a patriarchal sex–gender system – both reflecting and actively reproducing male and female behavior patterns. The economy then becomes complicit in reproducing sexism, a point insightfully explored by Batya Weinbaum, for example in her South End Press book, *Curious Courtship of Women's Liberation and Socialism.*

Parecon's impact

In parecon the reproduction of sexist relations emanating from a patriarchal sex-gender system disappears. It isn't just that a parecon works nicely alongside a liberated kinship sphere. It is that a parecon precludes, or at least militates against, non-liberated relations among men and women. Parecon contradicts sexism.

A parecon will not give men relatively more empowering work or more income than women because it cannot provide such advantages to any group relative to any other.

Balanced job complexes and self-management require adults who are able to engage in decisions and to undertake creative and empowering tasks regardless of gender or any other biological or social attribution.

Parecon cannot respect or incorporate hierarchies born in gender relations because there are no hierarchies in a parecon that men can dominate. Women cannot earn less than men, nor have less empowering jobs, nor have less say over decisions.

But many feminists may ask at this point, what about household labor? Parecon claims to remove the differentiation at work and in income required by contemporary sexism, but is household labor part of the economy? Why or why not?

My inclination is to say that there is no one right answer to this question. I can imagine a society that treats household labor of diverse types as part of its participatory economy. I can also imagine one that doesn't. With my current state of understanding, I would prefer the latter for a few reasons, but neither choice is ruled out or made inevitable purely by the logic of parecon.

There are a few reasons why I tend to think household labor shouldn't be considered part of the economy subject to the norms of productive labor with remuneration for effort and sacrifice, balanced job complexes, etc.

First, I don't think parenting the next generation is like producing a shirt, stereo, scalpel, or spyglass. There is something fundamentally distorting, to my thinking, about conceptualizing household childcare and family maintenance on the one hand, and workplace production on the other, as the same type of social activity. As much as I celebrate and respect workplace labor, I think this equilibration undervalues what goes on in families.

Second, I think household labor should not be counted as part of economic production because the fruits of much of household labor are largely enjoyed by the producer him or herself. Should I be able to spend more time on household design and maintenance or even on interacting with my kids, and receive more remuneration as a result of that? If so, I will get at least the lion's share of the pleasurable output of the work I do, or my kids will, and I will then get more income too. This is different than other types of work where there is a consumer who benefits, and it seems to me that for this reason changing the design of my living room or keeping up my garden is more like other consumption I do than it is like production. In the same way, tending my children's sickness at night, preparing meals for them, or cleaning up their messes fails to resemble production.

Suppose I like to play the piano, or to build model airplanes, or whatever. The activity I engage in for this hobby has much in common with work that others do in workplaces and could even be identical in its step by step actions – but we call it consumption anyhow because I do it under my own auspices and entirely for myself. What we call work, in contrast, is what we do under the auspices of workers' councils to produce outputs that are enjoyed by people other than just ourselves, in part in accord with their influence, and only to the point of utilizing assets socially beneficial and not beyond. We don't view either raising our children or cleaning our kitchens in these ways.

What about the opposite option? Is there a problem in saying that raising children is fundamentally different than producing cars or screwdrivers or even teaching public school or working day care? Is there a problem in saying that maintaining a household is different in its social relations and benefits than working in a factory? Is there a problem in concluding from these differences that we shouldn't count household labor as work to be remunerated and to occur under the auspices of parecon's workplace and allocation institutions?

I guess if we think it is impossible to transform sex–gender relations themselves, then, yes, there is a problem with this choice. If we assume, that is, that the norms and structures of households and living units will inevitably remain highly sexist at their core, and if we then decide as well that a parecon shouldn't incorporate household labor as part of the economy subject to its norms, then it would follow that household labor would be done overwhelmingly by women and would as a result reduce their leisure or time for other pursuits relative to men.

But why would anyone assume unchanged kinship relations? Why couldn't transformed norms for household labor arise from a transformation of sex–gender relations themselves, based on new aspirations that include but also transcend economic insights, rather than only due to calling household labor part of the economy?

Take it in reverse. If this were a book about feminism and the rest of society, and if I had mapped out a convincing and worthy feminist sex–gender vision, I don't think many people would urge that we then count the workplace as a household and run it under the same auspices as families operate so that the economy gets the benefits of the innovative relations that new families and living units have. We would assume, instead, that there would need to be a revolution in the economy as well as in kinship, so that the best economic as well as the best kinship results could arise, and we would rely on the economic revolution for the chief redefinitions of life at work even as we also anticipated and required that the new economy abide and abet kinship gains.

In any event, whatever any particular good society decides about household labor, clearly a parecon militates against sexism because on the one hand it is structurally incapable of incorporating sexist hierarchies into economic relations, and on the other hand it empowers and remunerates women in ways that obstruct their subordination in any other realm.

Economics and sexuality

Perhaps it is the paucity of my understanding showing, but other than in direct analogy to the above discussion, I honestly don't see a deeper systematic relation of economics and sexuality. If there is homophobia or other forms of sexual hierarchy in a society, and if the economy is capitalist, then the economy will – to the extent owners are able to do so – exploit whatever differentials in bargaining power they are handed. Beyond this, the capitalist economy may also incorporate gay and straight behavior patterns into economic roles and consumption patterns. If the economy is pareconish, however, no exploitation of sexual difference is even possible because there is one norm of remuneration and one logic of labor definition that applies equally and equitably to everyone, and that fact intrinsically forecloses options of sexual hierarchy.

More positively, it seems to me that whatever liberated sexuality will mean in a future society, it can only be hastened by economic relations that bestow self-managing power on everyone and thereby tend to generate people who expect to be creative, initiating, and self-managing in other spheres of their lives, not just in the economic one.

In other words, what healthy sexuality requires of an economy, to be consistent and even supportive of its outcomes, a parecon can and automatically does deliver: people prepared to partake of life fully and equally to others, utilizing their capacities, enjoying dignity and equity of conditions, and self-managing their options. What precise outcomes will emerge from this, or even what broad outcomes, others will have to conceive or more likely discover though future life experiences. Will there be a variant on prostitution in a desirable future? A variant on pornography? Anonymous sex? Likely there is no single answer to questions like these.

Economics and intergenerational conflict

Capitalism exploits age differentials by remunerating the young and the old reduced amounts due to their having lesser bargaining power. It exploits different capacities related to age, and will rush labor entry into the work force or speed or delay labor withdrawal from the workforce compared to humane choices, again for exploitative reasons. A parecon, in contrast, will literally make such behaviors impossible due to their contradicting essential parecon norms and structures.

Societies with a parecon will decide the economic role of the elderly via retirement ages and other age-related policies, and will likewise set norms for young people's entry into economic responsibility. And while extra-economic intergenerational relations will be affected by a host of variables, including new kinship and gender forms, by requiring participatory self-managing workers and consumers parecon will impose a respect for all people and give everyone material equality and behavioral wherewithal contrary to any kind of ageist subordination.

We don't yet know beyond broad strokes what liberated gender, sexual, and intergenerational relations will be like in a new society, but there is no reason to think parecon won't be compatible with and even nurture them.

4 Community

BEING HUMAN INCLUDES situating oneself in the cosmos and having collective identifications, linguistic relations, and social celebrations. Humans create diverse communities, each enjoying a shared culture that typically differs in its artistic, linguistic, and spiritual preferences from the rest. The problem of cultural communities is that along with generating desirable diversity, different cultural communities can for many reasons exploit one another, attack one another, or even obliterate one another, as we have seen time and again throughout history. Community hierarchies, whatever their origins, entail for their justification cultural denigration, which in turn survives even beyond initial motivations.

In a good society presumably the largely one-way or sometimes mutual inter-community assault and destruction common throughout history would be eliminated.

What relations do economies, and in particular, parecons, have to cultural communities, whether those communities are warring or are mutually respectful?

First let's consider, however briefly, at least some attributes of the kinds of cultural relations we would like to have in a good society. Then we can on that basis address the relationship of economics and cultural communities, both now and in the future.

Cultural vision

We will not be magically reborn in a desirable society. We will not be free of our past and unaware of our historical roots. On the contrary, our historical memory, our sensitivity to past and present social process, and our understanding of our own and of our society's history, will all be enhanced during the process of reaching a desirable future. Instead of our diverse cultural roots being submerged by a process of winning a new society, they will grow in prominence.

So while, as Einstein pithily put it, "nationalism is an infantile sickness. It is the measles of the human race", still, the point of cultural vision is not to erase diverse cultures or reduce them to a least common denominator, but to enjoy their benefits while transcending prior debits.

As Arundhati Roy argues referring to fundamentalist inclinations to homogenize India, "Once the Muslims have been 'shown their place', will milk and Coca-Cola flow across the land? Once the Ram Mandir is built, will there be a shirt on every back and a roti in every belly? Will every tear be wiped from every eye? Can we expect an anniversary celebration next year? Or will there be someone else to hate by then? Alphabetically: Adivasis, Buddhists, Christians, Dalits, Parsis, Sikhs? Those who wear jeans, or speak English, or those who have thick lips, or curly hair? We won't have to wait long ... What kind of depraved vision can even imagine India without the range and beauty and spectacular anarchy of all these cultures? India would become a tomb and smell like a crematorium."

Instead of the transition to a better world having the effect of homogenizing cultures, historical contributions of different communities should in the future be more appreciated than ever before. They should enjoy greater rather than lesser means for mutually compatible development.

Trying to prevent the horrors of genocide, imperialism, racism, jingoism, ethnocentrism, and religious persecution by attempting to integrate distinct historical communities into one melting pot has proved about as destructive as the evils it seeks to eliminate.

Cultural homogenization annihilates diverse cultural self-management even as it heightens exactly the community anxieties and antagonisms it claims to diminish. Cultural homogenization, whether racist, fundamentalist, or leftist, ignores how cultural differences give people a sense of who they are and where they come from.

Yes, in a competitive and otherwise mutually hostile environment, religious, racial, ethnic, and national communities often develop into sectarian camps, each concerned first and foremost with defending itself from real and imagined threats, even to the point of waging war on others.

And yes, in other contexts, more subtle and less blatant racist expressions occur, as Al Sharpton noted, commenting on racism's changing face in the U.S. after the gains of the civil rights movement: "We've gotten to an era where people are much more subtle and more manicured. Jim Crow is now James Crow, Jr., Esquire".

But the near ubiquitous presence of racial and other overt and covert cultural hierarchies throughout society and history no more means we should eliminate cultural diversity than the existence of overt or covert gender or sexual hierarchies means we should eliminate diversity in those realms. The task is to remove oppression, not obliterate difference.

Racism certainly often has a very crass and material component, as evidenced by Desmond Tutu's comment on the South African experience: "When they arrived, we had the land and they had the Bible and they told us to close our eyes to pray. When we opened our eyes, they had the land and we had the Bible". But economics is not always the dominant theme of racism, and even when economics is highly operative, it is generally only one part of the racial picture. Much of racism, ethnocentrism, nationalism, and religious bigotry emerges from cultural definitions and beliefs that operate beyond material differences.

Dominant community groups rationalize their privilege with myths about their own superiority and the presumed inferiority of those they oppress. These myths attain a life of their own and often transcend material relations. The effects are brutal and distort the views of not only the racist, but also the oppressed. In the American novelist Ralph Ellison's words, "I am an invisible man. No, I am not a spook like those who haunted Edgar Allan Poe; nor am I one of your Hollywood-movie ectoplasms. I am a man of substance, of flesh and bone, fiber and liquids – and I might even be said to possess a mind. I am invisible, understand, simply because people refuse to see me. Like the bodiless heads you see sometimes in circus sideshows, it is as though I have been surrounded by mirrors of hard, distorting glass. When they approach me they see only my surroundings, themselves, or figments of their imagination – indeed, everything and anything except me."

Some elements within oppressed communities internalize myths of their inferiority and attempt to imitate or at least accommodate dominant cultures. As Native American activist Ward Churchill has explained, the white supremacy doctrines in the U.S. are so pervasive that often even American Indian children want to be cowboys. Many in oppressed communities respond by defending the integrity of their own cultural traditions while combating as best they can the racist ideologies that justify their oppression. But as W.E.B. Dubois notes, "It is a peculiar sensation, this double-consciousness, this sense of always looking at one's self through the eyes of others, of measuring one's soul by the tape of a world that looks on in amused contempt and pity". Frederick Douglass made a similar point, arguing that while for a white man to defend his friend unto blood is praiseworthy, for a black man to do precisely the same thing is criminal.

In any event, cultural salvation does not lie in trying to obliterate the distinctions between communities. Instead the only real cultural salvation lies in eliminating racist institutions, dispelling racist ideologies, and changing the environments within which historical communities relate so that they might maintain and celebrate difference without violating solidarity.

An alternative to racism, ethnocentrism, religious bigotry and other forms of community oppression is therefore what we might call "intercommunalism" or "multiculturalism". This alternative emphasizes respecting and preserving the multiplicity of community forms by guaranteeing each of them sufficient material and social resources to maintain itself confidently.

Not only does each culture possess particular wisdom and often language that are unique products of its own historical experience, but the intercommunalist interaction of different cultures enhances the internal characteristics of each in ways that no single approach could ever hope to attain. Negative intercommunity relations are replaced by positive ones, a change that eliminates the threat of cultural extinction faced by so many communities by guaranteeing that every community has the means necessary to carry on its traditions and self-definitions.

Individuals should choose the cultural communities they prefer rather than have elders or others of any description define their choice for them, particularly on the basis of prejudice. While those outside a community should be free to criticize cultural practices that in their opinion violate humane norms, external intervention that goes beyond criticism should not be permitted except to enforce that all members of every community have the right to dissent and to leave without personal loss.

Most important, until a lengthy history of autonomy and solidarity has overcome suspicion and fear between communities, under intercommunalist norms the choice of which community should give ground in disputes between two should be determined to protect whichever of the two is less powerful and therefore, realistically, most threatened. Intercommunalism of this sort would make it incumbent on the more powerful community, with less reason to fear being dominated, to begin unilaterally the process of de-escalating disputes. This simple rule is obvious and reasonable, despite being seldom practiced.

The goal of intercommunalism is to create an environment in which no community will feel threatened so that each will feel free to learn from and share with others. But given the historical legacy of negative intercommunity relations, there is no pretense this can be achieved overnight. Intercommunalist relations will have to be patiently constructed, step by step, until a different historical legacy of behavioral expectations is established. Nor will it always be easy to decide what constitutes the necessary means that communities should be guaranteed for cultural reproduction, and what development free from unwarranted outside interference means, in particular situations.

But the intercommunalist criterion for judging conflicting views seems likely to be that every community should be guaranteed sufficient material and communication means to self-define and self-develop its own cultural traditions and to represent its culture to all other communities in the context of limited aggregate means and equal rights to those means for all.

Race and capitalism

There is nothing in capitalism's defining institutions that says that people in one cultural community should be treated by the economy differently than people in any other, any more than there is anything in capitalism's defining institutions that says people of different heights or with differently pitched voices should be treated differently.

On the contrary, capitalism, unto itself, is what we might call an equal opportunity exploiter. If you have the requisite luck, brutality, or, in rare instances, talents, plus the needed callousness to rise in power and income, then, regardless of any cultural or biological features, you will get to own and profit capitalistically or you will get to monopolize empowering circumstances and enjoy the fruits of being in the coordinator rather than the working class.

On the other hand, if you have none of the requisites of success in capitalism, then regardless of your race, nationality, or religion, you will get to sell yourself as a wage slave doing overwhelmingly rote and obedient work, taking orders, and pocketing only small change.

The less derogatory presentation of this insight is made, for example, by the Nobel prize-winning economist Milton Friedman when he says, "The great virtue of a free market system is that it does not care what color people are; it does not care what their religion is; it only cares whether they can produce something you want to buy. It is the most effective system we have discovered to enable people who hate each other to deal with one another and help one another".

The first part of Friedman's observation is true of capitalism per se, but not of capitalism amidst people who hate each other, which makes the second part of his statement a manipulative lie.

The flaw in Friedman's analysis is that capitalism is not race blind, or religion blind, or ethnicity blind, or blind to any other cultural feature, whenever a society's broader social structures outside the economy consign the holder of the feature to a subordinate or to a dominant cultural position. In such cases, the economic logic of capitalism will notice the extra-economic hierarchy and will operate in light of it rather than ignoring it. Hate outside the economy is not overcome by capitalism, as Friedman implies, but is reproduced and enlarged by capitalism.

If racism in a society, for example, or religious bigotry, or whatever other cultural hierarchy, consigns some community to having less status and influence, in a capitalist economy that community's members will not in general be elevated above their "superiors", but will, instead, generally be made subordinate to them. The economy will use the existing expectations of community members – such as the racist expectation that whites are superior to blacks – to enforce, and, where possible, to enlarge its own economic hierarchies of exploitation. It will not choose to violate those external hierarchies at the potential expense of its own operations.

Thus, the capitalist employer – even one who is personally hostile to racism – will not, in general, if racism is ascendant in the broader society, hire blacks to rule over whites as managers or in other positions of relative influence, but will instead hire whites over blacks. The first choice is rejected because it risks disobedience and dissension. Capitalism, in other words, uses accustomed patterns from cultural life to enhance desired patterns in the economy.

Similarly, if, due to its cultural position, a community can be paid less, it will be paid less in light of market competition to reduce costs, even if that goes against some employer's personal preferences.

At the same time, it is also true that to the extent that growing opposition to racism begins to make racial hierarchies discordant with expectations and conducive to dissent and resistance, capitalist employers will shy away from overt exploitation of race but continue to try to extract any pound of flesh that they can get away with when selling products or buying people's ability to work. Thus in the case of heightened opposition to racism in society, we will see a shift from Jim Crow racism to James Crow Jr. Esquire racism, as noted by Sharpton earlier.

How, then, does a desirable economy reverse such phenomena?

Race and parecon

If a parecon exists in a society that has cultural hierarchies of race, religion, ethnicity, or nationality, what does it contribute? If it instead exists within a society that has desirable communities without hierarchies, what then? In general, does a parecon's needs regarding its own economic operations impose any constraints on cultures?

Change the U.S. economy to a parecon without altering the U.S. racial, religious, and ethnic landscape and you will have a contradiction. Persisting racial and other dynamics will still pit cultural communities against one another and give people expectations of superiority and inferiority. The participatory economy, will, however, violate these expectations tending, instead, to produce solidarity.

Parecon provides income and circumstances inconsistent with cultural hierarchies. It tends to overthrow cultural hierarchies by empowering everyone equally.

People in a parecon can't systemically exploit racism and other cultural injustices economically because there are no economic hierarchies to invest with a racist cast. Individuals in a parecon could try to do this, of course, and they could harbor horrible personal attitudes, of course, but there is no mechanism for racists to accrue undue economic power or wealth, whether as individuals or as members of some community.

If you are black or white, Latino or Italian American, Jewish or Muslim, Presbyterian or Catholic, southerner or northerner – regardless of cultural hierarchies that may exist in the broader society, in a parecon you have a balanced job complex and a just income and self-managing power over your conditions, like everyone else.

Lingering racism or other cultural injustices could penetrate a parecon in the role definitions of actors, but not in a manner that would bestow economic power or material wealth or comforts unfairly. Thus, blacks, Latinos, or Asians in a transformed United States might have statistically different characteristics in their balanced job complexes, but these differences could not violate the social balance of their work. Such culturally-defined job features might have otherwise denigrating attributes, it is true, though one would think that if they did, the self-managing dynamics of the economy would allow those who suffer them to undo the injustices.

Indeed, one can imagine, and even anticipate, that in a parecon, members of minority communities in workplaces would have means to meet together in what are typically called caucuses to guard collectively against denigrating dynamics that might otherwise arise, or to fight against denigrating dynamics that are present as residues from the past or as outgrowths from other spheres of social life. Eliminating income and power hierarchy and respecting cultural caucuses would seem to be about the best one can ask of an economy regarding obstructing cultural injustices.

What about desirable cultures in a desirable society affecting parecon? There is no reason cultural norms established in other parts of society cannot affect economic life in a parecon, and we can predict, I think, that they will. The daily practices of people from different cultural communities who have different customs, religions, ways of celebrating, and moral beliefs, could certainly differ not only in what holidays their members take from work, but in their daily practices during work or in consumption, such as incorporating periods of prayer, or disproportionately engaging in particular types of activity that are culturally proscribed or preferred, or having different diets, etc. There could be whole industries or sectors of the economy that members of a community would avoid for cultural reasons, as with the Amish in the U.S., for example.

However, the special economic needs of cultural communities would have to be consistent with the self-managing desires of those outside those communities as well as within them.

One possibility, for example, is that in more demanding cases it might make sense for members of a workplace to nearly all be from one community so that they can easily share holidays, workday schedules, and daily practices that others would find impossible to abide. Self-management doesn't preclude such arrangements and may occasionally make them ideal.

Alternatively, a workplace may incorporate members of many diverse communities, as will larger and sometimes also smaller consumer units. In such cases there may be very minor mutual accommodations – some members will have days off to celebrate Christmas and others to celebrate Hanukkah or other holidays, or perhaps there would be more extensive accommodations having to do with more frequent differences in schedule or with practices affecting what type of work some people can undertake.

The point is, parecon's workplaces, consumer units, and planning processes provide a very flexible infrastructure whose defining features are designed to be classless, but whose details can vary in endless permutations, including accommodating diverse cultural practices and beliefs.

Finally, how does parecon impose on cultures? Do the needs and requirements of the roles of worker and consumer in a parecon put limits on what practices a culture can use in its own internal affairs?

Cultural communities in a society with a parecon cannot without great friction incorporate internal norms and arrangements that call for material advantages or great power for a few at the expense of many others.

Take for example a culture that elevates priests, artists, soothsayers, elders, or whoever else, and that requires other members to obey these celebrated individuals or even to shower them with gifts. The likelihood that such a cultural community would long persist in a parecon is quite low. This is because people will be spending their economic time in environments that produce personal inclinations for equity, solidarity, and self-management, as well as for diversity.

These environments will school people in respecting but not blindly obeying others. Why would such people then submit to inequitable conditions and skewed decision-making in other parts of their lives?

Assuming that in a good society people will be free to leave cultures – and it is hard to imagine a parecon arising in a society that forbid such personal freedom, since people would have both the economic wherewithal and the knowledge and disposition to manage themselves – we might guess that most people would exercise their freedom to leave any cultural community that denied them the fruits of their labors or denied them their personal empowerment and equality with others. That, at least, is my expectation.

Addendum: Religion and the left

Before closing this chapter, I would like to comment very briefly on the relation between religion and parecon and between religion and the good society.

The interface between religion and parecon adds no complications to what I have said above. All religious people in a society that has a parecon, will, of course, be treated the same by the parecon. They will all enjoy balanced job complexes and just remuneration, and have self-managing decision-making influence.

A parecon will have no economic reason or means to elevate or denigrate people on the basis of any cultural commitments they may have, nor will it be easy, or even possible, for people with hostile cultural intentions to manifest them in a parecon. Likewise, there is nothing in a parecon that says the economy can't respect the holidays and practices of particular communities within the broader framework of attaining economic cooperation. But the question of religions and a good society, as compared to the question of religions and a parecon, is more complex.

Many on the left think this combination is simply impossible. They believe that religion is intrinsically contrary to justice, equity, and, particularly, self-management. Critics of religion think that parecon won't interface with good religions in a good society, because in a good society there won't be any religions at all, good or otherwise.

The anti-religion argument first looks at history and finds an endless procession of religious violations of humane behavior – and no one can deny this sad story. Some anti-religion critics then go another step and look at various scriptures showing all manner of explicitly ugly prescriptions and claims. The critics may highlight instances of religion obstructing reason or art, violating not only free social relations, but honesty and dignity. Finally, at their strongest, the critics will claim to clinch their case by arguing that once one invests extreme powers in a god and requires obedience unto those powers, it is but a short and virtually inexorable step to counterposing one's own god against others' gods and counterposing one's own fellow believers against believers of some other faith, finally moving from obedience to a god, to obedience to agents of a god, and then to obedience to authorities of all kinds.

This argument, one has to admit, is not weak, either in its predictive logic or in its historical explanatory power or predictive verification, but I think it is also, in the end, overstated because it generalizes about all religions based on the actions and beliefs of some religions, and it applies its condemnation of organized authoritarian religions to spirituality of all kinds.

My own inclination is to think that a good society will have good religion, but not no religion, just as a good society will have good economics, but not no economics, and will have good politics, but not no politics, and so on.

As to what shape such good religions will have – I would imagine they will vary widely, emerging from religions we now know as well as arising in new forms, but generally having in common a desire to establish rich and robust morals and an inspiring sense of place in the universe without, however, violating the morals and roles of the rest of a just society.

I can't say more about what that will look like. But though it is outside the bounds of this chapter, and certainly an area where my views are far from carefully developed and tested, I would like to say one more thing about religion and the left.

In my view a movement in the U.S., and no doubt in many other countries around the world as well, in which members are dismissive of, and even hostile toward, religion, is simply a losing movement.

Even if one isn't convinced that a good religion in a good society will be a positive thing in many people's lives, and if one thinks instead that the best stance is to be agnostic or even highly critical of religion in any form, and even if one is not humble enough to hold that view and yet simultaneously respect that others will differ with it and deserve respect in doing so, surely a serious leftist ought to be able to see that denigrating all things religious is strategic suicide in a society as religious as the U.S. Whatever views one may have, if one wants to help build a large participatory and self-managing movement in the U.S., one must find a way to function congenially and respectfully with those who celebrate and worship in a religious manner. The alternative is to close off not only religion, but a huge proportion of the population that one is presumably trying to relate to. Trying to be an organizer in the U.S. if you denigrate religion is not much wiser than trying to be an organizer in France if you denigrate people who speak French.

In any event, even short of having a full and convincing vision for a future cultural sphere of life, it seems that we can deduce with good confidence that parecon will compatibly foster and benefit cultural innovations, rather than obstructing them.

5 Internationalism

For this chapter, to take a different angle on things, let's begin with what we currently endure internationally and ask what changes we would like to win with our activism, short and mid term. Then we can see what our aspirations for international relations imply for economics per se, and, in turn, what our proposed new economic vision implies for international relations.

Rejecting capitalist globalization

Current international market trading overwhelmingly benefits those who enter today's exchanges already possessing the most assets. When trade occurs between a U.S. multinational and a local entity in Guatemala, Kenya, or Thailand, the benefits do not go more to the weaker party with fewer assets, nor are they divided equally, but they go disproportionately to the stronger traders who thereby increase their relative dominance.

Opportunist rhetoric aside, capitalist globalizers try to disempower the poor and already weak and to further empower the rich and already strong. The result: of the 100 largest economies in the world, over half aren't countries, they are corporations, and tens of millions of people throughout the world not only live in abysmal poverty, but starve to death each year.

Similarly, international market competition for resources, revenues, and audience is most often a zero sum game. To advance, each market participant preys off the defeat of others, so that capitalist globalization promotes a me-first attitude that generates hostility and destroys solidarity between individuals, corporations, industries, and states. Public and social goods are downplayed, private ones are elevated. Businesses, industries, and nations augment their own profits while imposing losses on other countries and even on most citizens of their own country. Human well-being is not a guiding precept.

Moreover, in current global exchange structures, whether they are

McDonaldsesque or Disneyesque, or even if they instead derive from worthy indigenous roots, cultural communities and values disperse only as widely as their reach permits them to, and worse, are routinely drowned out by other communities with greater reach.

Capitalist globalization swamps quality with quantity. It creates cultural homogenization, not diversity. Not only does Starbucks proliferate, so do Hollywood images and Madison Avenue styles. What is indigenous and non-commercial must struggle even to survive. Diversity declines.

In the halls of the capitalist globalizers, only political and corporate elites are welcome. The idea that the broad public of working people, consumers, farmers, the poor, and the disenfranchised should have proportionate say is actively opposed. Indeed, the point of capitalist globalization is precisely to reduce the influence of whole populations, and even of state leaderships, save for the most powerful elements of Western corporate and political rule. Capitalist globalization imposes corporatist hierarchy not only in economics, but also in politics. Authoritarian and even fascistic state structures proliferate. The number of voices with even marginal say declines.

As the financiers in corporate headquarters extend stockholders' influence, the earth beneath is dug, drowned, and paved without attention to other species, to by-products, to ecology, or even to humanity. Only profit and power drive the calculations.

Anti-globalization activists oppose capitalist globalization because capitalist globalization violates the equity, diversity, solidarity, self-management, and ecological balance that activists favor.

Capitalist globalization also establishes norms and expectations of international dominance and subordination. To establish, enforce, defend, and punish violations of those norms, the strong will often use violence against the weak. Domestically this means larger police state apparatuses and more repression. Internationally it means local, regional, and international hostilities and war.

So the question naturally arises, what is the alternative to capitalist globalization violating, as it does, virtually all norms of civilized and mutually beneficial exchange and development?

Supporting global justice

What do anti-globalization activists propose to put in place of the institutions of capitalist globalization, most prominently the International Monetary Fund, the World Bank, and the World Trade Organization?

The International Monetary Fund, or IMF, and the World Bank were established after World War II. The IMF was meant to provide means to combat financial disruptions adversely impacting countries and people around the world. It initially used negotiation and pressure to stabilize currencies and help countries avoid economy-disrupting financial machinations and confusion.

The World Bank was meant to facilitate long-term investment in underdeveloped countries and to expand and strengthen their economies. It was set up to lend major investment money at low interest to correct for the lack of local capacity.

Within then existing market relations, these limited IMF and World Bank goals were progressive. Over time, however, and accelerating dramatically in the 1980s, the agenda of these institutions changed. Instead of facilitating stable exchange rates and helping countries protect themselves against financial fluctuations, the IMF began bashing any and all obstacles to capital flow and unfettered profit seeking, despite the fact this was virtually the opposite of its mandate.

Instead of facilitating investment on behalf of local poor economies, the World Bank became a tool of the IMF, providing and withholding loans as carrot or stick to compel open corporate access. It financed projects not with an eye to accruing benefits for the recipient country, but with far more attention to accruing benefits to major multinationals.

In addition, the World Trade Organization (WTO) that was first proposed in the early postwar period actually came into being only decades later, in the mid 1990s. Its agenda became to regulate trade to the ever greater advantage of the already rich and powerful.

Beyond imposing on third world countries low wages and high pollution due to being able to coerce their weak or bought-off governments (as IMF and World Bank policies were already achieving by the 1990s), the idea then emerged that the rich could also weaken governments and agencies that might defend workers, consumers, or the environment, not only in the third world, but everywhere. Why not, wondered the truly powerful, remove any efforts to limit trade due to its labor implications, its ecology implications, its social or cultural implications, or its developmental implications, leaving as the only legal criterion of trade's regulation whether there are immediate, short-term profits to be made? If national or local laws impede trade – say an environmental, health, or labor law – why not have a new organization of world trade to adjudicate disputes, and to render an entirely predictable pro-corporate verdict in all cases? The WTO was thus added to the IMF/World Bank team to trump governments and populations on behalf of corporate profits.

The full story of these three centrally important global institutions is longer than this brief synopsis can present, of course, but even with only an overview, improvements are not hard to conceive.

First, why not have, instead of the IMF, the World Bank, and the WTO, an International Asset Agency, a Global Investment Assistance Agency, and a World Trade Agency? These three new (not merely reformed) institutions would work to attain equity, solidarity, diversity, self-management, and ecological balance in international financial exchange, investment, development, trade, and cultural exchange.

They would try to ensure that the benefits of trade and investments accrue disproportionately to the weaker and poorer parties involved, not to the already richer and more powerful.

They would not prioritize commercial considerations over all other values, but would prioritize national aims, cultural identity, and equitable development.

They would not require domestic laws, rules, and regulations designed to further worker, consumer, environmental, health, safety, and human rights, animal protection, or other non-profit centered interests, to be reduced or eliminated, but they would work to enhance all these, rewarding those who attain such aims most successfully.

They would not undermine democracy by shrinking the choices available to democratically controlled governments, but would work to subordinate the desires of multinationals and large economies to the survival, growth, and diversification of smaller units.

They would not promote global trade at the expense of local economic development and policies, but vice versa.

They would not force Third World countries to open their markets to rich multinationals and to abandon efforts to protect infant domestic industries, but would facilitate the reverse.

They would not block countries from acting in response to potential risks to human health or the environment, but would help identify health, environmental, and other risks, and assist countries in guarding against their ill effects.

Instead of downgrading international health, environmental, and other standards to a low level through a process called "downward harmonization", they would work to upgrade standards by means of a new "upward equalization".

The new institutions would not limit governments' ability to use their purchasing dollars for human, environmental, and worker rights, and other non-commercial purposes, but would advise and facilitate doing just that.

They would not disallow countries treating products differently based on how they were produced – whether they were made with brutalized child labor, with workers exposed to toxins, or with no regard for species protection – but they would instead facilitate just such differentiations.

Instead of bankers and bureaucrats carrying out policies of presidents to shape the lives of the very many without even a pretense at participation by the people affected, these new institutions would be open, democratic, transparent, participatory, and bottom up, with local, popular, and democratic accountability.

These new institutions would promote and organize international cooperation to restrain out-of-control global corporations, capital, and markets by regulating them so people in local communities could control their own economic lives.

They would promote trade that reduces the threat of financial volatility and meltdown, expands democracy at every level from the local to the global, defends and enriches human rights for all people, respects and fosters environmental sustainability worldwide, and facilitates economic advancement of the most oppressed and exploited groups.

They would encourage domestic economic growth and development, not domestic austerity in the interest of export-led growth.

They would encourage the major industrial countries to coordinate their economic policies, currency exchange rates, and short-term capital flows in the public interest and not for private profit.

They would establish standards for, and oversee the regulation of, financial institutions by national and international regulatory authorities, encouraging the shift of financial resources from speculation to useful and sustainable development.

They would establish taxes on foreign currency transactions to reduce destabilizing short-term cross-border financial flows and to provide pools of funds for investment in long-term environmentally and socially sustainable development in poor communities and countries.

They would create public international investment funds to meet human and environmental needs and ensure adequate global demand by channeling funds into sustainable long-term investment.

And they would develop international institutions to perform functions of monetary regulation currently inadequately performed by national central banks, such as a system of internationally coordinated minimum reserve requirements on the consolidated global balance sheets of all financial firms.

These new institutions would also work to get wealthy countries to write off the debts of impoverished countries and to create a permanent insolvency mechanism for adjusting debts of highly indebted nations.

They would use regulatory institutions to help establish public control and citizen sovereignty over global corporations and to curtail corporate evasion of local, state, and national law, such as by establishing a binding Code of Conduct for Transnational Corporations that would include regulation of labor, environmental, investment, and social behavior.

And beyond all the above, in addition to getting rid of the IMF, World Bank, and WTO and replacing them with the three dramatically new and different structures outlined above, anti-globalization activists also advocate a recognition that international relations should not derive from centralized but rather from bottom-up institutions. The new overarching structures mentioned above should therefore gain their credibility and power from an array of arrangements, structures, and ties enacted at the level of citizens, neighborhoods, states, nations and groups of nations on which they rest. And these more grassroots structures, alliances, and bodies defining debate and setting agendas should, like the three described earlier, also be transparent, participatory and democratic, and guided by a mandate that prioritizes equity, solidarity, diversity, self-management, and ecological sustainability and balance.

The overall idea is simple. The problem isn't international relations per se. Anti-corporate globalization activists are, in fact, internationalist. The problem is that capitalist globalization alters international relations to further benefit the rich and powerful.

In contrast, activists want to alter relations to weaken the rich and powerful and empower and improve the conditions of the poor and weak. Anti-corporate globalization activists know what we want internationally – global justice in place of capitalist globalization. But if that is what we want internationally, what implications does it have for what we want domestically, inside our own countries?

Participatory economics not capitalist greed

There is still a vision problem for anti-globalization activists, even after we describe alternative global economic institutions. Everyone knows that international norms and structures don't drop from the sky. It is certainly true that once in existence they impose severe constraints on domestic arrangements and choices, but it is also true that global relations sit on top of, and are propelled and enforced by, the dictates of domestic economies and institutions.

The IMF, World Bank, and WTO impose capitalist institutions such as markets and corporations on countries around the world, of course. But the existence of markets and corporations in countries around the world likewise propels capitalist globalization.

So when anti-globalization activists offer a vision for a people-serving and democracy-enhancing internationalism in place of capitalist globalization, we are proposing to place a very good International Asset Agency, Global Investment Assistance Agency, and Global Trade Agency, plus a foundation of more grassroots democratic and transparent institutions, on top of the very bad domestic economies we currently endure. The problem is that the persisting domestic structures inside our countries would continually work against the new international structures we construct on top of them. Persisting corporations and multinationals would not positively augment and enforce our preferred new international structures, but would at best temporarily succumb to pressures to install them and then perpetually exert pressures to return to their more rapacious ways.

So when people ask anti-globalization activists "what are you for?" they actually aren't asking only what we are for internationally. They also mean, what are we for in place of capitalism?

If we have capitalism, they reason, there will inevitably be tremendous pressures for capitalist globalization and against anti-capitalist innovations. The new IAA, GIAA, and GTA sound nice, but even if we put them in place, the domestic economies of countries around the world would push to undo them.

Capitalist globalization is, after all, domestic markets, corporations, and class structure on a large scale. To replace capitalist globalization and not just mitigate its effects, we would have to replace capitalism too. Reducing or ameliorating corporate globalization via the proposed new international institutions shouldn't be an end in itself, but should be part of a larger project to transform the underlying root capitalist structures as well.

If we have no alternative to markets and corporations, many feel, our gains would be at best temporary. This assessment is widely held and fuels the reactionary slogan that "there is no alternative".

To combat this mentality and underlying reality we need an alternative vision regarding international agencies and global economics, such as the proposed new institutions, but also an alternative vision regarding markets, corporations, and domestic economies.

Capitalist economics revolves around private ownership of the means of production, market allocation, and corporate divisions of labor. Remuneration is for property, power, and, to a limited extent, contribution to output, all causing huge differences in wealth and income. Class divisions arise due to differential property ownership and differential access to empowered versus obedient work. Huge differences exist in decision-making influence and in quality of circumstances. Buyers and sellers one-up each other, and the broader public reaps what self-interested competition sows. Antisocial trajectories of investment and personality development result. Decision-making ignores or exploits ecological decay. Reduced ecological diversity results.

To transcend capitalism, suppose we were to advocate the same values I proposed above for global assessments: equity, solidarity, diversity, self-management, and ecological balance. What institutions could propel these values in domestic economics, as well as admirably accomplish economic functions?

Of course in this book our answer is parecon and we don't need to repeat the first chapter's summary of its features save in a very abbreviated form.

In a new economy consistent with just international relations, all citizens own each workplace in equal part. This ownership conveys no special right or income. Bill Gates won't own a massive proportion of the means by which software is produced. We will all own it, or symmetrically, no one will own it. Ownership becomes moot regarding distribution of income, wealth, or power.

Next, workers and consumers will be organized into democratic councils that disperse information and arrive at and tally preferences in ways that convey to each participant influence over decisions in proportion to the degree he or she will be affected by them.

Councils will be the seat of decision-making power at many levels, including work groups and teams and individuals, and workplaces and whole industries. People in councils will be the economy's decision-makers. Votes could be majority rule, three-quarters, two-thirds, consensus, etc.

Next, we alter the organization of work by changing who does what tasks in what combinations. What changes from current corporate divisions of labor to a preferred future division of labor is that the variety of tasks each actor does is balanced for its empowerment and quality of life implications.

Balanced job complexes complete the task of removing the root basis for class divisions, begun by eliminating private ownership of capital. Balanced job complexes eliminate not only the role of owner/capitalist and its disproportionate power and wealth, but also the role of decision-making coordinator who exists over and above all other workers. Balanced job complexes apportion conceptual and empowering and also rote and un-empowering responsibilities more equitably and in tune with true democracy and classlessness.

Next comes remuneration. In this new vision we receive for our labors an amount in tune with how hard we have worked, how long we have worked, and what sacrifices we have made while doing our work. This is morally appropriate and also provides proper incentives, rewarding only what we can affect, not what we can't.

With balanced job complexes, for eight hours of normally paced work Sally and Sam receive the same income. This is so if they have the same job, or any job at all, because no matter what their particular job may be, no matter what workplaces they are in and how different their mix of tasks is, and no matter how talented they are, if they work at a balanced job complex, their total work load will be similar in its quality of life implications and empowerment effects, so the only difference specifically relevant to reward for their labors is going to be the duration and intensity of work done; if we assume these are the same, then the share of output earned will also be equal. On the other hand, if duration of time working or intensity of work differ somewhat, so too will the share of output earned.

There is one very large step remaining, even to offering merely a broad outline of economic vision. How are the actions of workers and consumers connected? How do decisions made in workplaces, and by collective consumer councils, as well as by individual consumers, all come into accord? What causes the total produced by workplaces to match the total consumed collectively by neighborhoods and other groups and privately by individuals? For that matter, what determines the relative social valuation of different products and choices? What decides how many workers will be working in which industry producing how much? What determines whether some product should be made or not, and how much? What determines what investments in new productive means and methods should be undertaken and which others delayed or rejected? These are all matters of allocation.

Suppose that in place of top-down imposition of centrally planned choices and competitive market exchange by atomized buyers and sellers, in accord with extending the logic of our internationalism into our domestic economies, we opt for cooperative, informed choosing by organizationally and socially entwined actors, each having a say in proportion as choices impact on them, each able to access needed accurate information and valuations, and each having appropriate training and confidence to develop and communicate their preferences. That would be consistent with council centered participatory self-management, with remuneration for effort and sacrifice, with balanced job complexes, with proper valuations of collective and ecological impacts, and with classlessness.

To these ends, global activists turning their attention to domestic economics might favor participatory planning – a system in which worker and consumer councils propose work activities and consumer preferences in light of accurate knowledge of local and national implications and true valuations of the full social benefits and costs of their choices.

The system utilizes a back-and-forth cooperative communication of mutually informed preferences, via indicative prices, which convey summary information about relative valuations; facilitation boards which process and communicate preferences and other data; rounds of accommodation to new information, in which actors cooperatively negotiate with one another; and so on.

Thus the core of a new economic vision, parecon, that is consistent with the aspirations of anti-corporate globalization activism, is:

- Democratic workplace and consumer councils for equitable participation;

- Diverse decision-making procedures seeking proportionate say for those affected by decisions;

- Balanced job complexes creating just distribution of empowering and dis-empowering circumstances;

- Remuneration for effort and sacrifice in accord with admirable moral and efficient incentive logic;

- Participatory planning, in tune with economics serving human well-being and development.

The implications of parecon for international relations

Now suppose we approach the problem of this chapter – the relations between a domestic parecon and international relations – from the opposite direction. What are parecon's implications for international relations?

First, the pressure of capitalism to conquer ever-expanding market share and to scoop up ever-widening sources of resources and labor is removed. There is no drive to accumulate per se, and there is no tendency to expand market share endlessly or to exploit international profit-making opportunities, because there is no profit-making. The sources of imperialism and neo-colonialism, not merely some of their symptoms, are removed, at least in the country with the parecon.

If the whole world has participatory economies, then nothing structural prevents treating countries like one might treat locales – neighborhoods, counties, states – within countries. And likewise, there is no structural obstacle to approaching the production side similarly, seeing the world as one entwined international system.

Whether this would occur or not, or at what pace, are matters for the future. It certainly seems to be the natural and logical international long-run extension of domestic advocacy of parecon. If balanced job complexes and equitable distribution in light of the total social output are morally and economically sound choices in one country, why not balance across countries and relate incomes based on effort and sacrifice to international output so as to attain international equity?

Likewise, if it makes sense to plan each country in a negotiated participatory manner, why wouldn't it make sense to do that, as well, for interactions from country to country?

Of course, even with the structural obstacles emanating from capitalist relations of production gone, and even assuming cultural and political forms would allow, or even welcome, extending the logic of domestic parecons to a worldwide participatory economy, the remaining difficulty is the magnitude of the inter-nation gaps that would need to be overcome.

Even if one wanted to, one simply cannot sanely equilibrate income and job quality between a developed and an underdeveloped society, short of massive and time consuming campaigns of construction, development, and education. Moreover, if there are some parecons, and some capitalist economies, the situation is still more difficult, with gaps existing in development and also in social relations.

So the real issue about parecon and international relations becomes: as countries adopt participatory economies domestically, what happens to their trade and other policies with still capitalist countries?

No outcome is inevitable. We can conceive, I suppose, of a country with a parecon that is rapacious regarding the rest of the world. It is difficult to imagine, yes, but not utterly inconceivable. What we are assessing is a policy choice.

How should a parecon interact with other countries who do not share its logic of economic organization and practice?

A good answer seems to me to be implicit in the whole earlier discussion of international global policies. The idea ought to be to engage in trade and other relations in ways that diminish gaps of wealth and power.

One obvious proposal is that the parecon trades with other countries at market prices or at parecon prices, depending on which choice does a better job of redressing wealth and power inequalities.

A second proposal would be that a parecon engage in a high degree of socially responsible aid to other countries less well off than itself.

A third proposal would be that a parecon supports movements seeking to attain participatory economic relations elsewhere.

There is every reason to think the workers and consumers of a parecon would have the kind of social solidarity with other people that would drive them to embark on just these kinds of policies...but such actions would involve a choice, made in the future, not reflect an inexorable constraint that is imposed on society by a systemic economic pressure.

The long and short of this chapter is that seeking just international relations leads, rather inexorably, toward seeking just domestic relations, and vice versa. Parecon fulfills both agendas.

 Ecology

Economies and the environment

Economies add new contents to the environment, such as pollutants. They deplete contents from the environment, such as natural resources. They alter the arrangement and composition of attributes in the environment, or the way in which people relate to the environment, for example, by building dams or creating changed patterns of human habitation, and countless other possibilities. And each of these and other possible ways of an economy affecting the environment can, in turn, have ripple effects on nature's composition and people's lives.

Thus, an economy can add economic byproducts to the environment – for example, exhaust fumes spew from cars; smoke stacks force chemicals to accumulate in the atmosphere. In turn these effluents can impede breathing or alter the way the sun's rays affect atmospheric temperatures. Both these economic implications can in turn affect people's health, or change air currents which impact on sea currents which in turn affect polar ice caps, altering weather patterns, sea levels, and crop yields, and dramatically affecting human options and conditions.

Or an economy can use up oil, water, or forests, leading to people having to reduce their use of depleted resources, thus affecting the total level of production and consumption around the world, or the availability of nutrients essential to life or of building materials needed for dwellings in many parts of the world.

Or an economy can alter the shape and content of the natural environment's dynamics, as for example when by reducing forests we reduce the supply of oxygen they emit into the atmosphere, or when by increasing the number of cows and affecting their eating patterns (to produce more tasty steak for ourselves) we increase the methane they expel, which leads to greenhouse effects that in turn alter global weather patterns, or when we alter human housing patterns and thus transport patterns and other consumption patterns and attitudes, affecting people's on-going relations to mountains, rivers, air, and other species.

In the above cases, and also countless others affecting the supply or the quality of weather, air, water, or even noise, globally or regionally, or affecting resource availability, or even affecting the availability of enjoyable natural environments, what we do in our economic lives affects, either directly or by a many-step process, how we prosper or suffer environmentally in our daily lives, as well as how the environment itself adapts.

In other words, economic acts have direct, secondary, and tertiary affects on the environment, and the changed environment in turn has direct, secondary, and tertiary effects on our life conditions.

Sometimes these effects are quite tremendous, as in seas rising to swallow coastal areas and even whole low-lying countries, or as in crop, resource, or water depletion causing starvation or other extreme widespread deprivations. Or maybe the effects are slightly less severe as in tornadoes and hurricanes devastating large swaths of population, or inflated cancer rates caused by polluted ground water, or escalated radiation cutting down large numbers of people early in life, or dams eliminating whole towns, or villages washed away by newly constructed lakes. Or maybe the effects are limited to smaller areas which suffer the loss of enriching surroundings when natural environments are tarred over or noise pollution arises from loud production methods.

It follows from all these possibilities that the relations of an economy to the surrounding natural environment are deadly serious, and that to fail regarding relations to the environment – even if succeeding on all other criteria – would be a damning weakness for any proposed economic model.

Capitalism fails quite miserably regarding the environment. First, capitalism's market system prioritizes maximizing short-run profit regardless of long-run implications. Second, markets exclude environmental effects from decisions and have built in incentives to violate the environment whenever doing so will yield profits or, for that matter, consumer fulfillment at the cost of others. And, third, there is the capitalist drive to accumulate regardless of effects on life.

In markets a seller encounters a buyer. The seller tries to get as high a price as possible for the object sold while also reducing costs of production. The goal is to maximize profits, which in turn not only yield higher income, but also facilitate competition-enhancing investments that win market share and preserve business.

The buyer, meanwhile, tries to pay as little as possible for an item and then to consume it with as much fulfillment as possible, regardless of the impact of these actions on others about whom little or no information is available.

For both parties, market exchange obscures the effects their choices have beyond the buyer and seller and prevents taking into account the well being of those who feel these external effects.

If some course of action will lower the cost of producing an item, or will increase the fulfillment of its consumption, but will also incur environmental degradation that affects someone other than the buyer or seller, that course of action will be undertaken. We routinely use production techniques that pollute, and we also routinely consume items with no regard for environmental impact.

Rock salt, it turns out, is a very effective tool for "keeping both private drive-ways and public highways from icing up". Andrew Bard Schmookler reports that "…the runoff of the salt…causes damage to underground cables, car bodies, bridges, and groundwater. The cost of these damages is twenty to forty times the price of the salt to the persons or organization buying and using it". In other words, rock salt has unaccounted adverse effects beyond the buyers and sellers who choose to produce it, sell it, buy it, and use it, to keep roads from icing up. Schmookler then reports that "there is an alternative product to rock salt that produces no such damage from runoff. It is called CMA, and it costs a good deal more than the salt. It costs less, however, than the damages the salt inflicts". But "no highway department, homeowner, or business would purchase large quantities of CMA today even if it were widely available, because the individual doesn't care about [social] cost, only [about private] price". In other words, markets create incentives to violate the environment, and anything else external to the buyer and seller, whenever doing so will enhance the producer's profit.

This is just one of countless examples, chosen for its clarity, and as Schmookler rightly concludes, it shows that market forces "will make changes flow in a predictable direction, like water draining off the land, downhill, to the sea". That is, sellers will use production methods that spew pollution but that cost less than using clean technologies, or they will use production methods that damage groundwater or use up resources but that cost less than methods that don't, or they will use production methods that build into products secondary effects which consumers who buy the product won't directly suffer but others will, and which cost less. And the same logic will typically hold for consumer choices about how to utilize the items they have bought. The impact of their use on others will most often be unknown and ignored.

And it isn't only that in each transaction the participants have an incentive to find the cheapest, most profitable course of production and the most personally fulfilling course of consumption; it is that markets compel the absolute maxi-mum of exchanges. There is a drive to buy and sell, even beyond the direct benefits of doing so, because each producer is weighing off not the benefits of a little more income versus a little more leisure due to working less but, instead, the benefits of staying in business versus going out of business. That is, each actor competes for market share to gain surpluses with which to invest to reduce future costs, pay for future advertising, etc., and these surpluses must be maximized in the present lest one is out-competed in the future.

The race for market share becomes a drive to amass profit without respite, which means to do so even beyond what the greed of owners might otherwise entail.

It is one thing to understand the above theoretically, and even to see the frantic, depleting, spewing results all around us. It is another thing to hear the impetus described by those who suffer its force, and I should like to relate such an experience.

I had lunch once with a fellow who had been, not that long before, a four hundred dollar an hour senior partner in a large and lucrative law firm in Boston, Massachusetts. He had quit his position to take a job with a non-profit organization that did fundraising and direct mail work for progressive clients, candidates, and others, which is what brought me and him together for lunch. At one point I asked him why he had made such a dramatic and income-reducing change. He replied that while it was in part due to wanting to do socially valuable work rather than winning large fortunes for already overly fortunate corporate clients, he could not claim that that was the only reason. He had been seeking to escape his old lucrative employment not just because he had lost a taste for the clients and their skullduggery, but also due to self-interest. He wanted a life.

He told me that in his prior job, while he had tremendous income, he had to work seventy and even eighty hours a week and more, which left him too little time to live. He wanted more time off.

But, I said – knowing the theoretical answer well – why didn't he just work less? He was a boss, after all. Why didn't he pack up and go home each week after fifty hours, or forty, or, jeez, given his income, after thirty or even twenty if he wanted more leisure time with his family?

He chuckled and said it was because his choice was always more work hours or no work hours, not more work hours or fewer work hours. The firm competed with other firms. The competition occurred not only in the obvious form of having excellent lawyers (by the standards of the clients, which included the lawyers being steeped in the ways and tastes of the clients and being able to wine and dine them, speak their language and hold their hands), but also in all the material accoutrements. If the firm started to take in less revenue and have less funds available for its lawyers to attain lofty living standards that marked them as rich and successful, and less funds for the firm to purchase rugs, wall hangings, high-end parties, meetings, high rent occupancy, and high-end travel costs, and to afford maximum expenditures on experts, and so on, in short order its clients would begin to switch to other firms better able to serve their every need. However slight it might be at first, this shift of clients would snowball over time. A few less clients means a little less surplus, which in turn means less wining and dining, and then more lost clients, and so on.

My friend explained to me, in other words, how even in competing law firms, not only in competing auto plants, the drive to amass revenues to retain, and if possible enhance, market share, was ever present and permanent. It could be bent somewhat, but only by pressures which worked equally across all firms, such as the collective bargaining power of workers. But wherever market pressure could bend people's wills to accumulate ever more via more intense and longer work, it would do so. In his case, if other bosses in other law firms would work longer – and surely there were many who had so reconstructed themselves that doing so was their reason for being – then he would have to do so in his firm as well. And the only way to break free of that pressure was to escape completely, as he had done, with another aspiring corporate climber taking his place.

In all market systems, and particularly in capitalist markets, growth is god. The guiding philosophy is grow or die, regardless of contrary personal inclinations. This not only violates attentiveness to sustainability of resources but also produces a steadily escalating flow of garbage and pollution. Transactions multiply, and in each transaction the incentive to pollute and otherwise violate the environment persists. In the end, what we get is an economy spewing into, using up, and damaging the environment on a massive scale – ranging from turning communities into dump sites, making cities sick with smog, polluting ground waters all of which escalate cancer rates, or causing global warming that threatens not only raging storms but even vast upheavals of ocean levels and agriculture, with untold costs to follow.

Parecon's alternative approach

Will a participatory economy be any better for the environment than capitalism? The answer is yes, for a number of reasons.

First, in a parecon there is no pressure to accumulate. Each producer is not compelled to try to expand surplus in order to compete with other producers for market share; instead, the level of output reflects a true mediation between desires for more consumption and desires for a lower overall amount of work.

In other words, whereas in capitalism the labor/leisure trade off is biased heavily toward more production at all times, due to the need for overall growth to avoid shrinkage and failure, in parecon it is an actual, real, unbiased trade off.

In a parecon we each face a choice between increasing the overall duration and intensity of our labor to increase our consumption budget, or, instead, working less to increase our overall time available to enjoy labor's products and the rest of life's options. And since society as a whole faces this exact same choice, we can reasonably predict that instead of a virtually limitless drive to increase work hours and intensity, a parecon will have no drive to accumulate output beyond levels that meet needs and develop potentials, and will therefore stabilize at much lower output and work levels – say thirty hours of work a week, and eventually, even less. Interestingly, and revealingly, some mainstream economists view the fact that in a parecon people will decide their work levels, and will likely decide on less than now, as a flaw, rather than celebrating it as a virtue, which is of course my view.

The second issue is one of valuation. Unlike in capitalism, as well as with markets more generally, participatory planning doesn't have each transaction determined only by the person who directly produces and the person who directly consumes, with each of these participants having structural incentives to maximize personal benefits regardless of the broader social impact. Instead, every act of production and consumption in a parecon is part of a total overall economic plan. The interrelations of each actor with all other actors, and of each action with all other actions, are not just real and highly consequential – which is of course always true – but are also properly accounted for.

In a parecon, production or consumption of gas, cigarettes, and other items with either positive or negative effects on people beyond the buyer and seller, take into account those effects. The same holds for decisions about larger projects, for example, building a dam, installing wind turbines, or cutting back on certain resources. Projects are amended in light of feedback from affected councils at all levels of society, from individuals and neighborhoods through countries or states to the whole population.

The social procedures which facilitate all this ecological rationality are summarized in considerable detail in the book *Parecon: Life after Capitalism*. The bottom line is relatively simple, however. By eliminating the market drive to accumulate and to have only a short time horizon, and by eliminating market-induced ignorance of economic effects that extend beyond buyers and sellers (such as on the environment) and the consequent market mispricing of items, parecon properly accounts for, and provides means to self-manage environmental impacts sensibly.

It isn't that there is no pollution in a parecon. And it isn't that no non-renewable items are ever used. These norms would make no sense. You can't produce without some waste, and you can't prosper without using up some resources.

Rather, what is necessary is that when production or consumption generates negative effects on the environment, or when it uses up resources that we value and cannot replace, the decision to do these things is made taking into account the implications.

We should not transact when the benefits don't outweigh the detriments. And we should not transact unless the distribution of benefits and detriments is just, rather than some people suffering unduly.

This is what parecon via participatory planning accomplishes ecologically and this is really all we can ask an economy to do by its own internal logic. We don't want the economy to prejudge outcomes through the pressure of its institutional dynamics that humans have no say in, as, for example, the accumulation drive propelled by markets decides the labor/leisure trade-off. We want a good economy to use its institutions to let people who are affected make their own judgments, with the best possible knowledge of true and full costs and benefits, and bringing to bear appropriate self-managing influence. If the economy presents this spectrum of possibility and control to its actors, as parecon does, what is left to assess is what people will then likely decide, and on that score all that we can ask of an economy is that people not be biased by institutional pressures or made ignorant due to institutional biases. Parecon guarantees both of these aims. Parecon also provides for people to be free and self-managing, and ensures that the logic of the economy is consistent with, and possibly even conducive to, the richest possible human comprehension of ecological connections and options.

Under these circumstances, it is reasonable to think that parecon's citizens will not only make wise choices for their own interests, but for their children and grandchildren as well, regarding not only direct production and consumption, but also the myriad ripple effects of economic activity on the environment.

Other species

We live on a planet – the earth – which is a gigantic rock swirling in space around an almost unfathomably larger and hugely energy generating sphere of combustion – the sun – in an even vaster sea of similar entities born billions of years ago and maturing ever since. We share the bounty or resources and energy of our planet and the sun's rays with a huge diversity of other species, who themselves contribute in a multitude of ways to defining how the planet produces, processes, and presents its assets to us.

Indeed, our own existence arose from a sequence of other species modified by chance occurrences and selected by dynamics of cooperation and competition, and our existence depends for its continuation on a vast number of current species as well.

A capitalist economy views other species as it does everything else, in terms of their profit-making possibilities. If directly preserving or nurturing a species is profitable, capitalists do it. If ignoring another species and leaving it to its own wiles is profitable, capitalists do that. If directly consuming or indirectly obliterating another species is profitable, again, that is the capitalist way to go.

Capitalist market competition looks around and assesses profitable possibilities and pursues them. If we add to capitalist economy governments or other agencies with priorities other than profit, they may ameliorate many ills, though if these bodies significantly defy or impede profit-making, it will be difficult for them to maintain themselves against the logic of capitalist accumulation. This occurs both because the economy fights back against efforts to restrain accumulation and because capitalism tends to produce a population unreceptive to even thinking about the long-term benefits of other species to people, much less the independent rights of other species.

These insights encapsulate the well known history of environmental concerns. The results we see around us are indicative of the destruction wrought by profit-seeking pressures.

What would replace capitalism's possibly suicidal and certainly horribly gory interspecies relations if we instead had a parecon?

First, a parecon would move us from profit as the guiding norm of economic choice to human fulfillment and well-being in accord with solidarity, diversity, equity, and self-management.

Second, parecon would move us from having a driving profit-seeking logic that constantly overpowers and undoes any ecologically or otherwise non profit-justified restrictions placed on the economy, to being instead flexibly responsive to constraints imposed by forces and concerns that are not economic.

Third, parecon moves its producers and consumers from having a very narrow and fragmented approach to economy, to comprehending instead the interconnectedness of all acts and their multiple implications.

And fourth, parecon moves us from a me-first, anti-social interpersonal mindset that can easily extend beyond relations to people toward relations to nature, to a solidaristic interpersonal mindset, which can plausibly extend to nature and species as well.

The first point is a change of guiding logic or motivation. The second point is a change in its intensity. Together they ensure that parecon doesn't have the negative impetus toward other species typical of capitalism. The third and fourth points bear upon a less structural issue, more conjectural, which is whether people who operate as workers and consumers in a parecon are likely to be more receptive to arguments regarding the rights of other species.

Regarding its guiding logic, a parecon intrinsically and inexorably views other species at least as it views everything else, which is in light of pursuing human fulfillment and development possibilities consistent with promoting solidarity, advancing diversity, maintaining equity, and ensuring self-management. In a parecon, if directly preserving or nurturing a species is humanly beneficial, the incentives will be strong to do it. If leaving a species to its own devices is humanly beneficial, again, the incentives will point in that direction. If directly consuming or indirectly obliterating a species by taking away its habitat is humanly beneficial, again, that is the purely economic path that a good economy would intrinsically arrive at.

Parecon, via its participatory planning, looks around and assesses humanly beneficial possibilities, and provides means and reasons for producers and consumers to pursue them. It does not, of its own accord, incorporate the interests of non-human species. And, regrettably, such species cannot be incorporated as decision-makers to attend to their own interests.

However, a parecon's citizens can decide that they want to add to parecon governmental or other responsible agencies to act on behalf of species, and these structures can be smoothly incorporated even if they defy or impede possible human benefits in favour of the rights of other species. Indeed, even in such cases, while such structures or agencies will need to be added to parecon because a parecon has no planning procedure that allows species other than people to express their intentions and desires, and while these structures will therefore presumably need to have popular support manifested through, say, political choices, maintenance of such restraints on economic activity will not require a continuous and difficult struggle against the continually re-impinging logic of capitalist accumulation because the latter is absent.

In a parecon, that is, once there is a restriction placed on the economy – let's say, the economy is not to interfere with the nesting habitats of caique parrots, or the economy must, if altering those habitats, move all potentially affected caiques to new and at least as sustainable environments – the economy functions thereafter in accord with the external ruling and it does not continually produce structural pressures and practices that try to overcome or remove the restriction. Individuals might try to reverse such a decision, but the system as a whole has no built-in tendency to do so.

Where capitalism has an accumulation process that propels each producer to try to maximize profits regardless of external restraints, parecon functions well in a context of external restraints and has no built-in tendency to aggressively seek to overcome or thwart them.

The question remains, can we expect the kinds of external constraints I have mentioned so far to arise in a society with a participatory economy? Will producers and consumers who use self-managed councils, balanced job complexes, equitable remuneration, and participatory planning be inclined to stewardship for species other than their own and therefore to incorporate rules and norms on behalf of such species on top of the economic means they share to manifest their own preferences? That is, will the populace in a parecon be more or less receptive to arguments on behalf of other species than they would be if their economy were instead capitalist?

It is hard to answer a question like this definitively before the fact, of course. But it seems quite plausible that, whatever factors tend to cause people to become concerned for other species, they will be less thwarted and more enhanced in a system that promotes solidarity, as does a parecon, than in a system that promotes anti-sociality, as does capitalism.

Similarly, a parecon exalts not only the benefits that accrue from variety, but also the need to avoid narrow scenarios that eliminate options we might later find superior. We can expect parecon's respect for diversity in social situations to extend to a popular awareness of the richness of biodiversity and its intricate interconnectivity. Hurting or eliminating species curbs diversity and risks long-term currently unknown losses to humanity as well.

In sum then, parecon removes capitalism's accumulation drive for corporate profit which compels behavior that hurts and even decimates other species. It puts in its place a concern for human well-being and development that doesn't forcefully a priori preclude harming other species, but which is receptive to and respectful of governmental or other social or ecological restraints on behalf of other species. If other species had votes, in other words, they would vote for parecon.

7 Science/Technology

Defining science

LIKE EVERY LABEL for a complex personal and social practice, the word science is fuzzy at its edges, making it hard for us to pin down what is and what isn't science. Nonetheless, for our broad purposes, we can assert that science refers to an accumulated body of information about the components of the cosmos, to testable claims or theories about how these components interact, as well as to the processes by which we add to our information, claims, and theories, reject them as false, or determine that they are possibly or even likely true.

My personal knowledge that the grass I see from my window is green is not science, nor is my knowledge that my back was hurting an hour ago, or that my pet parrot Zeke is on my shoulder. Experiences per se are not science, nor are perceptions, though both can be valid and important.

It isn't by way of science that we know what love is or that we are experiencing pain or pleasure. It isn't science that tells a Little Leaguer how to get under a fly ball to catch it. Science doesn't teach us how to talk or what to say in most situations, nor how to add or multiply numbers.

Most of life, in fact, including even most information discovery and communication, occurs without doing science, being ratified by science, or denying, defying, crucifying, or deifying science.

And yet, most knowing and thinking, and especially most predicting or explaining is much like science, even if it is not science per se.

What distinguishes what we do every day from what we call science is more a difference of degree than a difference of kind. Perceiving is perceiving. Claiming is claiming. Respecting evidence is respecting evidence. What distinguishes scientists doing these things in labs and libraries from Mr. Jones doing these things to choose the day's outfit and stroll into town is science's personal and collective discipline.

Science doesn't add new claims about the properties of realities' components to its piles of information and its theories, nor does it assert the truth or falsity of any part of that pile, without diverse groups of people reproducing supporting evidence and verifying logical claims under very exacting conditions of careful collection, categorization, and calculation. Nor does science advance without reasons to believe that what is added to the scientific pile has significant implications vis à vis the pile's overall character, history, and development.

As Einstein taught, and as is generally agreed, what makes a theory more impressive is greater simplicity of premises, more different kinds of things explained, and its range of applicability. What is most happily added to science's knowledge pile are checkable evidence, or testable claims, or new paths connecting disparate parts that verify or refute previously in doubt parts of the pile, or that add new non-redundant terrain to the pile, in turn giving hope of providing new vistas for further exploration.

If we look in the sky and say, hey, the moon circles the earth, it is an observation, yes, but it is not yet science. If we detail the motions of the moon and provide strong evidence for our claims about its circling the earth that is reproducible and testable by others, we are getting close to serious science, or even contributing to it. If we pose a theory about what is happening with the moon, and we then test our theory's predictions to see if they are ever falsified or especially if they predict new outcomes that are surprising to us, then we are certainly doing science.

Webster's Dictionary defines science as "the observation, identification, description, experimental investigation, and theoretical explanation of natural phenomena".

The *Concise Oxford Dictionary* defines science as "the intellectual and practical activity encompassing the systematic study of the structure and behaviour of the physical and natural world through observation and experiment".

Seventy-two Nobel Laureates agreed on the following definition: "Science is devoted to formulating and testing naturalistic explanations for natural phenomena. It is a process for systematically collecting and recording data about the physical world, then categorizing and studying the collected data in an effort to infer the principles of nature that best explain the observed phenomena."

And Richard Feynman, one of the foremost physicists of the twentieth century, pithily sums up the whole picture: "During the Middle Ages there were all kinds of crazy ideas, such as that a piece of rhinoceros horn would increase potency. Then a method was discovered for separating the ideas – which was to try one to see if it worked, and if it didn't work, to eliminate it. This method became organized, of course, into science."

Science motives

We can say with confidence that the type of economy a society has can affect science by affecting the information that is collected and the claims about it that are explored, the means and procedures utilized in the collection and exploration, and who is in position to participate in these processes or, for that matter, even to know about and be enlightened by science's accomplishments.

There are at least two individual and two social motives that propel science.

First there is pure curiosity, the human predilection to ask questions and seek their answers.

Why is the sky blue? What happens if you run at the speed of light next to a burst of light? What is time and why does it seem to go only one way? What is the smallest piece of matter and tiniest conveyor of force? How do pieces of matter and conveyors of force operate? What is the universe, its shape, its development? What is life, a species, an organism? How do species form, persist, get replaced? Why is there sex? Where did people come from? How do people get born, learn to dance, romance, try to be a success? What is a language and how do people know languages and use them? What is consciousness? When people socialize, what is an economy, how does it work, and what is a polity, culture, family, and how do they work?

Inquiring minds passionately want to know these things even if there is nothing material to be gained from that knowledge, rather like someone passionately wanting to dance even if no one is watching, or someone passionately wanting to draw even if no one will put the results on a wall.

A second personal motive for science is individual or collective self-interest. Knowledge of the components of reality and their interconnections sufficient to predict outcomes and even to affect outcomes, cannot only assuage our curiosity, it can increase the longevity, scope, range, and quality of our lives.

What is the cause and cure for polio or cancer? How do birds fly? How does gravity work? Curiosity causes us to open the door to the unknown with gigantic desire and energy; but we drive whole huge caravans through the doors of science, in part because of the benefits we gain.

The benefits can come from the implications of the knowledge itself, but also from remuneration for scientific labors or achievements. There can be material rewards for gathering information and for proposing or testing hypotheses about reality. Pursuit of these rewards is also a motive for doing science.

Likewise, the benefits to be had beyond the satisfaction of fulfilling one's curiosity are not confined to material payment. One can attain status or fame, and doing science is often at least in part driven by pursuit of the social prizes, notoriety, stature, and admiration that accompany discovery.

Science and economics

An economy can plausibly increase or diminish people's curiosity, or just push it in one direction or another. It can affect as well the ways that scientific know-ledge can directly benefit people, and, of course, it can affect the remuneration and other material rewards bestowed on people for doing science as well as the social rewards they garner.

We can see all of this in history too. For a long time science as we define it did not even exist. There was mysticism and belief, sometimes approximating truth and sometimes not, but there wasn't an accumulation of evidence tested against experience and guided by logical consistency.

Later, societies and economies propelled science and oriented it in various ways. At present, tremendous pressures from society, and particularly from capitalist economy, both propel and also limit the types of questions science pursues, the tools science utilizes, the people who participate in science, and the people who benefit from or even know of science's results.

In the U.S. science has become ubiquitous, revealing the inner secrets of materials, space, time, bodies, and even, to a very limited extent as yet, minds. But science has also become, in various degrees and respects, an agent of capital. Distortion arises when the different methods and problems scientists utilize are biased by motives other than scientific inquiry undertaken for its own sake.

British journalist George Monbiot reports that "34% of the lead authors of articles in scientific journals are compromised by their sources of funding, only 16% of scientific journals have a policy on conflicts of interest, and only 0.5% of the papers published have authors who disclose such conflicts".

In the pharmaceutical industry, circumstances are arguably worst, in that we find that "87% of the scientists writing clinical guidelines have financial ties to drug companies".

More subtly, commercial funding and ownership affect what questions are raised and what projects are pursued. If patent prospects are good, money flows. If they are bad, even when reasons of general curiosity or improving human welfare warrant a line of inquiry, funding is hard to come by.

At the most horrific extreme, citizens may wind up "guinea pigs as in the Tuskegee Syphilis Experiment between 1932 and 1972, or in experiments between 1950 and 1969 in which the government tested drugs, chemical, biological, and radioactive materials on unsuspecting U.S. citizens; or [as in] the deliberate contamination of 8000 square miles around Hanford, Washington, to assess the effects of dispersed plutonium". On a larger scale, in the U.S. the Pentagon now controls about half the annual $75 billion federal research and development budget, with obvious repercussions for the militarization of priorities.

I recently sat on an airplane next to an MIT biologist interested in human biological functions and dysfunctions. He was not at all political or ideological, but he had no confusion about the way things work. "What we do, what we can do, even what we can think of doing," he told me, "is overwhelmingly biased by the need for funding which, nowadays, means the need for corporate funding or, if government, then a government that is beholden overwhelmingly, again, to corporations or to militarism. More, the corporations plan on a very short time horizon. If you can't make a very strong case for short run profits, forget about it. Find something else to pursue, unless, of course, you can convince the government your efforts will increase killing capacities." My travel neighbor's attitude shows the deadly combination of market competition and profit seeking plus militarist governments at work (and anecdotally reveals as well, that everyone knows what's going on).

Parecon and science

What would be different about science in a parecon? Four primary structural things would change, which in turn have a multitude of implications.

Each parecon scientist will work at a balanced job complex, rather than occupying a higher or lower position in a pecking order of power.

Each parecon scientist will be remunerated for the duration, intensity, and, to the extent relevant, harshness of their work, not for power or output, much less for property.

Each parecon scientist, with other workers in his or her scientific institution – whether it's a lab, university, research center, or other venue – will influence decisions in proportion as he or she is affected by them.

The level of resources that parecon's scientists are allotted to engage in their pursuits will be determined by the overall economic system via participatory planning, again with self management.

As a result pareconish science will no longer be a handmaiden to power and wealth on the one hand – indeed these won't even exist in centralized forms – nor will those involved in scientific pursuits earn more or less remuneration or enjoy more or less power than those involved in other pursuits.

A scientist who makes great discoveries within a parecon will no doubt enjoy social adulation and personal fulfillment for the achievement, but will not thereby enjoy a higher level of consumption or greater voting rights than others. Likewise, a scientific field will not be funded on grounds of benefiting elites as compared to advancing human insights for all.

Will there be huge expenditures on tools for advancing our knowledge of the fifteenth decimal point of nuclear interactions or the fourteen billionth light year distant galaxy even before we have figured out how to reduce the hardships of mining coal or containing or reversing its impact on the ecology, or before we develop alternative energy sources?

Will research be undertaken on grounds of military applications instead of on grounds of implications for knowing our place in a complex universe?

These are questions that will arise and be answered only when we have a new society. What parecon tells us is the broad procedure, not the specific outcomes that people will choose, though we can certainly make intelligent guesses about the latter, too.

When the latest and greatest particle accelerator project was being debated in the U.S., a congressman asked a noted scientist who was arguing for allocating funds to the super collider, what its military benefits would be. The scientist replied it would have no implications for weaponry, but it would help make our society one worth defending. The scientist's motivations and perceptions failed to impress the Congress, which voted against the project.

Do we know that in a parecon the participatory planning system would have allotted the billions required? No. We don't know one way or the other. But we do know that the final decision would be based not on the project's military benefits, but rather on how the project would contribute to making society a more desirable and wiser place.

So parecon in no way inhibits scientific impulses. Instead it is likely to enhance them greatly, through an educational system that will seek full participation and creativity from everyone, and because parecon will allot to science what a free and highly informed populace agrees to. Science, in the sense of creatively expanding the range and depth of our comprehension of the world, depends on real freedom, which is to say real control over our lives to pursue what we desire – which is what parecon provides.

Technology

Technology is similar to science in its means of pursuit and logic of development. Those who work to produce technology or applied science in a parecon will have the same influence, conditions, and income as those who do other endeavors. The critical difference will be how society decides which technologies are worth pursuing.

Capitalism pursues technologies when they can yield a profit or help elites maintain or enlarge their relative advantages. As a result, capitalist technological innovations reflect the priorities of narrow sectors of the population, not generalized human well-being and development.

In the U.S., for example, technological nightmares abound. Indeed, the whole idea of high tech and low tech is revealing. Something is high tech if it involves huge apparatuses and massive outlays of time and energy, thus generating many opportunities to profit. Something is low tech if it is simple, clean, and comprehensible, and generates fewer possibilities for profit. Why can't we change the standards so something is considered high tech if it greatly enhances human well being and development, and something is considered low tech if it tends toward the opposite effect?

Smart bombs, in their deadly majesty, are now considered the highest of high tech. The sewage system, mundane and familiar, is considered low tech, at best. Yet the former only kills and the latter only saves.

The pursuit of new drugs with dubious or even no serious health benefits is considered high tech. Working to get hospitals cleaner and bug free is considered low tech – relying largely on medical hygiene norms. The former helps the rich and powerful accrue more wealth. The latter would help all of society accrue longevity and a better quality of life, but might actually diminish profits. Capitalism celebrates the former and prevents the latter.

In the U.S., the pursuit of industrial technology is overwhelmingly about profits. This has diverse implications. U.S. technology seeks innovation to lower market-determined costs, which in any event ignore the adverse effects of production on environment and workers. Thus technologies that use fewer inputs at lower costs are sought, but technologies that spew less pollution or impose less stress on workers are not sought unless owners are forced by social movements to pursue them.

U.S. technology seeks to increase market share by convincing audiences to buy products regardless of the value of the innovation or its social cost in byproducts. Gargantuan resources and human capacities go into designing packaging and producing advertising, often for entirely interchangeable and utterly redundant or even harmful products. Everyone knows this. Within our system, it is just another nauseating fact of life.

U.S. technology likewise seeks to increase coordinator class and capitalist domination of workplace norms by imposing divisive control and fragmentation, regardless of the harsh implications for subordinated workers. The point is that under capitalism there won't be funds to research new workplace organization and design aimed at workplace well-being and dignity. There will be no effort to enhance the knowledge and power of workers, but exactly the opposite.

U.S. technology also seeks to ward off avenues of innovation that would diminish profit making possibilities for the already rich, even at the expense of lost public and social well-being for the rest of society. Don't even think about replacing oil as our main source of fuel as long as there are profits to be extracted from its use. The economy will rebel against serious pursuit of wind, water, geothermal, and other approaches that would decentralize control and diminish specialization that benefits elite sectors, and that would challenge the current agendas of major centers of power.

U.S. technology also seeks to implement the will of geopolitical war-makers by providing smarter bombs, bigger bombs, deadlier bombs, and vehicles to deliver them. So if you are a young potential innovator, there will be enormous pressure on you to study certain disciplines, develop certain skills, and nurture certain aspects of your personality, if you want to make it. And then once you have accumulated these talents, there will be enormous pressure to utilize them. It is even evident throughout popular culture just how much this is all taken for granted. The only thing people doubt is that there is any alternative.

Economics and technology

As historian and philosopher David Noble urged in an interview with *The Chronicle of Higher Education*, "No one is proposing to ignore technology altogether. It's an absurd proposition. Human beings are born naked; we cannot survive without our inventions. But beneficial use demands widespread and sustained deliberation. The first step toward the wise use of our inventions would be to create a social space where these can be soberly examined". Additionally, this space has not only to prepare people to soberly examine options and welcome them doing so, it has to remove the incentives and pressures that prevent people applying as their norms those that support human well-being and development. Does parecon do all that and therefore contribute to desirable technological development?

Imagine a coal mine, a hospital, and a book publishing house in a society with a participatory economy. Inside each there are people concerned with evaluating work conditions and proposing possible investments to alter production relations and possibilities. These are not being done in pursuit of greater profit – a goal that doesn't exist in a parecon – but in pursuit of more efficient utilization of human and material inputs to provide greater fulfillment and development among those who both consume and produce workplace outputs.

The coal mine has a proposal for a new technique, made possible via new scientific or technical insights, that would ease the difficulty of coal mining and increase its safety, or, if you want, that would reduce the pollution effects of coal mining.

The hospital has a proposal for developing a new machine that would make healing more effective in certain cases, or one that would make certain hospital tasks easier.

The book publishing house has a proposal for a technological change or new equipment that would make the work of preparing books a bit easier.

And let's add two more proposed innovations, as well: a social investment that would allocate resources to some military experiments and the implementation of a new weapons system on the one hand, and, on the other, the allocation of resources to an innovative set of machines and work arrangements that would produce quality housing at low cost with reduced environmental degradation.

What are the differences between how a capitalist economy and capitalist workplaces and consumers address these possibilities, and how a participatory economy with pareconish workplaces and consumers addresses these possibilities?

In capitalism, as we have seen, various affected parties will weigh in on the choice, to the degree they even know the decision is being made. Capitalists and coordinators will be privy, and will have access to the levers of power. They will consider immediate implications for themselves – largely in terms of profit possibilities but partly, particularly for the coordinators, in terms of implications for their conditions and status. They may also consider longer run implications of their decision for the overall balance of class and social forces.

Innovations bettering the situation of workers or even consumers will be rejected unless, and to the extent, they are also profitable for owners and to the degree the more general benefits don't raise profitability problems. Technical innovations will be appreciated for lowering costs incurred by the owners – perhaps by dumping costs on others – and for increasing control and sub-ordination on behalf of the lasting preservation of favorable balances of power.

In the capitalist workplace, in fact, innovations that cost more and generate less gain in output, but that provide greater control from above, will often be preferred over innovations that yield more output per asset, but empower workers. The reason is that in the latter case the gains may ultimately be distributed, due to workers' increased bargaining power, such that the overall result for owners is a loss rather than a gain, even though the result for productivity as a whole is positive.

Or take another case. Why is there such a disproportionately large allocation of social resources to military expenditure and research in the U.S., as compared to what is spent on health care, low income housing, roads, parks, and education? Diverse explanations are offered for this bias. Some say it is because military expenditures provide more jobs than social expenditures, and therefore are better for the economy. But this is clearly wrong; in fact, the reverse is overwhelmingly the case. The technology-laden production of bombs and planes and associated research requires only a fraction of the labor per dollar invested that producing schools and hospitals requires.

Others say it is because of the massive profits that accrue to aerospace and other militarily involved industries, which obviously lobby hard for government support. But this too is false. The same, or indeed equally large other industries, would make the same kind of profits if expenditures went to housing, road repair, and other infrastructural work undertaken to fulfill government contracts. It is highly interesting that in the aftermath of obliterating the social structure of Iraq, there is a tremendous flurry of interest among multinationals to rebuild that country, yet there is no similar flurry to rebuild the inner cities of the U.S. itself. What makes blowing up societies, or even just stockpiling the means to do so, or reconstructing societies other than our own – at least up to a point – more attractive as a path of major social commitment than reconstructing and/or otherwise greatly improving the social conditions of poor and working class communities throughout the U.S.?

The answer is not short-run profits. These can be had in all the competing pursuits. The same companies or equally large ones could make huge profits building schools, roads, and hospitals in cities throughout the U.S., just as in Iraq.

What causes the military investment to be preferable to the social investment isn't that it is more profitable, or that it employs more people – both of which are false – but that the product of military investment is less problematic. While social investment betters the conditions, training, confidence, health, and comfort of most working people, it also contributes to their ability to withstand unemployment and to form and advocate their own interests, and it thereby increases their bargaining power. In turn, having increased bargaining power means workers will be able to extract higher wages and better conditions at the expense of capitalist profits – and that's the rub.

It isn't that owners are sadists, who would rather build missiles that sit in the ground forever than build a school that educates the poor because they revel in people being denied knowledge. It is that owners want to maintain their conditions of privilege and power, and they know that distributing too much knowledge or security and well-being to workers is contrary to doing so.

Parecon's technology

How is parecon different? In a parecon, proposed technological investigation, testing, and implementation are pursued when the planning process incorporates a budget for them. This involves no elite interests, only social interests. If military expense will benefit all of society more than schools, hospitals, and parks, so be it. But if the social expenditures would benefit society more, as we can reasonably predict, then priorities will shift dramatically.

But that is the relatively obvious part. What is really instructive is to look at the other choices mentioned earlier. In a parecon how do we assign values to the costs and benefits of an innovation in a workplace?

A new technology can have diverse benefits and costs. If it doesn't require any inputs or expenditure but it does have benefits, of course it will immediately be adopted. But suppose there are high costs for materials, resources, and human labor. We can't afford to do everything, so choices must be made. If we produce another toothbrush, something else that would use the same energies and labors goes unproduced. On a larger scale, if we make one resource and labor-claiming innovation, some others will have to be put off. How is the choice made?

The claim is that in a parecon the criteria for evaluating expenditures are that they will increase human fulfillment and development and that people must have a say proportionate to the degree they are affected. Without re-describing participatory planning in full, it may help to point out one very revealing aspect.

If I am in a capitalist coal mine contemplating an innovation that would make coal mining less dangerous, and you are in a capitalist book publishing house contemplating an innovation that would make work there more pleasant, we each want the innovation in our own workplace for our own well-being. Neither one of us has any reason at all to be concerned about conditions beyond our work-place, nor do we have any means to know what is going on regarding worker fulfillment in other firms. We battle for our investment – actually, we try to accrue profits to pay for it. We don't give a damn about other firms and, indeed, if we are to gain maximally, we should waste no time fruitlessly worrying about them.

Now suppose the workplaces are in a parecon. Things change very dramatically. The coal miners have a balanced job complex, as do the publishing house workers. It isn't just that each person in the coal mine has a job comparable to all others in the coal mine, or that each person in the publishing house has one comparable to everyone else in the publishing house, it is that all of us, taking into account our work inside as well as our work outside our primary workplace, have a socially average job complex. I do some coal mining and some quite pleasant and empowering work in my neighborhood, and you do some publishing house work and some largely rote and tedious work in your neighborhood, and we have, overall, comparably empowering and fulfilling labor.

How do we benefit from innovations in our workplaces? We all wind up with a balanced job complex. Benefits don't accrue only in single workplaces, but average out over society. If the innovation in the coal mine makes the work there less onerous, the time I spend outside will change in accord. Likewise if the innovation in your publishing house makes work there even more pleasant than it already was. We all have an interest in technological investments that maximally improve society's overall average job complex because that's what determines the quality of the job we each wind up with. This means we have to be concerned with what occurs outside our workplace if we are to advocate what is, in fact, most in our own interest.

In a parecon, what is best for society and what is best for oneself are essentially the same thing, and the norms guiding choices among technological possibilities are, therefore, in accord with all people's self-managed desires rather than reflecting the preferences of a few who enjoy elite conditions and circumstances. People might have different opinions and estimates of implications, but the underlying values are consistent. Parecon establishes the kind of context that both benefits and is benefited by technology in precisely the humanistic sense one would rationally prefer.

Health as a further indicator

A particularly graphic example of the entwined logic of both science and technology and their interface with economics is the issue of health in society. In discussing health and the economy, on the one hand there is the issue of health levels and health care. How do we organize care giving, pharmaceuticals, and associated research? Before that, even, what is the relation of economic life to the degree of health enjoyed or the degree of illness and harm suffered by the population?

On the other side of the same coin, there is the issue of receiving care. Who is eligible, to what degree, and at what personal and/or social cost? What happens economically to people who are unable to work, whether temporarily or even long term or permanently? And finally, does having a worthy approach to health place any undue pressure on economic life that parecon is unable to abide? The logic of all this is very like the logic of our other chapters, however, so we want to stick to a few indicators that bear not only on health, but also on the larger science and technology realm.

There is a sense in which the situation of capitalism is well summarized by this quote from Andrew Schmookler: "Which entrepreneur will the market reward better? The one who sells a device that will give many hours of joy over a few years before, for a pittance, it needs to be replaced? Or the one who sells an addictive substance that must literally be 'consumed' to be used, and that itself consumes the life of its devotee?"

In capitalism, not only accounting but also markets favor accumulation and profit making. Not only pharmaceutical companies but even hospitals are generally seeking market share and profit. Potential patients without money get short shrift. Potential patients with money should be separated from it. Those who own, whether it be the pharmaceutical companies or the hospitals or medical groups, benefit. Profit is always the operating principle. Gains that aren't profitable only occur if someone puts up a hard fight against profit-making pressures. Ironically, everyone who reads popular medical suspense novels or who even watches the better legal or medical dramas on TV knows all this.

At any rate, borrowing from Yves Engler's research, we note that "a report by Health Grades Inc. concludes that there were an astounding 575,000 preventable deaths in U.S. hospitals between 2000 and 2002, many from hospital-acquired infections". Likewise, "an American study reported in the *Chicago Tribune* concluded that up to 75 per cent of deadly infections caught at hospitals could be avoided by doctors and nurses using better washing techniques".

As Engler concludes, "Billions of dollars are spent annually on the development of new drugs and medical technologies, but little is spent on basic hospital infection control – even though this would save a greater number of lives – because there has been little economic incentive to do so. Some company makes a profit when a new MRI machine is purchased, but the bottom line that benefits from better hand-washing techniques is only measured in lives".

Everyone knows as well, for example, that the AMA exists largely to protect the monopoly on skills, knowledge, and particularly the credentials of doctors, keeping the total number of doctors down to keep each doctor's bargaining power up, not least against aspiring nurses.

Engler, again, notes that, "recent American data, reported in *New Scientist* July 2003, shows that more than 70 per cent of hospital-acquired infections are resistant to at least one common antibiotic. Infections resistant to antibiotics significantly increase the chance of death". From where does this resistance come? It is "in large part, attributable to our overuse of antibiotics, which is connected to drug companies' bottom lines". To sell product there is great pressure to give the drugs even when not warranted, so antibiotics are routinely over-prescribed. This facilitates "the growth of multi-resistant organisms".

Even more dramatically, "half of all antibiotics sold each year are used on animals, according to *New Scientist*. Industrial farmers give their animals constant low doses of these drugs to treat infection but also as a growth hormone. The administration of low doses is especially problematic since it becomes a feeding ground for organisms to mutate. Data shows a strong correlation between increased use of antibiotics on animals and the emergence of resistant strains in the animal population with mirrored increases amongst people". Profits of major food companies run up against the health of the populace...and in capitalism the former are likely to win.

To offer one final case study, it turns out that, as Stephen Bezruchka reports, "about 55% of Japanese males smoke, compared to 26% of American men". Nonetheless Japan has the greatest longevity for its citizens on the planet, and the U.S. comes in nearly 30th. Bezruchka asks, "How do [the Japanese] get away with winning both Gold Medals? What is loaded in Japan's smoking gun?"

One explanation would be that while smoking is certainly bad for people, other prevalent health conditions, in which Japan scores better than the U.S., are significantly more important.

Bezruchka reports that "research has shown that status differences between the rich and the poor may be the best predictors of a population's health. The smaller the gap [in status] the higher the life expectancy. The caring and sharing in a society organized by social and economic justice precepts produces good health. A CEO in Japan makes ten times what an average worker makes, not the 531 times in the USA reported earlier this year".

The point here is that an economic system affects health in numerous ways. Perhaps the most important effect the economy has on our health via the environment is the overall environment it establishes for us to live in, endure tension and pain in, or thrive in.

In contrast to understanding the overarching impact of economies, people commonly equate health with health care. But the U.S. spends almost half of all money spent world-wide on health care to serve less than 5% of the planet's people. Despite this, health in the U.S. is not even top notch, much less proportionately better than in other countries. This is partly due to the expenditures mostly benefiting a few rather than all citizens. It's also due to much of the expenditures being guided by profit motive rather than a desire to improve people's health. And partly it is due to the fact that other effects of the economy – pollution, tension, inequality – are so harmful. The U.S., for example, with the most prized implementation of corporate capitalist logic worldwide, is also first in voter abstention, homicides, incarceration, teen births, child abuse leading to deaths, and child poverty, as well as in mental illness, and, of course, in the number of billionaires.

What all this has to do with science and technology is that it demonstrates, again, how science and technology can be misdirected, biased, and perverted by profit and market pressures. What will be different in a parecon?

All of it will be different. Parecon firms won't operate in a market and will have no incentive to sell other than to meet needs and develop potentials. Addiction will not be profitable; it will only be socially destructive. Deaths that can be prevented will be prevented – people will not be left to die because curing them isn't profitable.

Research and technology will be directed where it can do the most good, not where it will be most profitable to a few. Parecon will reduce deaths in hospitals due to insufficient attentiveness to hygiene, or lack of staff, and reduce deaths in society due to pollution, dangerous means of transport, insufficient attention to workplace health and safety, addictive consumption of cigarettes or alcohol, and most dramatically, class difference.

There will not only be no impediment to addressing real areas of benefit, there will be every incentive to solve social ills in proportion to benefits that can thereby accrue, not to individuals hoarding property, but to all society.

In a parecon we will have the number of doctors that health warrants. No doctor will have any incentive to try to inhibit the number of people who get medical training. There will be no coordinator class interest to protect at the expense of society losing the productive capabilities of its populace.

Similarly, in a parecon there will be no drive toward workplace speed up and cost-cutting that destroys health. People throughout a parecon will choose to work longer, or less long, in accord with the quality and richness of the lives thereby afforded, including attention to the health effects. And similarly, the huge gaps in income between owners, coordinators, and workers that generate so much ill health in capitalism won't exist in a parecon. Everyone will have a balanced job complex and exercise self-managing decision-making influence. Nor will there be billionaires and paupers due to ownership differences ... because no one will own means of production in a parecon.

In a parecon, whether we are talking about the direction or the scale of basic research, or about the technology of health care, or the social structures that make either science or technology beneficial or harmful, the guiding precepts are the same as exist for other parecon institutions: self-management by affected parties in pursuit of well-being and development, and in accord with equity, solidarity, and diversity.

8 Education

PART OF EDUCATION is intrinsic to the task of accruing knowledge and skill and is best oriented to the individual. To think about education from this angle, we examine the process of conveying information and skills and developing talents in each student. We ask, what is the best way to educate students given the exigencies of what is taught, the attributes students have, and the abilities teachers offer?

But part of education is also contextual and social. To think about education from this angle, we examine the process of transferring information and skills and developing talents from the point of view of society's needs. We ask, what is the best way to educate students consistent with accomplishing what society seeks?

This polarity between enforcing society's agenda and nurturing the freedom and fulfillment of the individual is captured by the pedagogic revolutionary, Paulo Freire, when he writes, "There is no such thing as a neutral educational process. Education either functions as an instrument which is used to facilitate the integration of the younger generation into the logic of the present system and bring about conformity to it, or it becomes the practice of freedom – the means by which men and women deal critically and creatively with the reality and discover how to participate in the transformation of their world".

Freire is right about education today, but in a better future, society's interests should be the same as those of each new generation of students. The former should not limit the latter. In that case we will have a clear educational agenda. If that isn't accomplished, we will have to choose between serving students' needs and capacities and serving society's dictates.

Education now

Most readers of this book live in societies that have capitalist economies with private ownership of productive assets, corporate divisions of labor, authoritarian decision-making, and market allocation.

Because of these institutions, capitalism has huge disparities in wealth and income. About two per cent of the population, called capitalists, own most of the productive property and accrue profits from it. What parecon's advocates call the coordinator class – empowered lawyers, doctors, engineers, managers, and other empowered employees – comprises roughly 20 per cent of the population and largely monopolizes empowering tasks and the daily levers of control over their own and over other people's economic lives. Coordinators enjoy high incomes, great personal and group influence over economic outcomes, and great status. In contrast, the bottom 80 per cent of producers do largely rote work, take orders from those above, barely influence economic outcomes, and receive lower income. This is the working class.

This threefold class division is brought into being by the key institutions of capitalism. First, private ownership of productive property demarcates the dominant capitalist class. Markets structurally impose on owners a need to accumulate profits. The corporate decision-making structure gives owners their ultimate power over property.

Second, owners can't oversee their wide-reaching assets without assistance. The low number of owners, and the large requirements of control, propel the creation of an intermediate coordinator class. The corporate division of labor defines the coordinator class as those monopolizing empowering work and dominating daily decision-making. The requisites of legitimating control by managers and other coordinator class members ensures that this class monopolizes advanced training, skills, and knowledge – as well as the confidence that accompany these.

Third, all these features ensure that the largest portion of citizens will be left with little or no individual bargaining power, having to work for low wages at rote, tedious, and overwhelmingly obedient jobs.

These features will vary, in the suffering they impose as well as in the options they permit, depending on the relative bargaining power of the three classes. But in every instance of capitalism, the broad scaffolding of the economy's defining institutions will be as indicated. What implications does all this have for education?

If an economy has 2 per cent of its members ruling its outcomes through their ownership of property, 18–20 per cent administering and defining economic outcomes due to monopolizing empowering circumstances, and 80 per cent obeying due to doing only rote tasks, then each year's new recruits to the economy arriving from the educational system must be prepared to occupy their designated slot in one of these three classes. Recruits must be prepared to exercise assigned functions, pay attention to designated responsibilities, and ignore distractions. This is true for those who will rule, for those who will have great, but less than ruling power, and for those who will overwhelmingly obey.

A useful word for all this educational preparation is "tracking". Each new generation is divided into segments, and each segment is tracked into its appropriate destination. The educational system processes the incoming population so that about 80 per cent lose any inclination to affect events. Their confidence is obliterated. Their knowledge is kept minimal and narrow. The main skills they learn are to obey and to endure boredom. As Bertrand Russell often joked, people are born ignorant, not stupid; they are made stupid by education.

Another 20 per cent are tracked to expect to have a say over their own and other people's lives. They become confident and enjoy a monopoly on various skills and insights. The upper reaches of this privileged group learn how to have dinner with one another and to otherwise comport themselves in accord with their lofty station at the major societal "finishing schools" such as Harvard and Oxford. They become ignorant of and oblivious to social relations that run contrary to their advantages and callings.

The point is simple. If a society requires its population to have three broad patterns of hopes, expectations, and capacities, its educational system will provide precisely these differentiated outcomes. In that context, any effort to look at education as a system by means of which each individual can maximally develop their potentials and pursue their interests will either be mere rhetoric or will be limited by the presupposition that most people possess no serious potentials or interests. Of course, whether as students or as teachers, people can try to attain better educational outcomes against the economy's needs, but this entails acting against the logic of capitalism.

Regarding the largest part of the public, as the great satirist H. L. Mencken summarized, "The aim of public education is not to spread enlightenment at all; it is simply to reduce as many individuals as possible to the same safe level, to breed and train a standardized citizenry, to put down dissent and originality. That is its aim in the United States, whatever the pretensions of politicians, pedagogues and other such mountebanks, and that is its aim everywhere else".

Mencken misses some subtleties, but you get the point. Is there a worthy alternative? Will society's hierarchies always largely crowd out pedagogy aimed at the development of each student's potentials and aspirations? Will gains for students only arrive as a result of struggle against systemic dictates and be periodically obliterated by economic pressures whenever student vigilance diminishes?

When the Carnegie Commission on Education considered the state of U.S. education as part of a government effort to understand what "went wrong" in the 1960s, it decided that the problem was too much education. The population, the Commission reported, expected to have too much say in society, too much income, too much job fulfillment, too much dignity and respect – and upon getting ready to enter the economy many members of the population had had their high expectations trashed, and as a result rebelled. The solution, the Commission reported, was to reduce the tendency of education to induce high expectations in too large a proportion of the population. It was necessary to cut back higher education and make lower education more rote and mechanical – save for those who were destined to rule, of course. The result of this inclination has been a steady diminution in the quality and degree of education available for most citizens in the U.S., even more so than elsewhere in the world.

Future education

If we look at education from the angle of the person to be educated, we may differ over preferred methodology, of course, which is quite appropriate, as there is unlikely a universally optimal approach. I bet we would agree, however, on broad aims.

Students should be assisted to discover their capacities and potentials, explore them, and fulfill them, while simultaneously becoming broadly confident and able to think, reason, argue, and assess in ways needed to function effectively among socially aware and caring adults.

Other people might formulate this mandate somewhat differently, but one thing is quite clear: for this type of education to happen, society must need this type of adult. It must not want wage slaves who are obedient and passive, and elite coordinators who are callous and commanding.

So to be compatible with worthy pedagogy conceived from the angle of the student, an economy needs to call forth from each participant nothing less than the fullest utilization of their capacities and inclinations, whatever those capacities and inclinations may turn out to be. What kind of economy would do this?

Eighty per cent of us are presently taught in schools to endure boredom and to take orders, because that's what capitalism needs from its workers. Another eighteen per cent are made ambitious, as well as callous to the conditions of those below, and ignorant about their own callousness. At the very top, two per cent are made cruel and greedy. Of course it isn't perfectly cut and dried, as portrayed, but this is the overall, average picture.

In a parecon, education will also be compatible with society's broad defining institutions, since that will always be true in every society. But in a society with a parecon – assuming that other spheres of social life are comparably just and equitable – society will want us to be as capable, creative, and productive as we can be, and to participate as full citizens.

Participatory economics is a solidarity economy, a diversity economy, an equity economy, and a self-managing economy. It is a classless economy. In these respects, its educational system will be based on, and generate, solidarity, diversity, equity, and self-management – as well as rich and diverse capacities of comprehension and creativity. Everyone in a parecon benefits from each of society's workers and consumers being as confident and educated as possible.

Under capitalism, talk of desirable pedagogy may on the one hand mean pedagogy that is consistent with the desire to reproduce the hierarchies of society. In that case, it is more about control and tracking than it is about what most of us mean by good education: edification and fulfillment. On the other hand, pedagogy in capitalism could be about edification and fulfillment, but if so it would contradict the basic needs of the capitalist economy because it would be trying to establish outcomes contrary to the market, private ownership, remuneration for property and power, and the corporate divisions of labor. In capitalism one only gets desirable education by contesting against undesirable economic pressures.

With participatory economics, good education isn't something we win and then perpetually defend because the underlying institutions of society are at odds with it. Good education for the individual in a parecon is part and parcel of the logic of the society's collective economic and social life.

Are there implications for the actual structure and procedures of schooling and education implicit in the structures of parecon? I would guess the answer is yes, not least of all because – but also not confined to the fact that – educational institutions would themselves be self-managing, interface with participatory planning, and incorporate balanced job complexes.

There would not be staff of schools and universities who only teach, some who only administrate, and some who only clean up. But the specific meaning of changes in methodology of training, learning, and sharing will no doubt emerge only from the actual experience of teaching and learning in a new society, and will no doubt also have a myriad of shapes and forms. Maybe sometimes the familiar memorization approach to learning will make sense. Other times an approach that emphasizes doing and interacting with those who can already do, through students learning from mentors, will make more sense. No doubt lectures will play a role, and certainly reading and collective projects will play a role. Perhaps some kind of evaluative grading will be sensible. Without doubt, however, there must be standards. A good economy does not have people who are poorly equipped undertaking tasks they are unlikely to do well, whether it be flying passenger planes, composing music, building houses, driving trucks, or conducting cancer research.

How much education will people get? How many years? What will be the balance between generalist preparation to be a full citizen and specialized training in a field of major pursuit? To what degree will resources go to raising the comprehension and capacity of less able students as compared to advancing students pursuing cutting edge intellectual insights? To what degree will resources go to expanding comprehension and capacity in any form, as compared to being allotted to other social ends? These choices and countless others are not a matter of a priori determination. They are what free people in the context of free institutions will decide for themselves in a better future.

The point here is that, save for a minority, capitalism annihilates aspirations for worthy education. In contrast, parecon actualizes educational aspirations for all.

 Art

ONE COULD EASILY anticipate that people who own factories would dislike participatory economics. Factory owners, after all, benefit greatly from capitalism's inequalities and tend to feel that they deserve their great wealth rather than that they benefit from institutional injustice. When capitalists look in the mirror, in most cases they preen and celebrate their socially valuable entrepreneurship.

Similarly, those in the coordinator class, or those who aspire to join it, will in many instances (at least for a time) dislike parecon. They tend to feel they are smarter, wiser, more capable, and more enterprising than workers below. They don't perceive the relative monopoly on training and empowering conditions and the morally bankrupt criteria of reward and decision-making they benefit from. When coordinator class members look in the mirror, they tend to see a superior person deserving disproportionate luxury and influence for his or her intelligence and greater capacity to enjoy a rich and varied life.

Oddly, it turns out that another group seems to have a more or less reflexive tendency to reject parecon – artists. In my experience, at least, this sector worries greatly on hearing about parecon's features and tends to doubt parecon without considering possible gains for others or even for themselves. Something deep within artists often seems to be threatened, and they respond with vigor.

So what is the situation of art and artists in a parecon? Will a parecon benefit artists and art, or will it degrade their lives and product? Put in reverse, would having an ideal environment for people to undertake artistic labors consistent with others having comparable conditions and opportunities impose needs and implications on the rest of economics that a parecon could not abide? Or is a parecon consistent with optimal art?

Artistic attitudes

It seems that artists' reactions to parecon are like those of coordinator class members more generally, but with a twist. Artists don't think all lawyers, doctors, and engineers are like them. They often think, instead, that there is something grand about art that distinguishes artists from all other members of society. And they fear, at least on first hearing about parecon, that parecon will interfere with their endeavors.

What is this artistic specialness? Creativity, the artists answer. We create, they say. We dredge something from nothing. And, more, we not only see what isn't and nurture it into existence; we often do this in advance of most people's preferences, only to their later benefit. Our work often takes time to even understand, much less appreciate.

Since that is all true, what is it about parecon that worries artists? Partly it is that artists will have to participate in balanced job complexes. And even more so it is that artists will have to operate in the participatory planning system, which means that other people, that is non-artists, will have an impact on whether artists can do their thing.

How will art be created in a parecon? What will be the implications for artists and their creations of having to participate in a balanced job complex and abide the participatory planning process? And, finally, is there anything special about artists' worries?

Parecon art

Artistic labor in a parecon – painting, sculpting, designing, writing, filming, directing, performing, dancing, conducting, and other activities – will be subject to the same structural impositions as all other paid labor. There will be workplaces for different types of art, workers' councils of those involved in artistic production, consumers who benefit from the art, self-managed decision-making, remuneration for effort and sacrifice, balanced job complexes, and participatory planning of allocation.

In capitalism, the artist of one kind or another attempts to earn income for their labors by appealing to a source of financing. Ultimately this will be property owners – capitalists – who may directly finance movies and plays, or who may have their publishing houses or foundations produce books or support a public symphony, or buy paintings, or whatever else.

The owners or administrators will hire an artist if they believe they can profit from the artist's labors, or, in some quite rare cases, if they like what the artist produces and are willing to subsidize it regardless of losses. The artist's income will depend on his or her bargaining power, in turn depending on many variables, including the popularity of the artist's work and the artist's relative monopoly on the talents that go into its creation.

What all this leads to in capitalist economies is that artistic labor largely revolves around helping owners sell commodities. More prose and poetry is written for jingles, manuals, and ads than for audiences reading novels. More pictures are painted, photos taken, films created, and sculptures carved to sell commodities for profit than to directly edify, inspire, or uplift audiences, much less express the deepest insights of artists.

What about in a parecon, then? What difference would a parecon make for artists and art?

First, a worker producing art in a parecon will get hired like other workers, be remunerated like other workers, have a balanced job complex like other workers, and influence decisions like other workers, doing all this through worker and consumer councils and via participatory planning.

This means to get a job in a parecon the artist has to convince other artists in an artists' work council that he or she is a worthy worker able to produce desirable art. This would seem like a gigantic improvement over having to convince an owner that one's work would profit him or her.

It also means the artist's income will reflect the effort and sacrifice expended in socially valued labor, which will certainly be less than a few artists earn under capitalism but will also be considerably more than most earn. This is a collective improvement for society by contributing to overcoming inequity. It will also most often benefit individual artists.

The transition to parecon also means each artist will have a combined job complex that has an average empowerment effect. Artists typically take considerable responsibility for all sides of their activity even in capitalist economies, cleaning their own brushes and studios, buying their own materials, and so on. As to how much other work they would wind up incorporating to balance their overall job complex, that is hard to predict. There is nothing new in artists' situations as compared to any other producers, however. The change from corporate divisions of labor to balanced job complexes is not only better for everyone on the whole by contributing to classlessness, but it is individually materially better for all but a very few elite artists in that for most artists it would mean considerably more time doing the type of art they prefer at a higher level of income.

What about artist influence over the artistic product? Hearing about parecon, many artists worry: will others be telling me what to paint, carve, or write? Will the population vote on whether my art is worthy?

In parecon, artists' councils are like all workers' councils. They won't get workplace inputs, electricity, equipment, clay, paint, stages, printing, and other supplies unless their workplace meets social needs. But within that constraint, like other workers, artists will self-manage their own activity.

The rest of the population, in other words, will negotiate with artists how much of the social productive potential should go to art, taking into account both the positive effects art can have on people's lives as well as how much work artists are willing to do. But once this overall level of art for society is established, it is workers' councils in art workplaces that determine the conditions under which artists will work and be evaluated.

So artists must convince fellow artists their work is worthy. Of course, even a good and worthy artist might on occasion fail to impress other artists, but surely it will be easier, less alienating, and more in touch with artistic sensibilities to convince fellow artists than to convince an owner of one's merit. More, if an artist fails to convince one artists' council of the validity of his or her efforts and artistic potential, that artist can apply to another, or they can do art on their own time until they're able to demonstrate the validity of their work. Actually, in this sense artists have a real advantage over people who fail to get jobs that entail huge outlays of material to conduct and who therefore cannot demonstrate their merits to a potential council by flying planes on their own time, building skyscrapers on their own time, or teaching students on their own time.

Some critics of parecon's relations to artists have worried that the population will be unable to see merit in artistic work that transcends current preferences. They fear that too little resources will be allotted to forward looking art. But this makes no more sense than the idea that the population won't see in advance the value of specific new ideas in science, engineering, or other walks of life, so they will under-resource these areas. The public has only to value innovation per se in a field that does work on the cutting edge and beyond. It is the councils of other artists that determine which aspiring artists can help produce such innovations.

Art is just like science, for example, in this respect. The public decides that society wants so much of its energies and labors devoted to scientific advance. The public doesn't need to judge, and in fact isn't able to judge, which specific pursuits are likely to be scientifically advantageous, only that scientific advance is advantageous. The details of which projects make sense and which scientists are able to conduct them are for scientists to judge. The same applies to art. The public says we want so much of this and that art that is within the current realm of popular taste, and we want so much innovation because we of course realize art must advance. The art councils then employ artists and distribute resources taking into account their best collective judgment about merit.

Another layer of resistance to parecon's implications for artists questions the merit of requiring artists to do a balanced job complex. Some artists feel this will take away from society's total art product due to their having to spend time at non-artistic labors. But this is quite like doctors, lawyers, or architects feeling similarly. And it is no less elitist than the idea that the 80 per cent of the population currently denied means and opportunity to develop its potentials to become doctors, lawyers, or architects, could not generate sufficient, medical, legal, or architectural product to replace anything that might not get generated due to some doctor, lawyer, or architect having to sweep up.

In fact, on two counts the claim is more dubious regarding artists than the other professionals mentioned. First, artists generally sweep up quite a lot now, even very successful ones, unlike current doctors, architects, etc. So in the switchover, less time given to current artistic labor is traded off to other tasks. And second, most people doing artistically creative work now are not, in fact, generating worthy art but are instead devoting their talents to generating packaging, advertising, and other less worthy pursuits, none of which will be required in a desirable economy like parecon. That is, in the switchover, current artists, even having to do a balanced job complex, will do more real art than now, not less.

So the bottom line is that a parecon does to and for art what it does to and for other pursuits. It removes class differences. It guarantees that social assets are used in accord with social desires. It inserts self-managing methods. It remunerates justly. It meets needs and fulfills potentials. It removes elitism and yet it retains and even enlarges quality and standards.

Artists' questions

For the purposes of rounding out this chapter, here are three questions explicitly put to parecon by artists, and my answers.

1. Wouldn't parecon limit individual artistic creativity by subjecting artists to referendums or committees?
If the questioner is worried that it would be within the purview of society to decree that some types of artistic innovation are unlikely to be successful, and that for that reason resources shouldn't be given over to them – yes, that is true for art in a parecon as it is also true for pareconish innovation in bicycle building, ladder construction, researching diseases, or flying to Mars. But the assumption is dubious that in a parecon the population would not want artists to pursue artistic innovations. I think the opposite would be true.

What people like at the moment of making planning decisions would be an issue in a parecon – for sure. A parecon isn't going to produce massive amounts of avant-garde books and films that nobody wants. But that isn't the end of the story. For one thing, smaller groups of people can like things a great deal, making certain products very worthwhile even though they are not widely appreciated. Only a small number of people appreciate advanced physics texts or heart transplants, but that doesn't imply that society won't produce these.

Also, at any moment in time, there are many pursuits – not only in art, but in science, engineering, product design, etc. – that are not yet appreciated except by those who are trying to explore them, and maybe even not entirely by them.

Art, despite what many artists might think, is not special in this respect. There is need for exploration and elaboration in art and music, and also in ideas and innovation more generally, all of which might not initially serve popular taste. But there is nothing about parecon that precludes or even impedes this exploration relative to any other economic model I am aware of, much less relative to capitalism.

Imagine a workplace for musicians. Society respects this workplace and includes it as part of the economy because society values music, including musical innovation. To work at this institution (and in different parecons we can imagine different approaches to all such issues) one has to be hired. This likely entails that prospective artists demonstrate to the workers' council of musicians certain knowledge, talent, or skills. The institution's socially determined budget is allocated internally by its members to various activities, and therefore certainly not only to what a mass audience outside already likes. A musician's workplace really isn't much different in these respects than a manufacturing workplace that is not only producing to meet current needs, but also investigating new products.

2. But aren't artists who have to answer to public controls not really artists anymore?
This notion that an artist is some special unique creature who should have special rights replicates a claim made by nearly all intellectual workers who are in or wanting to be in the coordinator class – each sees the claim as valid for themselves but not as equally valid for others. In fact, however, the claim is true for all and for none, depending on how you look at it.

There is a difference, that is, between being controlled by an external public or other authority – what artists and others reasonably fear – and being part of a society and operating in accord with its norms.

Parecon gives everyone in the economy self-managing influence over economic outcomes. This includes people who do science, engineering, administration, building, serving, and yes, also art as a part of their balanced job complex, each like all the rest. The artist has to function in society, affected by society's decisions, but in parecon the artist has as much influence over those decisions as everyone else.

3. The whole idea of being an artist seems contrary to the notion of producing "popular" art for mass appeal. What happens to an artist who makes unappealing art in parecon?

Suppose I happen to like some kind of weird arrangement of items in my living room, and I like the setup changed daily, and it takes me an hour each day to redesign my room, and it is hard work. Should I be able to earn my living in part for doing that? It has no value for anyone in society other than me and perhaps my family.

I think not. I shouldn't be forbidden from re-arranging my room, of course, but it is my private pursuit. It is more consumption than it is production, and as a result it isn't worthy of being called part of a job complex. Now this isn't by definition the case in a parecon – which could decide otherwise, for reasons I wouldn't personally agree with. That is, a particular parecon's participants could actually allow and incorporate this particular type of activity as socially useful work (though I doubt one ever would). Nothing structural forbids it.

Something similar happens for art, music, and also engineering, science, athletics, and really all pursuits. Insofar as society is going to allocate income to those doing some activity, it is going to want that activity to "count" as socially useful work. This means that overall, on average, an activity has to have socially beneficial outcomes. (There may be lots of misses on the road to some hits, and benefit may have many meanings … but still …)

So if I want to pursue some science, engineering, music, writing, building, landscaping, architecting, constructing, teaching, ball playing, cooking, or whatever, and I want this activity to be part of my balanced job complex, it has to be regarded by the economy as worthy.

But how does the economy determine worthiness? Most likely, for art as for engineering or other pursuits, it will do so by budgeting whole institutions that will in turn employ people who do this type of work based on employees' collective views of prospective workers' capacities and the estimated worth of proposed projects.

Could it be that some genius will propose to a music workplace, an art workplace, or a scientific research center, pursuits that others in the field wrongly feel deserve no time, energy, and resources? It could happen, of course. Einstein's PhD submission was initially rejected. But parecon is far less vulnerable to such problems than capitalism because profit and power no longer govern outcomes in a parecon.

Ignorance may still have an impact, or just plain human error, of course. No system can be immune from ignorance and error. But precisely because every system is vulnerable in these ways, one can at least roughly account for the likely distribution of ignorance and try to guard against its ill effects. This is just what parecon's elevating the value "diversity" to such a prime position helps achieve.

At any rate, the artist who makes currently unappealing art will either be respected by peers or not, permitted to utilize social resources and be remunerated for the activity or not, but the criteria will be broad and rich, not profit for a few, and the judges of merit will be artistic peers and not owners.

Artists' needs

As a last point, suppose we come at the problem from the opposite direction and ask, what does having the ideal system for artists require of an economy?

Of course the problem is arriving at what we mean by "ideal system for artists". Some might think the phrase is fulfilled if the system simply lets artists do whatever they want and gives them anything they want, both to do their art and to enjoy life as well.

But if we say instead that artists should have what will benefit their lives and their art consistent with all other people equally having what will benefit their lives and their preferred ways of expressing their capacities, then it seems that pareconish values arise quite directly, and in turn so do pareconish institutions.

Surely artists need to control their artistic endeavors and also their interactions in the world which inform their insights and communications. But to have this option consistently with others also having it means having self-managing say.

For the artist to be appreciated and to have a wide range of choices and to be able to maintain high standards and have access to needed tools and conditions – all consistent with others having the same benefits and costs when pursuing their life choices – requires remuneration for effort and sacrifice and balanced job complexes.

The point is, artists are people. Economically they produce and they consume. What they produce and how they produce it is different in its details from non-artists, but what everyone produces and how they produce it is different in its details from what others do. Artists conceive and originate, but so do all other social actors in the economy. To come up with product innovations, new techniques, new analyses in changing contexts, new basic theory, and so on, is also to conceive and originate new creations. Artists are worthy, inspirational, and valuable. They are not unique in these respects, however.

So, in sum, parecon creates conditions conducive to society benefiting from artistic talent and conducive to capable artists expressing themselves as they choose. More, parecon does all this consistently with economic equity and justice for all workers and consumers. Parecon is art friendly. It is an artistic economy.

10 Journalism

THE IDEA OF JOURNALISM is not overly complex. Societies involve huge ranges of activity and possibility. Each day events occur and processes unfold. The quality of our lives depends in two senses on news of these events and processes.

First, there is the simple benefit of knowing about, and vicariously enjoying, or feeling solidarity with, or otherwise partaking of information about events beyond the relatively narrow scope of our daily lives. If there is a new insight, achievement, or benefit, or if there is new suffering, struggle, challenge, or possibility – whether we are talking about scientists unearthing news about human origins or cosmic foundations, or about inventors scaling new heights of speed or size, or about a disease or a natural disaster, or about new medicine or energy provision, or about new national policy, interpersonal conflict, social possibilities, or social problems – people benefit from knowing about it. There is curiosity. There is vicarious pleasure. There is edification.

But second, what happens in the world, and knowledge of it, can also affect what we can do, wish to do, or need to do because of the ways events change the world around us or because of the ways events call on us to do things to affect conditions, policies, choices, and other matters.

The above refers to news, of course, but also to analysis of events, trends, and possibilities, to what is called commentary, and even to fiction, entertainment, etc., at least to a degree. It refers, that is, to everything that is included in a good news program or newspaper.

By journalism, in other words, we refer to information transferred from people who investigate and accumulate data and who also have time to think about it and make predictions, evaluations, and judgments about it, to other folks.

Capitalist media

In a capitalist economy, information-conveying media such as newspapers, periodicals, TV, and radio, are, like other corporations, profit-seeking firms with corporate divisions of labor and products to sell to consumers. Oddly, however, in many cases, what media institutions sell isn't always precisely what it seems.

Information firms sell information to their consumers, yes, but more so they sell their consumers to advertisers. And the information that flows is often highly contoured to purposes other than meeting consumers' needs. In examining capitalism's journalistic institutions, Edward Herman and Noam Chomsky developed what they called the Propaganda Model to explain its main features and operations.

"What is the propaganda model and how does it work?" Herman answers his own question by telling us that the model's "crucial structural factors" arise from the fact that "the dominant media are firmly imbedded in the market system". Newspapers, periodicals, TV news, radio, and the rest are all profit-seeking businesses, "owned by rich people (or companies)" and "funded largely by advertisers who are also profit-seeking entities, and who want their ads to appear in a supportive selling environment".

"Media institutions … also lean heavily on government and major business firms as information sources." Operating in society, both "efficiency and political considerations", as well as "overlapping interests, cause a certain degree of solidarity to prevail among the government, major media, and other corporate businesses".

Like all institutions, media are affected not only by internal requisites but also by demands and impositions from without. "Government and large non-media business firms" are best positioned (and sufficiently wealthy) to "pressure the media with threats of withdrawal of advertising or TV licenses, libel suits, and other direct and indirect modes of attack".

Internal profit-seeking and external stability-maintaining factors "are linked together, reflecting the multileveled capability of government and powerful business entities and collectives (e.g., the Business Roundtable; the U.S. Chamber of Commerce; the vast number of well-heeled industry lobbies and front groups) to exert power over the flow of information".

Chomsky and Herman's Propaganda Model emphasizes five factors involved in constraining and determining media output: "ownership, advertising, sourcing, flak, and anticommunist ideology". The last of the five factors was influenced in its description by the time at which the model was developed. It could be called "prevailing ideology" to make the list more general, or nowadays, it could be called "antiterrorist ideology," to make the list more timely.

The five factors, as Herman expresses it, "work as 'filters' through which information must pass, and that individually and often in additive fashion greatly influence media choices".

The model stresses "that the filters work mainly by the independent action of many individuals and organizations; and these frequently, but not always, have a common view of issues and similar interests".

"In short, the propaganda model describes a decentralized and non-conspiratorial market system of control and processing, although at times the government or one or more private actors may take initiatives and mobilize coordinated elite handling of an issue."

The point is, in contemporary society, journalism and information are constrained by capitalist economic dictates and a concordance of interests between the state and other powerful social institutions. That journalism reflects imposition of content by corporate and state power is evident every day all around us.

In American media, for example, news is routinely delimited by what is called contextual spin, verbal and visual coloration, and contextual biasing. Some matters are emphasized to the point of endless repetition. Some are excluded to the point of literal disappearance. Much is "misstated". As one analyst, Danny Schechter of Media Watch, put it in his book of the same name, as a result, "the more you watch the less you know".

In the U.S. it is not unusual for people to believe what amount to fairy tales about the issues of the broader society and even their own daily lives. The average citizen may believe the government budget spent on poor people's welfare dwarfs the government budget spent on armaments and other subsidies to rich corporations, or that more foreign aid and police and military aid goes to countries that are free and that care for their citizens than to countries that are repressive and routinely violate the rights of their citizens. Or the average citizen may believe that crime is rising when it is falling, or that guns in the home protect citizens, or that danger from street thugs should be their main worry, or that blacks receive an unreasonable percentage of social aid at the expense of whites, or that Iraq, or earlier Nicaragua, Libya, or Grenada, are serious threats to U.S. citizens that must be stopped lest our population suffer.

Here is the way media critic and linguist Noam Chomsky summarized the information problem some years ago:

"An academic study that appeared right before the presidential election reports that less than 30 percent of the population was aware of the positions of the candidates on major issues, though 86 percent knew the name of George Bush's dog. The general thrust of propaganda gets through, however. When asked to identify the largest element of the federal budget, less than one fourth give the correct answer: military spending. Almost half select foreign aid, which barely exists; the second choice is welfare, chosen by one third of the population, who also far overestimate the proportion that goes to blacks and to child support. And though the question was not asked, virtually none are likely to be aware that 'defense spending' is in large measure welfare for the rich. Another result of the study is that more educated sectors are more ignorant – not surprising, since they are the main targets of indoctrination. Bush supporters, who are the best educated, scored lowest overall."

Due to the tireless and relentless efforts of dissidents, it is no longer the case – particularly among the less wealthy and powerful sectors – that there is as much confusion about the basic character of U.S. society and life as in decades past, though the problem is still extensive, especially in times of crisis such as when the government is building up to a war. And the dictates of capitalist journalism have only intensified another problem that more than offsets moderately diminished public confusion – the feeling on the part of the public that horrible problems are a part of history and society that we cannot avoid. There may be more understanding of what's wrong than in the past, and at some deep level everyone may even realize that everything is broken, but there is also much more cynicism about the possibility of things becoming sane and whole. Margaret Thatcher's dictum that "there is no alternative" is believed because what the media reports and ignores and what it ridicules and celebrates daily hammers home the viewpoint that horrible problems are a fact of life.

How would media differ in a parecon?

Parecon and journalism

First, in a parecon, within journalistic and information handling institutions there are no hierarchies of wealth and power. Those working in the industry, whether writing or otherwise, do not occupy dominant and subordinate positions that they rationalize and justify. They work at balanced job complexes. They have self-managing power. They earn for socially valued work according to the duration, intensity, and onerousness of their labors. They have no structural reason to see themselves as systematically morally better or worse than others, and no hierarchical position to defend. They have no elite class allies and advantages to hide or defend or enlarge against subordinate classes. Parecon removes the key biasing variables present in capitalism by eliminating personalities and consciousnesses systematically bent on protecting and defending elite interests at the expense of subordinates. Parecon has no privileged class.

Second, the education people experience does not curb their curiosity or systematically bias their knowledge of history and social relations. In this dimension, too, there is no social structural force bending people's experience against the honest portrayal and assessment of events. There is no myopic and elitist education to limit those writing or disseminating information.

Third, in a parecon, there is no paid advertising, no sale of audience to advertisers. Media workplaces do not seek profits or other surplus, either. The media don't sell audience to producers. They amass, generate, and disseminate information, analysis, and vision.

The media's motive is communication. Incomes are earned for work socially valued by free and capable audiences. Media workers earn equally with everyone else throughout the economy.

Finally, there are no centers of disproportionate power that bend events to their will and compel coverage to accord with external requirements.

At the same time, there is no reason to expect ideological uniformity.

In a good society with a parecon and other innovative structures, different people will no doubt have different views, and sometimes there will be alignments of groups that have socially contrary beliefs and desires, and similarly, journalists and other information workers will have conflicting views, too. Information consumers will sometimes prefer magazines or shows more about science than about sports or vice versa, but will also sometimes seek writers who share values and conceptual frameworks they respect as compared to writers whose views they disagree with or find abhorrent.

Values of journalists and of media institutions will certainly affect what they cover, judge, and propose, and how they do all three, and why a given individual will favor one commentator over some other. The difference in a parecon isn't that conflict disappears, or subjectivity, for that matter, far from it, but that their roots are in honestly different perceptions and values, not in structural biases imposed by massive centers of power and wealth.

Still, there is another special feature that will most likely characterize pareconish media: diversity in valuing dissident views and minority opinions. Pareconish media can be expected to allot space and resources for viewpoints that are not widely, or are even only very marginally, supported.

In fact the logic and methodology of fostering diverse information flow is not much different than the logic and methodology of research and exploration in any field. Consumers negotiating with producers may want to allot significant amounts of socially productive potential to innovative investigation in technology, science, and art. They will argue that though this work has not been understood yet and hasn't demonstrated its intrinsic worth, it is worthy simply because overall such work generates what will be intrinsically worthy in the future. In the same way consumers can understand and support the importance of diverse and as yet even individually seemingly unworthy information sources on grounds of the need for overall innovation and exploration in, and continual diversity of, journalistic content.

Pareconish journalists may make mistakes, of course. They will misunderstand events at times, or miss things that are important, or exaggerate things that aren't important. One pareconish journalist will see things one way, another will have a different perception. The two will often be at odds and neither may be fully correct. Readers will pick and choose their sources, of course, and time and experience will clarify accuracy, values or even competence. But the key point is that variations won't manifest external pressures or even internally generated inclinations aimed to please particular constituencies regardless of evidence and logic.

Bias induced errors will be far more unusual in a parecon than under capitalism because in a parecon there is no income or power motive to bend perceptions. There will be no way to parlay readership or popularity into increased income or power. The impetus in journalism will be to capture reality accurately and to comment on it wisely. It isn't that people will all agree, or always be brilliant, or always escape personal habits or biases. It is that such problems will not be systemic and will therefore be less damaging.

In other words, the really key change is that in a parecon, even when bias does rear its head, it will have no particular structural longevity and will not be replicated widely. Bias due to the idiosyncratic views of particular writers rather than the interests emanating from structural centers of power is far less likely to spread throughout the media industry, unless there is widespread honest error. In that respect, pareconish journalism and information handling become much more like science at its best, undertaken without commercial pressures. The test of evidence and logic aggressively curbs escalating divergences from truth and sensibility regarding what is and what isn't the case.

The pareconish *New York Times* will print all the news, all the analysis, all the prescription, that its many writers choose to focus on, in a self-managing manner, with its resources governed by social negotiation in accord with the population's desires for news, entertainment, diversity, and dissent. And beyond the pareconish *New York Times* there will be diverse other sources of information, including, one would guess, some that operate privately via volunteerism.

Instead of each writer being at risk of losing employment for being insufficiently profitable, and in self-defense becoming acclimated to the constraints of reproducing hierarchies of power and wealth as defined by owners and editors who try to sell maximum receptive audience to advertisers, each writer examines events and conveys what he or she finds important in light of feedback regarding the needs and desires of very diverse constituencies of readers, listeners, and viewers, as well as in accord with the collective constraints of budgets and the desire to stay in high regard among fellow workers.

Will all periodicals and TV shows operate identically? Not at all. Some will feature entertainment, others news, and others commentary or investigation. Some will feature sports, others international relations, economy, polity, family issues, science, and so on. But even more, parecon doesn't dictate the internal decisions of workplaces about their specific approaches or priorities. Parecon dictates only that there will be workers' councils, self-managed decision-making, and remuneration for duration, intensity, and onerousness of work, balanced job complexes, and participatory planning. Different media institutions, like different restaurants, research institutes, schools, playgrounds, distribution centers, hospitals, and assembly plants, will have different ways of implementing these structures and of pursuing their endeavors. This is particularly true for media, where product differentiation is greater than for many other domains and the different choices made by workers' councils will affect not only who wishes to work in which institutions, but also who finds them a desirable source of information and insight.

The main point is that, in the future as now, information media will remain part and parcel of the elaboration, protection, and correction of social practices and structures. What will change is the character of those practices and structures, which in turn will change the internal dynamics of the information media and their product.

In sum, parecon's requisites for working in and organizing media prove consistent with what are likely to be desirable media's needs regarding information product and process and vice versa. Parecon is an information economy.

11 Athletics

BY THIS POINT, talking about parecon's implications for athletics and athletes ought to be relatively easy. They barely differ than for science, art, and journalism. There is, however, one interesting new issue to address: competition.

Pareconish athletics

First, as with other realms of human endeavor, parecon ensures that those who do athletic activity as part of their balanced work responsibilities will be remunerated for their effort and sacrifice, will have balanced job complexes and will self-manage their work.

What the empowerment ratio of playing tennis, golf, chess, or soccer as a part of one's work might turn out to be, we can only guess. But various pareconish sports industries will have job complexes internally balanced among responsibilities such as playing, training, coaching, traveling, maintaining the fields and stadiums, transporting, cleaning, medically maintaining athletes, taking tickets, and so on, and then also between their broad industry and the rest of the economy.

Likewise the inputs and outputs of athletic industries will be negotiated cooperatively, in the planning process, by workers' councils in industries that provide bats and balls, food, bandages, bikes, and other inputs, by those that provide sports events and opportunities, and by consumers' councils expressing their preferences for athletic consumption.

It might be interesting to ask how a sports team will be redefined, including how coaching will be handled and tasks distributed and motivated. But just as it is beyond our current capacities to delve deeply into such matters for symphony orchestras, movie actors and crews, writers and directors, or, for that matter, for truck drivers, cooks, or metal workers, so too for athletes and others associated with delivering athletic performances. The details are matters for future experiment and diverse determination.

We can say a bit more, however, about athletic remuneration, and it is revealing to do so. After that we can also address a much broader question that may be troubling some readers: would athletics even exist as a part of a parecon to be remunerated and consumed? Would bicycle riding exist only as an enjoyable hobby and pastime, but not as the Tour de France with remuneration? Would people play chess with friends, but not in tournaments as part of their income-earning work? Would there be hobbyist leagues for hockey and cricket, football and soccer, tennis and golf, chess and bridge, bowling and car racing, maintained by people earning for their labors, but without people doing such sports activity itself for pay?

Assuming for now that people continue to earn income for playing sports, remuneration will be for effort and sacrifice, of course. But what does that mean in this context?

Consider a marathon race. Current total prize money might be a million dollars. If so, in capitalism the first place winner might win four hundred thousand, second place two hundred and fifty thousand, third place one hundred thousand, fourth place fifty thousand, and the remaining two hundred thousand dollars might be awarded in steadily diminishing increments to the next thirty or forty finishers, with another thousand or more finishers earning nothing for their efforts.

If we consider, instead, the whole baseball, golf, soccer, track and field, bowling, car racing, or chess industry, each rewards its players similarly over the course of a year, with participants going from tremendous earnings at the top performance levels down to near zero or even below zero (since many athletes pay their own fees, transport, etc.) for a huge majority of lower performance levels. What about this picture changes in a parecon?

Consider the marathon again. In a parecon, marathon remuneration isn't for where you finish in the race but for the effort and sacrifice you expend in socially valued labor. If society values your sport and its products enough to warrant its being a part of the socially planned economy, then as a participant (whether your main activity is athletic, organizational, maintenance, medical, or whatever) you will get remunerated for the duration of your socially valued work, for the intensity of your efforts, and for your work's onerousness above or below the social average, but not for output – such as where you finish in a race.

Indeed, suppose you are, among your other responsibilities, a runner. Suppose you come in first, or fifth, or one hundred and fiftieth (just how slow a runner can be and still be considered a producer of a valued output is a matter that will be determined by sports councils in their hiring practices and by participatory planning in establishing what is sought by audiences, just as with baseball, hockey, soccer, and other sports). What difference will your finishing position make to your income? The answer is it will make no difference unless you are doing better or worse in the race due to extra duration or intensity of work – not due to natural talent – since only duration and intensity are remunerated.

In other words, if you are a natural-born jackrabbit competing in a marathon, you can't waltz across the finish line first, expending little effort in the race and in preparing for it, and expect to get high remuneration. And even if you did exert more than the social average, and if you worked overtime to get ready, the extra income you would thereby earn would be proportionate to your effort and not to your results. Your income would therefore certainly not be humongous, but socially sensible.

And this remunerative approach is not only morally sound – which is to say one shouldn't be remunerated extra for natural born talent or even for the output of training as compared to the difficulty, intensity, and duration of training – but it is also economically sound, which is to say it has the appropriate incentives to elicit maximal performance.

What a runner needs as an incentive to run faster is not inordinate reward for natural born talent, because the runner can do nothing to enhance genetic talent, and rewarding talent actually provides incentive only to win (even if at a much slower pace than one is capable of). What provides incentive is remuneration for the extra effort that goes into running faster, or lower income for not expending full effort.

Athletics?

This is all well and good, and is also consistent with parecon more broadly, and so by this time this kind of logic is hopefully not surprising. But, the question still remains, will athletics exist as an economic industry at all – not just as a hobby – in a good economy?

Why not? Why won't future citizens of a classless economy want to watch runners, bikers, kickers, shooters, passers, and hitters just as we do now, as exemplars of human performance in their respective fields? In that respect, how is it different than people wanting to see the work of painters, poets, novelists, sculptors, singers, composers, or dancers?

If in a good economy we will want to have symphonies or other perform-ances, movies, or shows, with remuneration for their production and performance, why wouldn't we also want to have athletic events and remunerate their produc-tion and performance?

Many critics of capitalism will have doubts about this, I suspect. Leftists dislike sports for their macho dynamics, racial biases, violence, commercialism, and class inequalities. But all this will be gone, presumably, in a good society and economy. Nonetheless, many leftists will remain suspicious that competition fosters conflict among people, and that competition is in that sense detrimental.

Critics of competition may say that while an orchestra aspires to the highest quality it can attain, and while we admire performances in accord with quality, and while we likewise enjoy and respect some compositions more than others, and we admire and enjoy some paintings, poetry, and novels more than others, to succeed in one of these pursuits requires that another participant must fail. There is no intrinsic necessity for winners and losers. But with sports, this critic might add, winning and losing are intrinsic to the activity. In a good society, the critic argues, this quality should make sports unworthy of being an industry with remuneration for workers.

In reply, first, it is correct that a great many sports intrinsically involve competition. We can conceive of competition-free alternatives but they are not the same thing. In the late 1960s I used to play with friends a non-competitive brand of basketball. We did score and defend when playing the game. But the score wasn't germane and needn't even be kept. A very good offensive player who was defended by a not so good defender would try to play in such a way as to bring out the defender's best possible defensive effort. The expert on offense had the difficult challenge to elevate the defender's effort, rather than scoring easily over and over.

Similarly, a really good defensive player covering a not so great offensive player would not shut the player down over and over, but would, instead, play with just the right tenacity and intrusiveness to spur the offensive player to play his or her best.

Playing this way was fun and challenging, but it wasn't basketball of the sort people enjoy when watching competitive NBA, college, or high school games. And of course there are many sports and games in which there is barely even a way to imagine a non-competitive variant – say chess, the hundred yard dash, a marathon, car racing, or the pentathlon.

But what about the competition, urges the critic? We can't want to reward and esteem the competition, can we?

Well, it is true that a central virtue of participatory economics is that participatory planning removes competition from economic allocation and also makes remuneration non-competitive. There is no zero-sum contest in participatory economic remuneration in which if I win you lose. However, this is deemed a great economic virtue not out of an a priori rejection of competition per se, but for allowing the economy to propel, rather than violate, solidarity, diversity, equity, and self-management.

Competition

So is competition per se a problem? If we don't increase income for the winner of a contest and don't reduce income for the loser, and if winning and losing have no bearing on workplace influence and self-management and don't lead to benefits in job definition and conditions, would competition still be problematic?

Parecon doesn't deny that performers and producers have different capacities. On the contrary, parecon has standards and admires excellence. You can't get remunerated in a parecon for work that isn't socially valued. You can't play ball poorly, lay bricks poorly, or tend sheep poorly, for pay. To get paid for work it must produce socially valued output, which means it must be done at a rate and efficiency that isn't wasteful and inferior.

I may want to be the shortstop on a baseball team like the Yankees, but Derek Jeter is so much better that the public would not value, and indeed would be horrified by, my work at that position. My play is simply not good enough to be worthy of employment as a shortstop. There is a competition for any balanced job complex that includes shortstopping for the Yankees. Indeed, there is also a competition in this same sense for all jobs. You have to be good enough in any job, but your income isn't a function of how good you are.

Suppose, for example, that I want to be a physicist or an airplane pilot, or that I want to do heavy labor, or play the oboe as part of my balanced job complex. So do other people, and in some cases, many more people than society needs. There is competition, therefore, for the honor of being able to be socially remunerated for each type of work. One must fulfill the social standards to get hired by a workers' council. If I can't fulfill the social standards sufficiently to be producing desired output, I can read physics books, fly model planes, lift weights, or play oboe as a hobby, of course, but not for remuneration.

Thus, a parecon is not without competition. But in parecon's competitions, winning or losing doesn't determine a level of pay, a level of influence, or conditions of work. What the competition does, instead, is to generate, reveal, and utilize competence. The competition yields something that we all benefit from without denying values we hold dear.

Can athletic competition be similarly positive, without negative side effects?

Suppose you play a game of chess (and yes, I think chess is a sport with struggle, challenge, and endurance, but if you prefer to think of chess as just a game, for our purposes here, that doesn't matter) with an opponent. Does the quality of your chess playing experience depend on whether you win or lose? It certainly might. It could be that you get more pleasure out of winning against a weak opponent easily, for example, even if you have played mundanely and inattentively due to your being a much better player, than you get pleasure out of just barely losing a finely played and very challenging game, due to your opponent being a bit better than you but with you playing at your absolute best. If so, it is mostly winning and losing that affects your mood, not the quality of your play.

On the other hand, can we imagine a society in which you typically get more pleasure out of playing really well in a really challenging and exciting struggle that you lose than you get out of winning easily? Isn't this what we tell our kids, in fact, all the time – that it's how you play the game, not if you win or lose, that matters, and that this is true even though you must try to win for there to be a game at all?

The effect of parecon on sports would certainly be profound. It would not mean that teams and individuals wouldn't try to win. It would mean, however, that their incomes would not be pegged to winning or losing. We would want to see quality, as now, but we would not materially reward quality per se.

Would athletes and audiences celebrate winners, or celebrate people that manifest their capacities fully – or both? Would fans get more pleasure out of their team winning easily while playing poorly, or out of their team losing a close, hard-fought struggle, but playing well?

In a good economy, would people no longer be paid for playing chess because there must be a winner and a loser, or would competitive chess persist, including championships, because we value quality of play and wish to manifest, observe, study, and enjoy talent, endurance, and effort, in chess as in so many other areas – but without win-based reward or loss-based penalty?

What about golf, soccer, or basketball? For that matter, would boxing disappear for being too violent a competition? What would become of car racing, horse racing, or marathons? How about archery, javelin, or pole vaulting?

We can't know the answers to these questions (not least because different societies may answer differently), any more than we can know what will happen in other industries in the future. Nor is there any reason to be agitated about our inability to predict future preferences. A vision for an economy or for any other part of life isn't about figuring out what choices future workers and consumers will make. It is about figuring out what type of institutional relations will permit workers and consumers to make the choices they prefer while furthering values they hold dear.

We can confidently assert that parecon will make equitable the way athletes are remunerated, will balance their jobs, and will no doubt also impact on the way athletes are viewed and their influence in society. We can also assert that parecon will likely change the way people regard and enjoy competitions.

Today star athletes earn millions and lord it over most of humanity. In a pareconish future, star athletes will earn equitable incomes and have influence like all other citizens. Now, sports are subordinated to profit and power. In a pareconish future, sports will be like all other economic pursuits, solidaritous, diverse, equitable, and self-managed.

The precise details of the future content and texture of athletics, whether undertaken for remuneration or in leisure time, as with the precise details of the future content and texture of music, art, literature, transportation, education, dining, fashion, science, sex, or anything else, will be for future citizens to work out in their own free fashion.

What an advocate of parecon urges is only that people exercise their economic preferences through worker and consumer councils, using self-managed decision-making, being remunerated for effort and sacrifice, fulfilling balanced job complexes, and abiding participatory planning. But these features are enough, it seems, to guarantee that parecon will satisfy the requirements of enlightened athletics and vice versa. Parecon is a sports economy.

12 Crime

IT IS OFTEN SAID that how a society treats those it punishes graphically displays how civilized and humane that society is. If we look at how criminals are treated we see a portrait of a society's moral soul.

It might also be said, look at the numbers of prisoners and the basis for their incarceration to see whether a society produces more solidarity or divisiveness, equity or desperation, dignity or self hatred.

Does society increase crime by making it necessary or at least viable and attractive? Does society disproportionately impel some sectors to crime? Or does society deter crime by making a lawful life worthy and fulfilling, and by confining crime and long term incarceration only to sociopaths?

To investigate crime and economy, I come at the problem from two angles that are a bit different than our approach to other topics in this book.

Crime and punishment in capitalism

About 30 years ago I was at a dinner party with a bunch of leftist economics faculty and grad students, and I posed a hypothetical question to engender some dinner debate. If you had only two choices, I asked, would you open all U.S. prison doors and let everyone out, or would you keep everyone right where they are?

To my surprise there wasn't any debate. Only I was willing to entertain what everyone else saw as the utterly insane, ultra-leftist notion that opening the doors might be better than keeping everyone incarcerated with no changes. I then added the option of giving everyone who was let out a job and ample training, but still there were no takers.

Years later, would the result of such a query to leftists be the same? As context, this little experiment might best be undertaken in light of the popular notion that it is better to let ten criminals go free than to jail one innocent person.

Of course that may be just a rhetorical posture for gullible law students, but it is supposed to communicate that there is something utterly unthinkable about letting innocent folks fester in prison.

Okay, this implies some calculations. For example, what is innocence and what is guilt, and is it better to jail one innocent person so we can also jail 20, 50, 100, or 1,000 malevolent psychopaths who would otherwise run amuck hurting and killing way more innocent folks? On the other hand, what if the calculus is the opposite? What if the real question is, should we keep one criminal in jail along with five or ten innocent folks, or let them all go free?

The crime rate in the U.S. is approximately the same as in comparably industrialized and citified Western Europe. The number of inmates per hundred thousand citizens in the U.S., however, is as much as fifteen times greater than in Europe, depending on which country we compare with.

The rate of incarceration in Spain is a bit more than England is a bit more than France is a bit more than Germany is a bit more than Turkey ... and Norway and Iceland are relatively crime free by comparison. The U.S. rate of incarceration is about fifteen times Iceland's, twelve times Norway's, a bit over eight times the Turkish rate, and a little over six times Spain's.

The high U.S. rates began spiraling dramatically upward about 30 years ago in tune with political and media exploitation of a largely manufactured public fear of crime. Political candidates – Ronald Reagan being the game's most effective player – would drum up fear and then use it to propel programs for warring on drugs, expanding the number of prisons, extending minimum mandatory sentencing, and imposing three strikes you're out innovations.

When everyone from the cop on the beat, to the police chief, to the crime beat reporter, to the district attorney, to the judge hears nothing but an endless litany of lock 'em up and let 'em rot rhetoric, they all become predictably aggressive. As Manning Marable reports, approximately 600,000 police officers and 1.5 million private security guards patrol the United States. The U.S. has more than 30,000 heavily armed, military trained police units. SWAT mobilizations, or 'call outs,' increased 400 per cent between 1980 and 1995. And between 1972 and 1998 the number of people in prison in the U.S. rose by over five times to 1.8 million.

Most of the increase in U.S. incarcerations has been due to nonviolent crimes such as possessing drugs, whereas in Europe such "crimes" rarely lead to prison. So in the U.S. we jail 5, 6, 7, or even 11 or 14 people who would be seen as innocent enough to stay out in society in Europe, for every one person we jail whom the Europeans would also incarcerate.

In other words, if we opened the prison doors in the U.S. right now – a horrendous proposal in most people's eyes – for every person the Europeans would have us jail, five to ten whom they would deem innocent would be set free. This is rather sobering. If we would let out ten guilty inmates to free one innocent one, surely we ought to rush to let out one guilty inmate to free five to ten innocent ones? And then we ought to refigure our approach to laws, trials, and, especially, punishment and rehabilitation.

The data and most of the ideas above, by the way, did not come to me by way of a dinner party with radical leftists. Instead, I borrowed this material from an article in *Scientific American*, August 1999. The author, Roger Doyle, was examining some facts to see their numeric implications. Being honest, of course, means looking at facts and reporting them truthfully. Being leftist means looking a little deeper at problems to find institutional causes, and then proposing well thought out solutions that further egalitarian and humanist values.

Doyle went on in his *Scientific American* essay to point out that (a) a key difference between young whites and (disproportionately jailed) young blacks was that the whites are more likely in our current economy to get jobs enabling them to avoid the need to steal or deal, (b) income differentials are vastly greater in the U.S. than in Europe and, reading only a little into his words, that (c) incarceration may be seen as a tool of control against the poor, so that "high U.S. incarceration rates are unlikely to decline until there is greater equality of income".

Kudos for *Scientific American's* honesty and even radicalism, but what about our hypothetical leftist dinner party? If the difference between the U.S. and Europe isn't that Americans have genes causing them to be antisocial but, rather, that Americans, and particularly black Americans, are put into circumstances by our economy which virtually require them to seek means of sustenance outside the law, and if, to be very conservative, half the inmates in the U.S. are arrested for victimless "crimes" that would not even be prosecuted, certainly not provoke jail time, in Europe, doesn't it make sense to ask whether the entire U.S. prosecutorial and punitive legal apparatus is, in fact, largely counterproductive?

Finally, why are some leftists sitting around a table, whether 30 years ago or today, or why is anyone at all, anytime, for that matter, more worried about the occasional antisocial or even pathological thug/rapist/murderer who is caught and incarcerated going free, than they are worried by (1) the violent and willful incarceration of so many innocent souls who have worthy and humane lives to live if only enabled to do so; or (2) the gray flannel businessmen walking freely up and down Wall Street who preside over the misery of so many for their own private gain, each businessman a perfect biological incarnation of willful, self-delusional, and largely incorrigible antisocial behavior that operates at a scale of violence which the worst incarcerated thugs can never dream to approach, or (3) the government, which, on behalf of those gray flannel businessmen wreaks massive mutilation and devastation on whole countries, then calls it humanitarian intervention so that they can avoid the death penalty our society prescribes for murder of any kind, much less for murder most massive such as they commit?

Our jails are 10 to 50 times more crowded than they would be under a humane legal system, primarily because diminishing the gap would entail reducing income differentials and improving the lot of society's worst off. Businessmen won't tolerate that, at least not without a fight.

Why does a capitalist country produce crime in greater numbers than genetic endowment plus equitable social conditions would entail? Consider Groucho Marx's little joke that the secret of success is honesty and fair dealing. If you can fake those, you've got it made. Or consider Sinclair Lewis' description of one of his most famous literary characters, George F. Babbitt, as being nimble in the calling of selling houses for more than people could afford to pay.

In other words, we live in a society in which to win is paramount, and even in legal transactions mindsets geared to winning are barely discernible from those geared to fraud and theft. The fact that people excluded from legal means of survival or prosperity in considerable numbers opt for illegal means is hardly surprising.

Here is Al Capone, the famous, and, in some respects, lionized American thug, on the subject: "This American system of ours, call it Americanism, call it capitalism, call it what you will, gives each and every one of us a great opportunity if we only seize it with both hands and make the most of it."

First, capitalism produces poor and poorly educated people on one side, and rich and callous people on the other. In the U.S., upwards of 30 million people worry about falling into, or already suffer, socially defined poverty. More frequently, even larger numbers of people periodically find themselves unexpectedly desperate. Over the course of a lifetime, as many as a hundred million people will suffer unemployment or fear of it at some point. At the same time a few million people have so much wealth and power that they virtually own society and determine its course of development.

Next, capitalism imposes non-stop economic transactional requisites that convey invitations to lie, cheat, and otherwise fleece one's fellow citizens through such means as price gouging, dumping pollutants, and paying sub minimum wages. Further, largely to maintain a degree of order and, in particular, to protect the property and safety of the rich and powerful, as well as to provide a context of control over all others, capitalism elaborates a system of laws even as draconian as three strikes you're out. A largely callous and often corrupt police apparatus and jurisprudence system is added to the mix. And the result is not just massive, generally unproductive, and very often unwarranted and aggressively dehumanizing incarceration rates, with abominable prison conditions, but crime galore, plus rampant fear and hostility. Since it all persists with barely a nod to improvement, presumably this is what those at the top want and are satisfied with, from behind their gated communities.

Capitalism produces disparities in wealth, reductions of solidarity, imposed insecurities, and propulsion of a mindset that winning ought to be pursued by any means necessary. It creates an environment in which getting away with crime is commonplace, crime is profitable, and the repression of crime is not only profitable but an excellent means of social control. Capitalism makes the distribution of tools of violence profitable and even empowering, and induces conditions of cynicism that impede rational judgments about policies and practices. In light of all this, in capitalism we abide an absence of anything remotely resembling rehabilitation, and we celebrate, instead, punishments and incarceration that spur more crime.

To figure out a more desirable approach to uncovering crime, determining guilt or innocence, and administering justice for victims and perpetrators, will be no simple task. But to see some of the broad implications of capitalism for crime, as noted above, and of parecon for crime, as noted below, is much simpler.

Parecon and crime

In a parecon there is no impetus to reduce or expand wide disparities in wealth by cheating, because there are no wide disparities to reduce. People are never uncertain, unstable, unsettled, and facing destitution, with crime as the only way out. People do not choose between a criminal career and jobs that are debilitating and dehumanizing. But more, it is not solely absence of the conditions of poverty that induce people to commit crimes to survive or care for loved ones, and absence of the conditions of great advantage which instill callousness and a belief that one is above society, that diminish parecon's crime rates.

In a parecon no one profits from crime. There is no industry which benefits from crime control or punishment of criminals. No one has a stake in larger and larger prisons, police budgets, and arms sales, and thus in crime growing. If there are still workplaces producing guns, no one connected with them has any interest whatsoever in anyone owning them for anything but socially desirable purposes.

There is every reason for citizens to rationally and compassionately consider the well being of themselves and of all citizens and to pursue policies accordingly, rather than settling for personally and socially counterproductive policies in the cynical belief that there's no better choice.

So, in a parecon, equitable social roles and the socially generated values of solidarity and self-management, plus stable and just conditions, all make it unnecessary for people to try to enhance their lives through crime. To deter crime rooted in pathology, or to deal with social violations stemming from jealousy or other persistent phenomena, a good society would of course want to have fair adjudication and sensible practices that continually reduce, rather than aggravate, the probability of further violations.

But there is another feature that is quite interesting and instructive, insofar as we are talking about crime for personal material gain – as compared to talking about criminal pathology (crime for pleasure), or about crime for passion or revenge.

Under capitalism, how do self-aggrandizing thieves operate? They might engage in fraud or deception, or literally grab items that belong to others. They then either have more purchasing power, or they have items they have grabbed which they add to their possessions or sell to amass more purchasing power. Capitalism's thieves live at a higher standard, as a result of stealing. They climb the ladder of material well-being and in so doing they appear to have been the beneficiary of high pay, bonuses, or victorious gambling.

Now what about in a parecon? We don't know what type of criminal justice system it will have, though we know it will incorporate balanced job complexes. But we do know that some people will still be fraudulent, grab what isn't theirs, or commit other criminal acts. The question is, what happens next, assuming they succeed? How do they enjoy the material spoils of crime?

If the spoils are tiny, their consumption won't be particularly visible. But the kind of booty that motivates serious theft is substantial. We become self-aggrandizing criminals pursuing the kind of booty that pushes our income way up. How can one enjoy that in a parecon?

The answer is, one pretty much can't enjoy that kind of booty in a parecon; save perhaps in one's own basement, if one has stolen items like paintings. In a parecon, any consumption of significant criminally acquired income will be visible to others. In capitalism, there are all kinds of ways for people to have hugely disparate incomes, but in a parecon, that isn't the case. If in a parecon you don't work much longer or harder – and there are limits to what is possible – then the only way you can have significantly extra wealth is through illegal means.

In other words, parecon creates a context of income distribution that makes it impossible for anyone to benefit greatly, in public, from crime. This both reduces the appeal of crime and greatly simplifies its discovery.

Parecon thus reduces: incentives to steal, conditions that breed crime, reasons for needing crime, inclinations in people's consciousness consistent with or conducive to engaging in crime, and prospects for success at crime.

But, before I close this chapter, I should address one more point that some readers may be wondering about – does parecon add another possible avenue of crime, as well as curtail many that now exist?

Economic crime in parecon?

In any economy, it is a crime to operate outside the norms and structures of acceptable economic life. In capitalism, it is criminal to own other people as slaves, for example, or to pay sub minimum wages, or to have overly unhealthy workplace conditions. Likewise, in a parecon it will be criminal to hire wage slaves, or to use unbalanced job complexes, or even just to operate outside the participatory planning system to accrue excessive income. Have we reduced some avenues to crime in a parecon, only to open up others?

It turns out this is overwhelmingly an economic question, because the economic dictates of parecon establish a context in which violations of parecon's defining economic structures are so difficult and so unrewarding that, even without considering legal penalties, they would rarely, if ever, attract interest.

Take opening a workplace and hiring wage slaves. It is certainly possible to open a new workplace in a parecon. You establish a workers' council and receive sanction to proceed from your related industry council, and then enter the planning process to receive inputs and provide outputs so employees can earn income.

One cannot, therefore, employ wage slaves openly because there would be no acceptance of it. Can one claim to be a parecon firm in public, but behind closed doors have one or two people entirely running the show with all other employees receiving full incomes but then turning over large parts back to their bosses?

Even if we ignore the difficulty of turning over purchasing power, the image is, of course, absurd. Why would any worker submit to this sort of condition when the whole economy is full of balanced job complexes, self-managing positions, and, even more, when the merest whisper about the situation would immediately cause the workplace in question to be revamped into pareconish shape?

Similarly, suppose there is a parecon in some country and an overseas capitalist decides to open an auto plant inside its borders. He brings components into the parecon country and builds a plant – this is already quite impossible, but let's ignore that – and then he advertises for workers. Suppose he is prepared to pay much more than the country's average income level and he promises good enough work conditions that there are takers, which is also hugely implausible (rather like people now agreeing to be literal slaves for a foreign entrepreneur opening a shop in New York City in exchange for luxury accommodations in the slave quarters). Still, even assuming workers are ready to sign on, this is none-theless an impossible scenario because others involved in the planning process will neither deliver electricity, water, rubber, steel, or other essential inputs, nor buy the cars produced – not to mention imposing penalties against this anti-pareconish firm.

Obviously the above logic applies identically to violations of parecon short of wage slavery, such as unfair salary differences or unbalanced job complexes inside a particular firm. But another scenario has to be assessed as well.

Suppose I am a great painter, or cook. I work in an art council or cooks' council in my city and have a balanced job complex and get pareconish remuneration. But I am unusually good, highly admired and well known for the great quality of my creations, and I decide I want to parlay my talent into higher income.

I paint or cook in my spare time, in my home – in hopes that in short order I can leave the pareconish job and work only out of my home. To make enlarged income, I make the output of my private labors available through a black market. This violates the norms of parecon, but what stops me from doing it?

Well, first, if it so chooses, society can of course enforce penalties for this type of violation just like it does for fraud, theft, or murder. But even if there were no penalties, I would confront considerable economic obstacles to benefiting through a black market.

To ply my private trade in any great degree I have somehow to obtain all the supplies I need. But this isn't an insurmountable obstacle, since if I also have a pareconish income from a pareconish job, I can forego some personal con-sumption and use that income to get ingredients I need for black market endeavors. My tremendous talent guarantees that in short order the results will be worth much more than the cost. So far, so good, unlike, say, if I was trying to do something privately where I needed costly supplies or a large venue – such as if I was a pilot giving private flights, or a researcher trying to cure cancer on the sly and sell the results.

But there is still the problem of people buying my meals or paintings. How do they consume this illegal black market bounty? And how do I get purchasing power out of it? I can't. The best I can induce is for them to give me something for my output, such as a shirt, a meal, or a piece of furniture.

But to top off that complication, in addition to the difficulties of the whole endeavor, and the risk of being caught and at the very least suffering ignominy, how can I enjoy my material bounty? I can't enjoy it, except in private. I can't accrue a whole lot of payment in kind and then waltz around wearing, driving, and otherwise visibly consuming it, as that would be a dead giveaway that I was crooked. I have to take my bounty to my cellar, for private consumption.

So the whole picture is that I have to pay for ingredients and produce on the sly something I could be well paid and highly admired for producing in the real economy; find people willing to barter illegally even though they could get essentially the same goods in the economy legally and without hassle; and then enjoy the fruits of my deception in private. Even the easiest of all possible types of violation is in a parecon made structurally onerous and of limited benefit, in addition to being illegal.

Capitalism creates poor people who steal to survive or to garner otherwise absent pleasure. It creates wealthy people who steal to maintain their conditions against collapse. It creates anti-sociality that makes criminal mindsets prevalent. It makes crime's rewards unlimited. It makes revelation of even public crime unlikely. It hardens and even expands the criminal skills of those who commit crime rather than rehabilitating them.

In contrast, parecon makes crime unnecessary for survival or for gaining pleasures. It eliminates rich people needing to preserve their advantages. It creates conditions of solidarity that make criminal mindsets personally abhorrent. It minimizes crime's rewards, and it makes discovery of anything but the most secretive violation virtually inevitable. It rehabilitates those who do commit crimes.

The bottom line is that parecon tends not to produce crimes and would certainly be compatible with desirable ways of dealing with crime control in a new and improved society. Parecon is a just economy.

13 Questions

NEW IDEAS HAVE intellectual value largely in proportion to their impact on further new ideas. Does a new idea open doors? Does a new idea lead nowhere?

The main doors for innovative social ideas to open are practical. Parecon should provoke efforts to attain new institutional relations. But we can also ask whether parecon's insights propel an intellectual agenda. Do parecon's insights raise new questions to explore? Do intellectual tasks arise from parecon's claims?

Capitalism questions

One type of intellectual extension of parecon's insights will be to explore each new concept or claim it makes about capitalism more deeply and fully. For example, imagine looking more deeply at markets to discern the details of their attributes as highlighted by parecon – including their antisocial impact on personalities, distortion of public/private consumption ratios, constraining of the trajectory of investments, snowballing mispricing of items with external effects, coercive imposition on work duration and intensity, coercive imposition on work organization and divisions of labor, and coercive implications for class definition and rule. Studies inspired by pareconish thought could reveal the extent of these claimed features and uncover their deeper relations and dynamics.

Or one can imagine similar extensive explorations of capitalist workplaces and their divisions of labor and modes of decision making. For example, what is the relation between different modes of conveying and assessing information and the influence that different people have on decisions in capitalist firms? What is the relation between different corporate decision-tallying methods and people's influence? What capitalist decision patterns exist, and what properties and implications do capitalist decision patterns impose? In turn, what impact does the choice of corporate decision-making and division of labor in capitalism have on capitalist technological innovations and work methodologies, and what

131

effects do those implications have on profits, quality of output, and use of talents and resources?

One could also imagine examining how the coordinator class and its agendas affect capitalist dynamics. First one could seek to document the coordinator class's existence and shared properties, including circumstances, consciousness, and aims. Then one could investigate how coordinator agendas affect profit-seeking, market competition, workplace organization, workplace and market decision-making, and the interface between workers and owners. Understanding what typifies relations between the coordinator class and the capitalists on the one hand, and between the coordinator class and workers on the other, would be beneficial. What consciousnesses, preferences, and interests emerge in the respective classes due to their mutual relations, and how do these class characteristics affect economic motives, income distribution, consumption patterns, family relations, schooling, sports, culture, and so on?

Parecon questions

A second broad area for extrapolation of parecon's insights has to do with parecon itself. What are additional or deeper properties of parecon or of possible extensions and variations of parecon?

In exploring and refining parecon as an economic vision, however, we won't want to make either of two mistakes:

1. We shouldn't mistakenly think that all parecons will be alike and that by describing a possible feature of a parecon we are describing an actual feature that must always be present in all parecons. In other words, we should not seek homogeneity of economic vision. Future economics and societies will be diverse in their details.

2. We shouldn't mistakenly think that we have the means and information to closely predict the future, or, for that matter, that there is a good reason to want to closely predict the future. In other words, we don't need blueprints. The details of future economies and societies will emerge from the unpredict-able, and from the often varied choices of their citizens, not from prognos-tications, much less instructions, developed in advance.

In future economies, people will do what they want to do. But avoiding over-reaching into excessive detail should not prevent our addressing main features that can help inform and motivate efforts to move forward. So even while we avoid mistaking possibilities for inevitabilities or going overboard with details, it is certainly useful to explore the logic and implications of the key defining institutions of parecon, both intellectually and in practical experiments, and to use the resulting insights both to improve the vision (without over-specifying it) and to refine our comprehension of the vision and thus our ability to effectively advocate and seek it.

So, for example, what more can we say about the specifically economic implications of worker and consumer councils, of self-managed decision-making, of balanced job complexes, of remuneration for effort and sacrifice, and of participatory planning? Can we describe what they might be like in specific industries? Can we give insights into differences that might exist from country to country? Can we investigate more deeply the dynamics of information and voting, of work tasks, and of cooperative, collective, negotiation of outcomes?

The issue isn't trying to foresee tenth order, or even third or perhaps second order, properties and features. The issue is to elaborate and comprehend the main defining implications of proposed structural choices for liberating people's options, behaviors, views, fulfillment and development in order to test and investigate the worthiness and viability of the vision.

Likewise, what about demonstrating with more care various mechanisms that could facilitate desirable exchange of information and preference tallying, both in theory and empirically? That would enhance the case for participatory planning. One could imagine conducting not only practical experiments on various scales – such as creating pareconish workplaces or groups of them, and pareconish neighborhoods or groups of them – but also perhaps conducting a large scale simulation, whether in fictitious but carefully constructed computer form, or perhaps through a kind of parallel economic activity in the real world. The same holds for further exploring the interpersonal and psychological implications of all pareconish structures, as well.

How diverse might balanced job complexes have to be? Can we more compellingly investigate the impact of balanced job complexes on levels of output? How smoothly would participatory planning handle shocks and crises? What might be the pace and implications of overcoming disparities of wealth within and between countries, during the periods of disruption? For that matter, there are major questions of transition, of course.

Questioning today's society

A third broad area of parecon-informed research and intellectual innovation involves elaborating on what has been loosely discussed here in this book: the interface between economy and the rest of society; first regarding capitalism itself, and then regarding participatory economics.

For example, what are the deeper and more fundamental ways that capitalist economic institutions affect other realms of society, including gender, race, politics, ecology, international relations, education, science, art, and so on? And, likewise, how does the broader society affect capitalist economies?

How do capitalist markets, corporate divisions of labor, and the three-class economic division of capitalism affect family life, education, cultural communities, political parties, science and technology, and art and music?

Are families seriously constrained by the processes of market participation and competition? Do families deeply embody class consciousness, and if so, in what respect for each class? Do they internally mimic, in some degree, economic structures such as divisions of labor or class relations, and if so, with what implications for how children are raised and socialized? Do families today produce adults without economic categorization or do they produce members of classes? Is the sexism that exists in capitalism different than sexism in other systems? Is it molded and constrained by class and market pressures?

How does education in a society with capitalist economics reflect economic influences and constraints? Do the pedagogy, methodology, and roles of those who teach and learn intimately reflect capitalist pressures? Does the subject matter conform with capitalist dictates? Does the distribution of educational opportunities to different students abide capitalist class requisites?

Are racial, religious, ethnic, and regional communities structured differently than they might otherwise be due to existing in the field of influence of capitalist economics? Do they show significant influence from market competition and commercialization? Do they internally abide, incorporate, and even reproduce class divisions? Do their modes of self-definition, celebration, and mutual interaction embody features imposed by capitalist competition, class division, or pay structures?

Do the structure, role offerings, and programs of political parties, and the roles and practices of the state, reflect the pressures of capitalist competition, profit seeking, accumulation, and class division and rule? Does the state contradict the existence of classes, does it accommodate the existence of classes, or does it actually reproduce the class hierarchies of capitalism? Do government's internal methods embody corporate norms and logic?

Are science and technology affected by the processes employed, the roles available, the discoveries made and emphasized, the insights gleaned and communicated, and the products researched, conceived, designed, and widely implemented by capitalism? Does all this reflect economic pressures generated by the market, corporations, and profit seeking?

Are the production and enjoyment of art and music different within a capitalist economy than they would be without capitalist influences? Are the artist's choices, work conditions, and well-being affected? Are the remuneration for artistic work and the dissemination of its results affected? Are the music tastes of people freely arrived at, or do people's positions in the capitalist economy, and particularly their class, bias their preferences?

And what if I reverse the questions I just asked? In particular, how do sexism, racism, and political authoritarianism contextualize, constrain, shape, and even define features of capitalist economy?

Are workplaces to some extent like families, cultural communities, or political states in their operations, structures, and roles? Are classes affected by gender, race, and political divisions? Do the ways corporate divisions of labor play out vary due to influences from other parts of society? Are there counterparts of men and women, mothers and daughters, fathers and sons, in workplaces? Is there a racial community dynamic in work roles and products? Does market competition get altered by the state's intrinsic political logic?

Just a little thought reveals many examples of mutual implications – and, indeed, many different schools of thought have tackled questions like those raised above. Indeed, their insights have in many respects provided the impetus for the inclusion of these questions here and in earlier chapters of this book. But perhaps additional study that particularly incorporates and even emerges from parecon's insights and modes of thought can discern additional features, patterns, and dynamics that add to our understanding and, most important, that have strategic implications for activists seeking change.

Questioning future society

And finally, in accord with the intellectual priorities of the rest of this book, all the above issues bearing on the mutual relations of capitalist economics and other dimensions of life apply also to the future. That is, a pareconish intellectual agenda includes exploring further the relations between parecon's economic innovations and parallel, entwined dynamics in other parts of contemporary life – which is to say the implications of parecon for racism, sexism, political authoritarianism, and unconstrained growth, and vice versa – but, more, it also includes the further elaboration of vision for other spheres of life and the exploration of the interface between revolutionized other spheres of life and parecon.

In other words, a big parecon-related intellectual agenda is for activists and movements to generate a compelling vision for other parts of society, and in particular for kinship and gender/sexuality, for community and race/religion, for politics and the state and citizenship, and for relations to nature and relations among societies.

One possibility bearing on this desire for additional visions is that the path that has so far been used to conceive and advocate a parecon might be largely repeatable for other focuses. Perhaps we can set out key values for other spheres of life, refine those values somewhat for each, and then seek to conceptualize and comprehend new institutions for that sphere that are able to accomplish its key functions in accord with the preferred values. In other words, the intellectual steps associated with generating parecon could be done in turn, for gender, culture, polity, and perhaps other parts of life as well.

For example, a feminist intellectual agenda influenced by parecon's methods might start from the insight that the kinship sphere is concerned with procreation, sexuality, nurturance, socialization, and the handling of associated daily life relations. It might posit as guiding values solidarity, diversity, equity (meaning in this case that people should have kinship-related responsibilities free of gender, sexual, or age-related social hierarchies), and self-management. And it might then seek to describe feminist living and sexual arrangements – obviously celebrating a great diversity of types, but also including certain key defining structures able to accomplish kinship functions while advancing the guiding values.

Or, similarly, anti-racists and liberation theologists and others concerned about cultural and community liberation might note that community is about self-definition, communication, and celebration, and might posit values such as solidarity, diversity, equity (which might mean security for cultural communities), and self-management. They might then advocate multicultural (or perhaps it might be called intercommunal) ways for communities to define themselves and interact with one another to accomplish cultural functions without generating racial, ethnic, religious, national, or other cultural community hierarchies of security, status, freedom, wealth, or power.

Similarly, anarchists and others concerned about political relations might note that politics is about the legislation of shared norms, adjudication of disputes and violations, and implementation of collective projects and programs, and might pose as values solidarity, diversity, and equity (meaning a just distribution of accountability and responsibility), and self-management. They might then advocate liberatory new structures to accomplish political functions that enhance our political values, such as those of parpolity discussed earlier in this book. This would not be about eliminating polity, nor about capturing the current polity, but about conceiving and constructing a new polity in accord with the logic of a new society.

Finally, in all these cases of intellectual pursuit, beyond looking only toward the shape of a worthy future, another task would be to explore strategic implications of the visionary insights for the present, and to test and continually refine new insights in practical work. I begin to take up this task in the next chapter.

14 Strategy

THE EFFORT TO WIN a new economy will obviously have a great many facets. In a book called *Moving Forward* (AK Press), I discussed parecon related strategic issues in detail. A more recent book by Robin Hahnel, *Economic Justice and Democracy*, also addresses parecon related strategic issues and does so more historically.

Here I should at least note that pareconish movements will, in the process of struggling to win a new economy, likely build and then emphasize worker and consumer councils that will engage in wide-ranging pursuits for many years, continually enriching members' consciousness and advancing members' capacities for self-organization.

These worker and consumer councils, along with other related movement organizations, ranging from mass movements to unions to new rank and file organizations to local projects, will certainly struggle to win reforms – meaning to win gains in workplaces (such as better conditions and pay), in neighborhoods (such as pollution controls and public services), and in the whole economy (such as redirection of national budgets and expansion of democratic control over them). They will do all this, however, in a non-reformist manner, cooperating with movements seeking to win gains in kinship, cultural, political, international, ecological and other relations.

Non-reformist reform struggles

In other words, movements to win a new society, including, but certainly not limited to, a new economy, will not assume that existing defining social features will persist forever, but will seek reforms that will improve people's lives in the present as part of the process of replacing those defining features fully in the future.

A fight for higher wages will not be an end unto itself-but will seek to raise public consciousness of the worthiness and viability of later instituting a system of remuneration for effort and sacrifice. It will seek to win higher wages now, and also inform and enrich the means and desire to win full equity later.

A fight for better working conditions will not be an end unto itself, but will seek to raise public consciousness of the worthiness and viability of later instituting balanced job complexes. It may seek new forms of accountability, information transfer, job sharing, and job training, all moving toward classless workplace organization.

A fight over pollution controls and public services will not be an end unto itself, but will seek to raise consciousness of the worthiness and viability of later instituting the means for consumers as well as producers to influence all economic decisions that affect them through self-management. It may seek elements of collective consumption planning or other restructuring and restrictions on current consumption and production – its volume, content, by-products, methods, etc. – moving toward allocation in accord with true social costs and benefits.

A fight over winning less military spending and more social spending, or over democratizing control of collective consumption, will not be an end unto itself, but will seek to raise public consciousness of the worthiness and viability of transcending both market allocation and central planning with a new system of cooperative negotiated allocation called participatory planning, and will seek to win additional gains in that direction.

These and all other projects undertaken to improve lives now will always also seek to leave movements stronger, better organized, more committed, and even more desirous to win further changes as time passes, rather than leaving movements sated and inclined to call a premature halt to their endeavors.

There will be pareconist efforts to win immediate reforms, and then more reforms, and still more reforms, but all these efforts will not only continually respect the limits and contexts of current conditions, but also self-consciously lead toward future revolutionary goals.

Much of what this will look like can be known only through actual future experience because what movements for change will do will depend to a considerable degree on what agents of reaction do and on what future conditions make relevant and possible. Nothing about movement choices is set out inflexibly in advance, other than, arguably, a few very broad features that would be hard to do without if we are to win the new economy we seek.

Class maps: class struggle

In that light a key insight that emerges from what we might call a pareconish understanding of both economic vision and current economic relations is that movements can be anti-capitalist and even overcome capitalism, and yet none-theless not attain classlessness, equity, solidarity, diversity, or self-management.

The choice that faces social activists is not the two-way choice between capitalism and classlessness, that is, but is instead the three-way choice between capitalism, coordinatorism, and classlessness. And this means that anti-capitalist activism that seeks to attain a new type of economy needs to orient itself-very carefully to attain classlessness rather than coordinator class rule. More, this isn't only a matter of a movement's members having admirable wishes and hopes.

Coordinatorism is an economy in which a layer of people who, in capitalism, receive wages and are certainly not capitalists, become a new ruling class over the still subordinate working class. This layer I call the coordinator class. In capitalism, it holds a relative monopoly over daily decision-making and empower-ing work as compared to the working class, which performs overwhelmingly rote and obedient labor.

The coordinator class is, in other words, composed of managers, doctors, lawyers, engineers, and other people whose roles in economic life give them substantial control over their own conditions of work and over the conditions of work of those below. The coordinators earn more than those who labor below them. The coordinators have more status than those who labor below them. The coodinators see themselves and subordinate workers differently than capitalists see coordinators and subordinate workers, and, likewise, subordinate workers see coordinators differently than they see capitalists.

Coordinators legitimate their ruling position by claiming superior capacity and insight due to their having more training, schooling, and on the job empowerment. However, these advantages are not intrinsic to individuals, as coordinators tend to believe, but are socially determined and enforced. Holding a collective monopoly over empowering positions in the economy, not personal merit, distinguishes the coordinator class from the working class.

In coordinatorism, this third class that resides in capitalism between labor and capital becomes the ruling class above workers. Private ownership of the means of production is eliminated – a progressive step – but compromising this gain is the retention of corporate divisions of labor with top-down decision making and with either markets or central planning for allocation. Remuneration in coordinatorism is based on bargaining power, and, to a lesser degree, on output. Decisions are made overwhelmingly by the coordinator class. This is not a hypothetical scenario: coordinator class rule has existed under the names of market socialism and centrally planned socialism, both in actual practice and in textbook models.

And so arises the strategic point that I would like to make in closing this brief chapter. Anti-capitalist activism can have as its goal elevating the coordinator class or eliminating class differences. Movements of each type against capitalism will very often find themselves fighting for the same short- and even medium-term aims, including higher wages, better conditions, new property relations, and greater say for workers and consumers, as well as presumably supporting diverse struggles for gains in other dimensions of social life.

Their short-term demands will not differentiate movements likely to usher in classlessness from movements likely to usher in coordinatorism. Rather, key difference will lie in the arguments they offer on behalf of their typically similar short-term demands, the goals they say their similar short term demands are part of a process to reach, and the ways their respective movements are organized to "melt into" a new economy and society or, instead, to assume that the current one will persist forever.

Do movements tend to mimic corporate divisions of labor in their internal structure? Do they tend to employ competitive or authoritative remuneration? Do they implement authoritative decision-making, or even formally democratic decision-making that is always, however, dominated by a relatively few people who have coordinator class credentials or aspirations? Do movements not only utilize, but reproduce and even enlarge, advantages in knowledge and social skills that some members have as compared to others, and elevate coordinator class rather than working class values and preferences? Do they feel congenial to and empower coordinators more than workers, and even obscure the existence of a coordinator class, much less the importance of avoiding becoming subservient to it?

If the answers to these questions are yes, then, even if nearly all members of such movements sincerely want more than anything else to attain real class-lessness, the movements are, nonetheless – even despite the aspirations of their members – far more likely to usher in coordinator domination of workers. Their structures will override their members' desires.

On the other hand, do movements reject corporate divisions of labor in their structure, and instead opt for balanced job complexes? Do they reject old-style remuneration and instead value only effort and sacrifice in determining income? Do they reject authoritative decision-making, and even formally democratic decision-making that is always predictably dominated by a few members, and instead opt for real self-management by all members? Do they carefully, and as a high priority, work to reduce, and finally undo, advantages in knowledge and social skills that some movement members have as compared to others? Do they elevate working class rather than coordinator class values and preferences? Do they feel congenial to and empower working class members more than coordinator class members, and do they highlight not only the existence of a coordinator class, but also the importance of avoiding tutelage to it?

If the answers to these questions are yes, then we are likely talking about a movement that is headed toward classlessness not only in its claims, but in its definition and deeds.

Strategy for winning a new economy is most certainly contextual, and therefore, in many respects, unspecifiable in advance. But in the broad features noted above, we can distinguish between efforts to ameliorate capitalism while leaving the capitalist system in place, and efforts intended to win gains now but also, in time, replace capitalism completely. We can also distinguish between efforts to overcome capitalism to attain coordinator class elevation via market or centrally planned coordinatorism, and efforts to overcome capitalism to attain the elimination of classes via participatory economics.

I have a final point to make, also bearing on strategy.

Fighting to win

What if, some might reply to all this, victory is simply impossible? Yes, they say, after a full assessment of your arguments, we agree that you have made a case for a new type of economy vastly superior to capitalism and also to what has heretofore borne the name of socialism (but which should have been called coordinatorism). And yes, we agree that you have made a case that this new parecon would be compatible with, and even positively benefit, other dimensions of social life. And yes, we agree with you that you have indicated some of the properties a movement would have to incorporate to attain a parecon. But we think that your having described properties necessary to winning a parecon is a far cry from describing properties sufficient to winning one.

We wonder, therefore, what if there is no list of sufficient conditions? What if history has progressed so far and so long down oppressive paths that extrication from exploitation is no longer possible? What if there is no route from where we have journeyed thus far in history to the very different destination we would like to reach? What if the direct path from oppression to liberation is blocked, the path back and around is blocked, and the path forward and over is blocked? What if in every direction there are only insurmountable obstacles? Then aren't all your demonstrations regarding parecon's theoretical desirability irrelevant? Aren't we stuck, our aspirations aside, with capitalism forever?

My answer is that yes, if we are stuck, as this view assumes, then of course we are stuck, as it concludes. The depressing conclusion is true by virtue of the depressed assumptions. But the assumption of conclusions has never constituted an argument for them, and there is both no reason to assume the conclusions you list and no argument to justify their likelihood.

When someone says there is no alternative — which claim we have tried to erase — or says, maybe there is an alternative, but we cannot attain it because the obstacles are too great, the first thing to note is that the messenger ought to be crying.

Someone saying there is no better social future is like a biologist reporting we will never find a cure for cancer. Those who make such harmful claims with a smile on their face reveal by their demeanor that their logic isn't logic at all, but is, instead, wish fulfillment — which is to say, rationalization of horrible injustice in service of elite privilege and prejudice.

But okay, suppose a sober, serious, caring person is miserable over his or her conclusions, but nonetheless puts forth the claim that, though parecon and a better society are humanly conceivable and would be worthy and viable, nonetheless the forces reinforcing current relations are too great to escape. It is as if we can conceive a universe of possibility off the planet, this person says. We know it is out there. We even know what its main features look like. But, regardless of that knowledge, our planet's gravity is too great for us to break free and reach the new world. Analogously, the person argues, we can conceive of the better future that parecon promises, but the tentacles of the past are too strong to escape.

My answer is that being an activist is not rolling rocks up hills, digging useless ditches, blowing into the wind, or opposing gravity. It is part of the single most important, most courageous, and most productive undertaking in all human history, a project with deep roots and a winning future. I can't prove my claim. No one can prove claims about what people will achieve in the future. But I believe it.

In contrast, do those who think that resigning to capitalism, patriarchy, racism, and authoritarianism lasting forever makes sense, also believe that the abolitionists were wrong, that workers in daily struggles for better wages and conditions were wrong, that the advocates of women and blacks and Latinos being people were wrong, and that seeking liberation has been and will be wrong?

Do they really want to assert that wage slavery is forever? Do they really want to base their actions on believing that it somehow violates nature and reason, or even just the accumulated history of human engagements and traditional constructions, that human beings should collectively rise up to control their own lives rather than the majority of people being always and forever subject to the domineering will of an oppressive minority?

Do they really want to say that people can't devise and implement – even against stiff opposition and diehard habits – new systems in which poverty, starvation, death by preventable diseases, and systemic denial of dignity and personal stature are eradicated?

On what grounds do they proclaim such pessimism?

Once upon a time, when Pharaohs whipped and/or mesmerized slaves into building their gargantuan tombs and maintained their largely unchallenged dominance for thousands of years with marginal changes of any kind, or when emperors dragooned peasants into fighting lions for imperial entertainment, or when slave owners lynched growers into maximal output and minimal freedom, was it desirable to resign from opposition? Why is now different? Does someone, somewhere, suddenly have a crystal ball which says that no matter how hard humanity struggles, there will be no better future?

To win a better future we need to generate a trajectory of activism that elites cannot repress or manipulatively derail, which they can't calmly abide, and which, perhaps even more significantly, will not implode because it embodies values and dynamics that run contrary to its own aspirations.

But what dissident approach can't be repressed, can't be manipulated off course, and won't destroy or distort itself?

The only answer I know is rapidly growing numbers of dissidents with varied focuses for their dissent, and with steadily escalating commitment and militancy, all bound together by informed shared commitment to a sufficiently conceived and widely enough shared vision of the future to both motivate and make steadfast their efforts.

To succeed, we need not just growing numbers of dissidents, not just multiple focuses, not just growing commitment and militancy, and not just widely shared inspiring vision, but all these assets at once. To me, since our movements have never simultaneously long sustained all these features, past failures (and there have been many partial victories as well, of course) reveal only our need for comprehensive diligence. They do not convey that there is some impossible additional component of activism that we can never attain. The right response to the difficulty of social revolution is not doubt that it can happen, but persistence in making it happen.

15 Marxism

THIS CHAPTER ADDRESSES the relationship between participatory economics and the theory and strategy of social democratic, Leninist/Trotskyist, and libertarian Marxist frameworks. The next chapter addresses parecon and anarchism. Chapter seventeen addresses parecon and broader left perspectives.

My discussions of anarchism, and particularly of Marxism, are contentious and controversial. It seems that my past presentations of this material have often failed to communicate my actual thoughts. To correct misinterpretation, here I argue positions from multiple angles and in multiple ways. This lengthens the delivery, but I hope readers will bear with it.

Marxism's features

Marxism is a wide and deep toolbox of concepts that label aspects of history and provide claims about their interrelations. Key to Marxism are the ideas that production and consumption are central to human existence, that accomplishing economic functions entails institutions or modes of production, and that modes of production in turn impose requirements that delimit virtually all outcomes and possibilities.

As Engels famously summarized: "Just as Darwin discovered the law of evolution in organic nature, so Marx discovered the law of evolution in human history. He discovered the simple fact, hitherto concealed by an overgrowth of ideology, that mankind must first of all eat and drink, have shelter and clothing, before it can pursue politics, religion, science, art, etc. And that therefore the production of the immediate material means of subsistence and consequently the degree of economic development attained by a given people or during a given epoch, form the foundation upon which the state institutions, the legal conceptions, the art, and even the religious ideas of the people concerned have evolved, and in the light of which those things must be explained, instead of vice versa as had hitherto been the case".

Of course, for Marxists the economy isn't the only factor affecting society, nor does influence run only one way. Instead, again according to Engels, "political, juridical, philosophical, religious, literary, artistic, etc. development is based on economic development. But all of these react upon one another and also upon the economic base. It is not that the economic position is the cause and alone active, while everything else has a passive effect. There is rather interaction on the basis of economic necessity, which ultimately always asserts itself".

Thus, history unfolds in light of the pressures and conflicts occurring largely in society's technology and social relations of production. "At a certain stage of their development the material forces of production in a society come in conflict with the existing relations of production, or what is but a legal expression for the same thing, with the property relations within which they have been at work before. From forms of development of the forces of production these relations turn into their fetters. Then begins an epoch of social revolution. With the change of the economic foundation, the entire immense superstructure is more or less rapidly transformed."

Critical to the Marxist framework is the idea that in accomplishing economic functions the economy casts people into contending classes with different ownership relations to the means of production. Some people own means of production. They are capitalists and gain income as profit. Other people own only their ability to do work, which they sell for a wage to the capitalists. They are workers, also called wage slaves.

The conflict or class struggle between owners and workers in capitalism shapes all society's aspects, including politics, culture, and gender relations, so that "the history of all hitherto existing society is the history of class struggles".

In capitalism itself, capitalists seek to maximize their profit, both for their own direct benefit, and because to maintain their position entails that they compete for market share and for revenues to invest. Workers, by contrast, seek to earn as high a wage as possible, both to stay above destitution, and, when possible, to eke out a better existence. The capitalist pays as low a wage and provides the cheapest conditions for as much labor as he can extract. The worker seeks as good conditions for doing as little labor for as much wage as he or she can extract.

The conflict that ensues between owners and workers over wage rates, unemployment levels, work conditions, and broader cultural and political policies composes class struggle and in turn contours the unfolding logic of capitalism.

Capitalism thus reprises the class struggles of all past history in a specific and new manner. "Freeman and slave, patrician and plebeian, lord and serf, the guildmaster and journeyman, in a word, oppressor and oppressed, stood in constant opposition to one another, carried on an uninterrupted now hidden, now open fight, a fight that each time ended either in a revolutionary reconstruction of society at large, or in the common ruin of the contending classes." With the arrival of capitalism the class struggle becomes that of workers and owners.

On top of these core Marxist conceptual commitments there arise additional insights and interpretations which inform diverse Marxism-based strategies.

Marxist economism

Do Marxism's concepts highlight what's most important and leave out only what's peripheral? Do they reveal the roots of oppression? Do they conceive liberating relationships? Do they comprehensively inform activist interventions? Finally, is parecon entirely and comfortably Marxist, or is parecon a reaction to failings in Marxism?

Marxism's virtues include that it tells us that economics is important (with which parecon concurs), it rejects capitalist ownership relations and profit-seeking (as does parecon), it reveals many horrible effects of markets (which insights parecon extends), and it highlights the importance of class dynamics (which parecon also highlights).

So far, so good, but what are Marxism's problems?

First, when real existing people utilize Marxism's concepts, they tend to systematically under-value and misunderstand social relations of gender, political, cultural, and ecological origin. Used under trying circumstances, Marxism tends to exaggerate in its users' minds the centrality of economics and insufficiently to prioritize gender, race, polity, and the environment.

Most Marxists feel that race, gender, polity, and environment are of course important, and often even very important – but they also think that non-economic features attain their importance largely through their relations to economics.

The concepts Marxists use to understand society are not confined to but are certainly rooted in attention to class relations. Marxists examine how economic relations affect classes and how class relations in turn affect potentials for change. Marxists in turn examine how race, gender, sexuality, power, ecology, and other factors impact on class struggle by propelling or impeding working class gains, which, in turn, they believe, will induce gains of all kinds.

A pareconist perspective agrees that economics is a profoundly important aspect of society and that the class divisions and struggles economics produces are hugely instrumental in affecting the quality of our lives. But a pareconist, or at least this pareconist, also sees that the same claim can be made for cultural relations, for sexual and gender relations, and for political relations.

Rather than understanding the latter three arenas of social life and the divisions and struggles they engender largely, or even primarily, as they are affected by class, a pareconist perspective asserts that we need to understand each, and economics too, insofar as they are all affected by one another.

Put differently, Marxism says that the mode of production of a society emanates a force field that affects all of society, often very dramatically. I agree with this claim and to me, in fact, it seems utterly incontestable. But then I also agree with the feminist who says that the organization and relations of socialization and nurturance emanate a force field that affects all of society. And I agree as well with the multiculturalist who says the same thing about cultural and community relations, and with the anarchist who says the same thing about political and power relations.

All these viewpoints rightly identify a locus of important influence, but each is wrong whenever it (explicitly or even just implicitly) denies the comparable importance of the other loci of influence. The conclusion is that there are at least four sources of profound influence in society rather than only one, as Marxism typically concludes.

The claim is that giving attention to matters of race, gender, authority, not to mention ecology and international relations, primarily via examining their impact on and implications for class struggle, often undercuts seeing their importance in their own right, and compromises attention to their own dynamics, as well seeing their mutual interconnection with one another, not just with economics. It may emphasize them, but it will be mainly or even only in their economic implications.

The mistake of what is sometimes called "monism" – even when it is a very flexible and enlightened monism – is to tend, under pressure, to elevate one realm to predominance and lose track of the priority of other realms. The point is, if we prioritize economics and class as the primary focus of conceptual attention and raise these concepts above all others in importance, we will likely not only misperceive a more complex reality, we will also relegate other comparably important focuses to a wrongly subordinate position. This of course also holds for overly prioritizing gender, race, or power above the rest, or above economics.

The solution for Marxists isn't to reduce attention to economics, but to elevate attention to other spheres and to their mutually defining influences, without presupposing any to be prior or dominant. To overcome Marxism's over attentiveness and over elevation of economics would therefore require a twofold alteration in the way many Marxists construct and utilize their world view. They would need to admit:

1. That Marxism mainly conceptualizes economics and not all of society and history, and

2. That feminist, multiculturalist, and anarchist conceptualizations offer equally central insights into society and history, and in particular, that influences from other domains can centrally shape economic relations, just as the reverse can occur.

That is, for real world Marxist practice to be desirably multi-focused, Marxists would need to jettison their claims of an economic base pushing and pulling a social and cultural superstructure, and instead highlight that gender, race, and political dynamics can all affect what goes on in workplaces, allocation, and consumption, just as significantly as economics can affect what goes on in religions, racial communities, families, and governments.

Marxism would need to recognize all directions of causality instead of exclusively or even just primarily emphasizing only causality from economics to the rest of society, and would have to refine many of its concepts accordingly.

This type of critique has in the past propelled feminists to create socialist feminism (to try to merge insights from gender-focused and class-focused analyses), and has led as well to variants of anarcho-marxism, Marxist nationalism, and other approaches, right up to frameworks that centrally address economics, polity, culture, and kinship all on a par.

The upshot is that while the observation/criticism that Marxism has been overly economic is important, I don't think it is devastating. Many Marxists accept this criticism already, and all Marxists could relatively easily adopt the more complex formulation described above – that influences from race, gender, sexuality, and authority can mold the economy just as the reverse can occur, and that groups defined by those other core features can be as central actors in historical struggle and change as classes can. If insufficiently highlighting and comprehending other spheres of social life in their own right were Marxism's only problem, it wouldn't cause me to reject Marxism, but to try, as I have in the past, along with others, to incorporate new insights to it.

Marxism and class

But an overly economic emphasis is not the problem of Marxism that I wish to feature in this chapter, partly because it is relatively straightforward to correct and a great many Marxists have worked hard on doing so, and partly because it isn't as directly germane to concerns about parecon as matters that I will now take up.

Suppose all Marxists soon achieve an enrichment and diversification of their concepts to incorporate race, gender, power, and also ecological influences, as primary. Would I be satisfied with such a renovated Marxism and then urge that parecon is a Marxist vision?

I would certainly be happy about the change, yes, but no, I wouldn't yet celebrate Marxism, because the pareconist perspective indicates that Marxism has a much more damning and less tractable problem than over prioritizing economics. Marxism, ironically, not only over-prioritizes economy, it gets economics wrong.

On the one hand, the orthodox Marxist concepts for explaining how economic inputs and outputs exchange, misunderstand the determination of wages, prices, and profits in capitalist economies. Marxism's conceptualization of relative valuations and wages sometimes tends to direct activists' thoughts away from seeing how wages are largely functions of bargaining power and control, which are categories that the Marxist labor theory of value largely ignores, and toward accounts of labor hours and subsistence (which are categories the Marxist labor theory of value highlights), as if the latter are objective, numerical, factors.

Likewise, orthodox Marxist crisis theory often distorts understanding of capitalist economies and anti-capitalist prospects by theorizing intrinsic collapse where no such prospect exists, and by orienting activists away from the importance of their own organizing for change and toward presumed historic contradictions that will inevitably arise within capitalism itself.

But in both these instances, too, one can imagine Marxists transcending these orthodox ills, like they can overcome the monism described earlier – as indeed many have. So, just as we assumed away an overemphasis on economics, let's assume these two more economic problems away as well.

The remaining problem with Marxism is that in virtually every variant, however flexible and enriched it is, Marxist class theory denies the existence of what I call the coordinator (or professional-managerial, or technocratic) class and underemphasizes, or more often literally denies, its antagonisms with the working class as well as with capitalists. This failing obstructs class analysis of the old Soviet, Eastern European, and Third World non-capitalist economies, and of capitalism itself. Worse, it interferes with attaining worthy goals.

Marxism rightly reveals that class differences can arise from differences in ownership. Capitalists own means of production. Workers own only their labor power, which they sell for a wage. The capitalist pursues profit by trying to extract as much work as possible at the lowest expenditure possible. The worker tries to increase wages, improve conditions, and work for as few hours and at as low an intensity as possible. This is class struggle. What's the problem?

The problem is that while this Marxist picture rings true as far as it goes, it only asserts, and never really proves, or even argues, that we should see property relations as the only cause of class difference.

Marxism, in other words, never investigates the possibility that other relations of work and economic life can divide people into critically important opposed groups with different circumstances, motives, and means. Marxism's fatal weakness in this regard is that it ignores the possibility that factors other than ownership can also produce classes, and that its overlooking additional possibilities compromises many core insights of the Marxist framework.

In capitalism, for example, some employees monopolize empowering conditions and tasks and as a result have considerable say over their own jobs and the jobs of other workers below them. Other less powerful workers control virtually no assets beyond their own energies and as a result endure only disempowering conditions and have virtually no say over their own or anyone else's conditions. The more powerful employees try to maintain their monopoly on empowering circumstances and greater income so as to continue ruling over employees lower down the hierarchy.

Within capitalism, we thus have not only capitalists and workers, but in between these two classes, a group of empowered individuals who defend their advantages against workers below and struggle to enlarge their bargaining power against owners above. I call this the coordinator class.

A Marxist might reasonably look at this claim and ask why we should introduce a third class label for this intermediate group. Why not just say it is a stratum of one of the other two classes?

I respond that we should give it a new class name because the position of those who monopolize empowering work isn't just confused or contradictory. They aren't workers with a slight difference from most other workers. They aren't capitalists with a slight difference from most other capitalists. Nor are they some kind of amalgam of the two, or the bottom stratum of capitalists merging into the top stratum of workers, thereby occupying what some might call a contradictory position. Instead this group has its own well defined position, its own clear definition, and, as a result, its own views and interests.

Calling it the petite bourgeoisie, as some Marxists do, continues to narrow our thought in accord with the old ownership viewpoint. It pays attention to the wrong attribute of these people's position – that they in some cases own a little but not too much capital – and it overlooks that something other than ownership is the source of this group's class interests.

Parecon's view, in contrast to Marxism's, says that the coordinator class between labor and capital is defined by having a relative monopoly on empowering work. It controls its own situation to a great extent. It controls or defines the situation of workers below, to a great extent. It works to enlarge and defend its comforts and power against capital above, as well as against workers below even as it sometimes also does the bidding of those above, of course.

Wealthy and powerful doctors, lawyers, engineers, managers, and professionals of many kinds compose this class. They self-servingly see capitalists, by and large, as an annoying obstacle to the fullest elaboration of their personal genius. They self-servingly see workers, by and large, as more or less dumb folks to be taken care of, and, of course, kept below.

At this point, the Marxist might ask, "What could possibly be the basis for political and social unity between a high level supervisor of the production process, the comptroller for the same company, a creative director at the advertising agency hired by that company, an engineer designer of the tools of the workplace, a legal partner at the company's law firm, and the surgeon who works on them all, if they come to need it?"

My answer is that the coordinators all get their status, power, income, and identity from monopolizing empowering skills and knowledge, as well as from their access to daily levers of economic control and influence.

What they have in common is that on average they all tell themselves that they have their considerable material and social advantages not because they rip off their greater wealth and status from others by monopolizing domineering circumstances, but because they are smarter than others. They see capitalists as a painful impediment to the fullest manifestation of their capacities – though also, of course, they frequently have to serve capital (like workers often do, as well). They see workers as inferior and subordinate, as maybe worth saving and even lifting out of destitution, but not as worthy of having serious influence over economic life. And, under certain historical conditions, if they manage to eliminate private ownership, they can run the economy without capitalists above them and with workers still below them.

The still skeptical Marxist might then ask, "Under what circumstances would they all unite against both workers below and capitalists above? Surely you can't mean they would do that."

My reply is that yes, to adopt such a stance publicly would be suicidal, of course. Rather, what this class's foremost elements would do if they wanted to usher in a new economy in their own interests is wage a class war against capital by identifying capitalism's many horrors to appeal to all those who suffer capitalism's indignities and impoverishment. In the course of the ensuing anti-capitalist struggles, however, the coordinator class, seeking its own domination and not just an end to capital's rule, would monopolize control over institutions into its own hands, elevate its own culture and values, and impose its rule on more grass roots movements and new institutions, all as a kind of reflex of its self image and its image of others. In this way the coordinator class would wind up dominating the new society, not only theoretically as I have just described, but, as has actually occurred in historical practice, in all countries where Leninists have taken power.

The Marxist might then reply, "In the real world, you mean to tell me that you can actually imagine these coordinators uniting to overthrow capital and establish their own independent mode of production?"

Yes, I might then answer, I mean exactly that. Not in the trivial way that some might think, such as coordinators dressing up in fancy clothes and holding aloft their graduate degrees while standing behind banners saying capitalists suck and workers suck too, but in a social process that throws off the capitalists as the enemy due to the immoral exploitation capitalism wreaks on all citizens and particularly on workers, all while employing the working class as allies – really, as troops – and then selling out the working class once victory over capital is attained. Indeed, to my mind this is what Bolshevism did.

The key point of all this analysis regarding parecon's relation to Marxist perspectives, is that this coordinator class can actually become the ruling class of a new economy with capitalists removed but workers still subordinate. The key problem this analysis raises about Marxism, then, is that Marxism's concepts obscure the existence of a class which not only contends with capitalists and workers within capitalism, but which can become rulers of a new non-capitalist economy, most usefully called, I think, coordinatorism.

Finally, the absolutely damning point for Marxism is that this coordinator-class ruled economy is in fact historically familiar. It has public or state ownership of productive assets and corporate divisions of labor. It remunerates power and/or output. It utilizes central planning and/or markets for allocation. And it is typically called by its advocates "market socialism" or "centrally planned socialism". It is celebrated, that is, as the goal of struggle in every serious Marxist economic text that gets beyond glorious economic rhetoric to actual institutional prescriptions for economic life. It has been imposed by every Marxist party that has transformed a society's economic relations. Yet, although this coordinatorism is prevalent in history, nonetheless, in Marxist theoretical literature, from its origins to the present, coordinatorism is barely conceptualized at all. When the actual system we call coordinatorism is discussed by Marxists, its class features are obscured.

Marxism and vision and strategy

It turns out that Marxism is counterproductive to attaining a desirable society in several ways.

First, and most easily overcome, is Marxism's general taboo against "utopian" speculation. Interestingly, what this taboo tends to do in practice, like an ironically parallel anarchist taboo of the same sort, is to cause folks concerned about over-reaching into inaccessible details and about authoritarianism to forswear vision entirely, thus leaving coordinator-inclined folks to take up prescriptive tasks alone.

Second, and also manageably overcome, Marxism tends to presume that if economic relations are made desirable, other social relations will fall into place. This leaves activists without any reason to generate vision in other spheres of social life.

Third, and a bit more troubling, Marxism confuses what constitutes an equitable distribution of income. The instruction that we ought to strive for "from each according to ability to each according to need" is not only utopian in being unattainable; even if we could attain it, it would curtail needed information transfer and thereby obscure rather than reveal the relative preferences people have for different economic choices. Moreover, it has, in any event, never been more than rhetoric for empowered Marxists, whose operational priority has been that we should seek "from each according to ability" and remunerate "to each according to contribution" (if not power). This is not a morally worthy maxim because it would reward not just effort but also genetic endowment and advantages from tools, conditions, and even luck.

Fourth, and most damning and intractable, in practice and in its substantive prescriptions, Marxism approves hierarchical corporate divisions of labor for production, and either command planning or markets for allocation, thus imposing coordinator class rule.

In other words, the heart of the problem that should make those who favor parecon reject Marxism is that due to Marxism's underlying concepts, Marxism's economic goals amount to advocating a coordinator mode of economic organization that elevates to ruling status administrators, intellectual workers, and planners.

Marxism uses the label "socialism" for this goal, but this is to appeal to workers and other people of good will. When Marxists are in a position to affect societal outcomes, Marxism does not, in fact, structurally implement "socialist ideals," nor does it offer even in theory a vision that could do so.

The situation is analogous, Marx himself would surely point out, to how bourgeois movements use the labels democratic, free, and equitable to rally support from diverse sectors to their capitalist agendas – even though, when implemented, their agendas do not structurally engender truly democratic, free, or equitable outcomes.

Finally, Leninism, which is a strategic orientation to win change, is a natural, and by far the most frequent, activist outgrowth of Marxism in capitalist societies. Marxism Leninism, however, far from being the "theory and strategy for the working class," is, instead, the theory and strategy of the coordinator class, due to its focus, concepts, values, goals and organizational and tactical commitments.

Marxism Leninism employs coordinator class organizational and decision-making logic and structure. Even against its advocates' intentions, it imposes coordinator class rule.

Council self-management is what the Leninist Bolsheviks destroyed in the Soviet Union. Remuneration for effort and sacrifice is denied by rewarding power or output, the typical approach of coordinatorist models. Balanced job complexes are obliterated by corporate workplace organization which imposes the coordinator rule that is present in all actual Marxist economies and substantive accounts of Marxist economic goals. Participatory planning is destroyed by markets and or central planning, which are also present in virtually all Marxist programs and practice, thereby imposing the allocative basis for coordinator rule.

Coordinatorism has roots in various Marxist and Leninist theoretical concepts and strategic commitments, even counter to the broad aspirations of most members of Marxist and Leninist movements, which is why these movements need to be transcended.

What if a Marxist or Marxist Leninist disavows economism and additionally enriches their framework with concepts focused on other domains of life, rejects failed economic aspects of the framework, and in particular rejects its two-class conceptualization and adopts the three-class view and also parecon as a vision? Do I then say, okay, I embrace your type of Marxism?

Yes, I in fact would happily do just that – but for one problem. At that point, I would have to wonder what is gained by still calling the revamped framework Marxism or Marxism Leninism. These labels convey to virtually everyone who hears them very different views than this hypothetical person holds. Why not find a new label that can convey the new allegiances, instead of tainting the new allegiances with the associations conjured to mind by old labels?

I suspect the answer is that folks who call themselves Marxist and Marxist Leninist do so overwhelmingly to see themselves as part of a heritage – not the heritage of the actual systems that have been put in place and have brutishly curtailed options and even snuffed out lives and aspirations, and not the heritage of top-down authority and internecine sectarianism that often persist in Marxist Leninist oppositional organizations that have lacked power, but the heritage of courageous resistance and struggle from below, grassroots aspirations, and the solidarity and mutual support that have existed among large populations seeking change.

Well, I too wish to see myself in that grassroots heritage and to be worthy of helping it continue, but I am also concerned with the meaning of my words – not their meaning for me, and not their meaning for people who agree with me, but their meaning for the huge numbers of people who justifiably understand the words differently than I may mean them. And so, no, even if a particular Marxist or Marxist Leninist party makes all the changes noted above – something that could certainly happen – I would not join up because of their use of the label, however much I would feel affinity for their choice and happily respect them and presumably often ally with them.

Marxism indicts Marxism

Marx taught us, quite brilliantly, to look at ideologies or conceptual frameworks, and to ask of them, who do they serve? What are they suited for? What do they include and what do they exclude, and will their inclusions and exclusions make them suitable or unsuitable for us?

Marx was no one's fool, and these are very insightful instructions. If we apply them to Marxism, however, the instructions reveal that the framework leaves out important economic relations regarding the division of labor and relations of allocation, absences which benefit the coordinator class's agenda to overcome capitalism and allocate ruling status to itself.

Because of this we shouldn't tinker with, and otherwise minimally reform, Marxism, just as we shouldn't tinker with, and otherwise minimally reform, bourgeois economics. These are both frameworks bent to serve interests that we oppose. They have insights we can borrow, especially Marxism, since it is anti-capitalist, but, following Marx's own advice, we have to transcend Marxism's overall conceptual package.

A contemporary Marxist may say, wait, Marxist and Leninist movements espouse values much like the ones parecon celebrates. They urge the need for classlessness, for equity, for justice, for solidarity, and so on.

Yes, they often do, and when bourgeois elements railed against royalty they didn't do it in the name of their own future great wealth and power either, but in the name of freedom and justice for everyone. Their ideology was sharp in railing at the enemy, but very vague as to differences between themselves and "their troops". This is always true when an elite group contends for power.

Indeed, I have no doubt that many advocates of bourgeois ideology believe their own rhetoric, and I think understanding this phenomenon is one of the abiding accomplishments of Marxism, including seeing that the rhetoric, no matter how heartfelt, doesn't redefine the reality. The class position of corporate elites, the defining relations of their lives, and the attitudes, values, and modes of operation their position in society gives them, lead them, even despite their rhetoric, to implement enrichment for the few. This is true for capitalists and it is the same (in different ways) for coordinators.

It may be that even the people in leadership positions in a coordinator-class oriented movement have quite sincere and worthy aspirations. They rally workers below – who certainly are sincere about their positive aspirations – by railing against injustices perpetrated by a capitalist elite they seek to remove. At such moments, the leading coordinator elements no doubt feel real pain for the suffering of others and feel real solidarity in struggle with them. The "masses" in turn certainly want dignity and justice and expect it. But in spite of all these fine desires and relationships, the Leninist process leads good people to become nothing more than a new class taking the place of the old one in a position of authority over workers, because that's what's immanent in the ideology and in its institutional commitments.

The Marxist may reply that when such movements yield new oppressive relations they have failed to fulfill their true agenda and are instead violating its underlying conceptions. In reply, I think it is just apologetics to call every victory by a party full of people who call themselves Marxists and who can recite Marxism's concepts and theories inside out, who say they are applying those concepts and theories, and who certainly seem to be doing so, and who are admired while in opposition and praised as exemplifying the cause, not Marxist just a little while later, despite no discernible renunciations or conceptual turnabouts.

The Marxist might say that what stands out most about these so-called "socialist" societies is how much they resemble capitalism, so why not just call them capitalist or perhaps state capitalist? The new term, coordinatorism, just confuses the issue, argues the Marxist.

My reply is that this is like seeing the folks between labor and capital as part worker and part owner, rather than as a class unto themselves. The Marxist is saying the old Soviet economy can only be capitalism or socialism. Those are the only possible options, so since it isn't socialism, it must be capitalism. But this is a set of failed concepts at work. Concepts always organize our thoughts and provide categories we use. Sometimes concepts are useful in that they push us past what's commonplace and help us reach important insights we would otherwise overlook. Other times, however, as in the case of Marxism's obscuring co-ordinatorism from us, concepts hide the obvious from us by cluttering our perception with mistaken formulations. We miss what we ought to be attending to.

As Einstein put this general insight: "Concepts which have proved useful for ordering things easily assume so great an authority over us, that we forget their terrestrial origin and accept them as unalterable facts. They then become labeled as 'conceptual necessities,' etc. The road of scientific progress is frequently blocked for long periods by such errors. It is therefore not just an idle game to exercise our ability to analyze familiar concepts, and to demonstrate the conditions on which justification of their usefulness depends."

To say that the old Soviet economy was capitalist despite there being no private ownership of the means of production, is, to me, far less useful than realizing that it must have been, if not capitalism, and if not an economy in which workers self-manage, then something else instead, for which we will need another name that highlights its different defining features.

The absence of owners and the elevation of central planners, local managers, and other empowered workers to ruling status is what characterized these economies as different.

If we call the Soviet Union state capitalist, as many Marxists urge, one conclusion is that we don't have to worry that maintaining a division of labor that has some people ruling over others is part and parcel of ushering in a new economy that isn't in the interests of workers. If there is no such thing as an economy not in the interests of workers other than capitalism, and if we are certainly anti-capitalist, we must therefore be on a good path forward. In truth, of course, the whole point is that one can be anti-capitalist in ways that don't elevate workers but instead elevate coordinators. That is what parecon strives to avoid.

When I argue that coordinatorism is celebrated as the goal of struggle in every Marxist text that offers a serious economic vision, many Marxists are likely to reply that "that is utterly false. Instead, for Marx, and for every genuine Marxist who followed him, the 'goal of struggle' in every text that takes up this question is a society characterized by mass working-class participation, democracy, and freedom".

Well, I think that what this Marxist says is true about Marxist rhetoric, but I think that what I claim is true about Marxist reality.

I don't say, in other words, that Marxists never verbally advocate working class participation and control. Or even that they never seriously desire it, as individuals. I say that they don't offer a vision that yields that result. I say that very nearly every serious Marxist formulation of economic aims, including of course, what Marxists have done in practice, is intrinsically coordinatorist, whatever accompanying desires and rhetoric might say to the contrary.

Yes, there have been some Marxists, most particularly the "council communists" such as Anton Pannekoek, among others, who tried to describe a truly socialist – in the positive sense – vision. I feel that while their intentions and many of their insights were very admirable, they didn't get very far into the institutions of a new vision – though others might feel that is too dismissive. But the main point is that what we might call libertarian Marxists or anarcho marxists are the nearly imperceptible exception that proves the overwhelming rule. While they ought to be extolled as the best Marxism has had to offer, instead, they are literally ignored by large Marxist parties the world over.

Not people at fault, but institutions

Put another way, to highlight another component and dimension of the argument, the problem with Marxism isn't bad people. Yes, Stalin was a bad guy, to put it mildly. But the real and lasting problem was the institutions that selected and elevated a thug like Stalin. The problem with Marxism Leninism isn't that everybody in Marxist Leninist parties wants to trample workers on the road to ruling them. That is utterly false. The problem is that those parties and their core concepts, however well meaning most members' motives may be, lead to that outcome.

None of us is immune to the pressures of our circumstances. On average, the Marxist concepts that organize Marxists' thoughts, and the organizational structures and strategies that Leninists abide, together have a built-in logic that causes Marxist Leninists – even against their best inclinations and aspirations – to elevate coordinators.

Become a police officer or a prison guard in a capitalist society, even with the best of motives, and the odds are that you aren't going to serve the public with sympathy and respect, even if that was your initial intention. Moreover, some who take this route will become grotesque agents of repression.

Become a lawyer or a surgeon in a capitalist society. Again, even with the best of motives, the odds are that you aren't going to be a paragon of justice but an elitist, commercialized person, even against your best inclinations.

Become a Leninist, even with the very best of motives, and the odds are that you aren't going to make a revolution in our modern world for want of a sufficiently diverse focus and especially for want of true working class appeal. If you do make a revolution, however, the odds are that even against your hopes, your achievement will elevate coordinators, not workers, to economic rule.

Some Marxists find this claim personally insulting. I don't think it should be. It isn't a comment about particular people. It is a comment about concepts, methods, and institutional allegiances, and their predictable impact on groups of people.

I am saying, in other words, that I think certain concepts and views, even in the hands of sincere and wonderful people, lead to results that all people of good will, including themselves, would at the outset say they reject.

So do I think that parecon is contrary to many of Leninism's and even of Marxism's inclinations? Yes, of course I do. But that doesn't mean I think all people who call themselves Marxist will be blind to a good thing when it comes along. I expect lots of Marxists to become advocates of parecon. This is already, in fact, happening. I'll also be happy when a Marxist party decides to advocate parecon – something that may take longer, but will likely also happen, and perhaps repeatedly.

Concepts and collective behavior

First, Marxism's concepts tend to overemphasize the defining influences arising from economics, and to underemphasize the defining influences arising from gender/kinship, community/culture, and polity.

This doesn't mean that all (or even any) Marxists ignore everything other than economics, nor even that all (or even any) Marxists won't care greatly about other matters.

It means, instead, that when Marxists address the sex lives of teenagers, marriage, the nuclear family, religion, racial identity, cultural commitments, sexual preferences, political organization, war and peace, and ecology, they overwhelmingly highlight causes arising from class struggle and implications affecting class struggle, and they overwhelmingly de-emphasize concerns rooted in the specific features of race, gender, power, and nature.

This criticism predicts that Marxist movements may respect innovations coming from other viewpoints when movements force them to do so, but also that Marxists will not generate many original and useful insights regarding analysis and aims for polity, culture, and kinship.

It also predicts that Marxism's concepts will not sufficiently offset tendencies imposed by society, by circumstances of struggle, or by tactical choices that generate authoritarian, racist, or sexist trends – even against the best moral and social inclinations of most Marxists.

And it therefore also predicts that we will see some pretty horrible results in the areas of race, gender, culture, ecology, and political organization from Marxist movements in struggle and especially from Marxist movements in power (as we most certainly have in practice).

In other words, my claims about Marxism's "economism" do not predict monomania about economics, or even a universal and inviolable pattern of adhering too strongly to economics and not enough to everything else, but, instead, they predict a harmful pattern of imbalance on average.

Second, and less tractable, Marxism's concepts fail to highlight a (coordinator) class between labor and capital defined primarily by its position in the division of labor and not by matters of ownership or political bureaucracy.

Marxism inadequately understands the post-capitalist mode of production that it calls "socialist" or "state capitalist," and it fails to see that this type of economy elevates neither capitalists nor workers to ruling economic status, but elevates instead what I call a coordinator class of planners, managers, and other empowered participants in the economy.

Likewise, Marxism typically favors markets or central planning for allocation, public or state ownership for control of assets, remuneration for output or for power (and sometimes for need) to determine the distribution of income, plus corporate divisions of labor to define workplace organization. And regardless of hopes or intentions, these commitments all lead to coordinator outcomes.

Notice, this doesn't say that most (or arguably even any) Marxists are intentionally trying to advance the interests of managers and other empowered economic actors over and above workers. It says, instead, that the concepts within Marxism do little to prevent this elevation of the coordinator class and even propel it in various ways, so that we can expect to see coordinator economic dominance emerging from successful Marxist movements regardless of the sentiments of the movement's rank and file and the slogans of its leadership – as we have in fact seen historically in every Marxist society from Russia to China, and East Europe to Cuba.

A better Marxism?

What is an antidote for the two highlighted problems? Regarding economism, the problem is a conceptual framework that starts from economics and then enters into other realms incidentally, with the primary intention of seeing economic implications. I propose that we ought instead to begin with concepts that simultaneously highlight not just economics, but also polity, kinship, and culture. We ought to use concepts that first prioritize understanding each of these spheres' own logic and dynamics, and then prioritize seeing how each sphere influences and even limits and defines the others. Our new conceptual framework should not rank any one of these spheres of life above the others, but should instead see how they work out in practice. I have urged that this approach will more likely yield thorough insights about racism, ethnocentrism, sexism, homophobia, and authoritarianism (as well as about economics) than will starting with economics alone, or any other single sphere alone, as our foundation.

If a new Marxist, and there are many like this, renounces ideas of economic base and extra-economic superstructure, rejects that historical change is driven only or even overwhelmingly via modes of production, and transcends seeing class struggle as the sole dominant conceptual framework for identifying strategic issues – will still calling him or herself a "Marxist" continue to mean what it meant in the past? Will the label "Marxist" connote what the multi-focus activist intends his or her self description to connote? I don't think so, but I can imagine overcoming this communicative problem as well.

The class-definition difficulty of Marxism is more troubling. Marxists sometimes talk about a class between labor and capital – but they do so primarily in political terms, asserting that its roots derive from Stalinism. They rarely see a third class between labor and capital arising from the economic division of labor and from economic modes of allocation (not from ownership or politics). And they do not see, therefore, that markets, central planning, and corporate divisions of labor are a source of class division, and of a ruling class other than capitalists, even if private ownership is eliminated and the state remains or becomes democratic.

Marxists do not, in this regard, offer a clear statement of truly classless institutional aims for economic decision-making, divisions of labor, workplace organization, remuneration, and allocation.

Yes, Marxists often offer descriptions of the justice, equity, and dignity that "socialism" should usher in. And these descriptions are often eloquent and worthy statements that any advocate of justice can support. But, if we look at texts by Marxists to see descriptions of institutions that will propel these proposed values, we find either vague rhetoric that lacks institutional substance, or, when there is real institutional substance, we find advocacy of institutions that are properly labeled market coordinatorist and/or centrally planned coordinatorist. And when we look at Marxist practice, we find these same coordinatorist structures universally implemented.

But could a Marxist transcend this problem too, and yet continue to see him or herself as a Marxist?

I don't know – but, if a Marxist does follow that path, I think signs that it has occurred would be obvious. For example, such new Marxists would disavow what has been called socialism in countries around the world, not by calling it capitalism, or by calling it state capitalism, or by calling it deformed socialism, but by recognizing it as a third mode of production that enshrines a different class above workers.

More, such new Marxists would offer a new economic vision contrary to coordinatorism, and this new vision would explicitly dispense with markets, central planning, and corporate divisions of labor, since these provide more empowering work to some people and less empowering work to others. The new vision would also dispense with modes of remuneration that reward property, power, or output.

Additionally, to transcend merely negative rhetoric and to orient strategy, such new Marxists would not arrogantly present a full blueprint for the future but they would propose major defining institutions to replace rejected options.

And finally, such Marxists would also advocate internal movement organization, methods, and programs that would propel their new positive aims, rather than approaches that would obviously obstruct those aims.

Strategies for social change need self-consciously to overcome coordinator class rule. If they embody organizational choices and methods that elevate coordinator class consciousness and attitudes to central authority – such as employing centralist parties and advocating markets, central planning, and corporate divisions of labor – they will not only not eliminate coordinator class rule, they will entrench it. Regrettably, Marxism's flaws lead to this result regardless of the desire of many Marxists to end up someplace much nicer than coordinatorism.

But what about Marxists who seek to correct the error of ignoring coordinatorism?

Well, I doubt that such new Marxists would call themselves Leninist or Trotskyist, but even if they did, they would certainly disavow many ideas of these two schools of thought. Instead of always quoting Lenin and Trotsky positively, they would forthrightly and aggressively reject Lenin's statement that "it is absolutely essential that all authority in the factories should be concentrated in the hands of management". Advocating self-management, they would be horrified by Lenin's saying "any direct intervention by the trade unions in the management of enterprises must be regarded as positively harmful and impermissible".

Likewise, Lenin's formulation that "large scale machine industry which is the central productive source and foundation of socialism calls for absolute and strict unity of will… How can strict unity of will be ensured? By thousands subordinating their will to the will of one", would nauseate such new Marxists, being virtually the opposite of their sentiments.

The capstone might well be the apoplectic reaction such new Marxists would have to Lenin saying, "A producer's congress! What precisely does that mean? It is difficult to find words to describe this folly. I keep asking myself can they be joking? Can one really take these people seriously? While production is always necessary, democracy is not. Democracy of production engenders a series of radically false ideas". This is of course the antithesis of seeking classlessness and self-management.

Trotsky would come in for harsh criticism as well. What new Marxist of the sort envisioned here would do other than scowl and then marshal facts to reject Trotsky saying about workers seeking to control their own lives: "They turn democratic principles into a fetish. They put the right of the workers to elect their own representatives above the Party, thus challenging the Party's right to affirm its own dictatorship, even when this dictatorship comes into conflict with the evanescent mood of the workers' democracy. We must bear in mind the historical mission of our Party. The Party is forced to maintain its dictatorship, without stopping for these vacillations, nor even the momentary falterings of the working class. This realization is the mortar which cements our unity. The dictatorship of the proletariat does not always have to conform to formal principles of democracy."

What new Marxist could feel affinity with Trotsky saying that "it is a general rule that man will try to get out of work. Man is a lazy animal"? Who would ratify him saying, with pride, no less: "I consider that if the Civil War had not plundered our economic organs of all that was strongest, most independent, most endowed with initiative, we should undoubtedly have entered the path of one-man management much sooner and much less painfully."

More positively, if the topic came up, such new Marxists would indicate how they would have done things differently than the Bolsheviks and than every Marxist party since the Bolsheviks.

For example, regarding the Bolsheviks, they might point out that the shop committee movement in Russia was moving in 1917–18 towards a National Congress to take over grassroots planning and coordination of the economy, and note that, unlike the Bolsheviks, they would have seen such local agents as the best locus of planning, rather than the state. They might also note that "Power to the Shop Committees" was what the anarcho-syndicalists argued at the First All-Russian Trade Union Congress in January 1918, and indicate that they would have supported the anarchists in that, instead of opposing them, as the Bolsheviks did.

These new Marxists, noting that the Bolsheviks voted at that Trade Union Congress along with the Mensheviks and SRs to dissolve the shop committees into the trade unions and advocated "union management" of the economy, might say they would have at least stuck with that compromise instead of devolving by 1921 into advocating replacing union management with the still worse top-down "one-man management".

Instead of a hierarchical army, these new Marxists might indicate that they would have favored using a militia based on the mass organizations, like the Revolutionary Army of the anarchists in the Ukraine. They might note that arguing, as supporters of Bolshevism do, that this would have been ineffective against the Whites would be unreasonable, given that it was the revolutionary army of the Ukraine that saved the Bolsheviks during the winter of 1919, when they attacked the White army besieging Moscow from the rear and destroyed it.

And instead of invading the Ukraine with the Red Army to crush the People's Congress of the eastern Ukraine in 1921, as the Bolsheviks did, these new Marxists might indicate that they would have supported the Congress and helped it expand into the western Ukraine.

These new Marxists would note that instead of invading Kronstadt in 1921 and crushing the Soviet there, they would have agreed to the Kronstadters' demands for new elections to the Soviets, even if this meant that the Bolsheviks would have to go into opposition.

More, these new Marxists would note more generally that hierarchical structures in political institutions risk ushering in coordinator rule (as well as creating an environment uncongenial to widespread worker involvement) and also provoke political authoritarianism, and if they wanted to argue that in some difficult contexts such structures had to be employed, they would urge using them only as a temporarily imposed expedient; in all other respects, they would try to pave the way for non-hierarchical relations, now and in the future.

And, finally, being attuned to the broader comprehension of class definition and working class liberation, these new Marxists would not say that everyone who sees vision and strategy differently than them but calls themselves a Marxist is a Stalinist. They would instead recognize that Marxism is a very incomplete framework that leads most people who adopt it to unworthy positions, even against their personal inclinations.

Getting personal about it

Those I would label as good and admirable Leninists and good and admirable pareconists each oppose capitalism and seek just and equitable improvements against current oppressions. We each advocate worker and consumer councils. We each oppose markets and also hierarchical planning. We each believe that movements should prefigure alternative goals even in current work.

We also agree that beyond capitalism there exists, not only a desirable economy, but also economic systems that we disavow. A difference between us is that pareconists tend to think the rejected systems elevate an economic co-ordinator class to ruling status, whereas what we might call good Leninists tend to think of this same group as a political product having to do with Stalinism.

We both oppose, at least as an end, authoritarian political structures. We also oppose, or feel we have to be very careful with, economic structures that create and elevate the in-between group that I call the coordinator class and that the good Leninist views as a bureaucracy. This means we both should advocate not only replacing markets and/or central planning with a new allocation system, but also replacing the current division of labor with balanced job complexes.

We both think allocation should be consciously, cooperatively undertaken by workers and consumers in a horizontal manner. Parecon proposes participatory planning for this kind of self-management. Hopefully many Leninists, even all Leninists, will, in time, agree.

All of this is, or should be, congenial and mutual. Yet the good Leninists are in a Trotskyist Party, or in a Leninist party, or in some tiny sect, all in the Marxist Leninist tradition. In contrast, I and pareconists more generally, still fewer in number, tend very strongly to reject such parties and their tradition, and are quite critical of Marxism as well.

A reader might reasonably wonder how this is possible. How can rank and file, and even many leading Leninists and pareconists, line up shoulder to shoulder in what they reject, differ almost indiscernibly in the economic values they espouse, agree up to what appear to be fine points regarding economic aims, and yet still have such contrary allegiances?

The questioner might ask me: "Albert, how can you think that Marxism Leninism yields outcomes you aggressively reject, and yet you so often interact congenially with people who identify with that heritage?"

To conclude this chapter, I hope to explain why this seemingly self-contradictory picture is accurate, possible, and not even unusual.

Imagine you were at a public talk given by Karl Marx. It is a wondrous tour de force in which he rails at capitalists for gouging workers while they pile up wealth at the expense of humanity. He explains how ownership imposes on capitalists a view of their employees and a set of interests that provoke their heinous behavior even against their own better natures. He says it is a systemic phenomenon that derives from capitalists' position in the economy and that manifests as members of the class collectively and individually carry out their economic functions. He calls capitalists "moneybags," for short, urging the need to eliminate them as a class.

The talk ends and Marx exits, stage left, of course. You go out for a bite and, lo and behold, there in the next booth at the local eatery is Karl Marx having his own snack while chatting with his close friend and lifelong ally, Frederick Engels. Yes, that's right, there with Marx is the Engels who owns a factory. How is that possible? Why is Marx not spitting in the face of this owner of capital?

The chummy session is possible without contradiction because Marx's class analysis never says that every person who occupies a certain position will inexorably hold certain views. Class analysis says, instead, that the class position people occupy tends to impose certain broad behaviors and views on them over time, especially in demanding circumstances. In the clash and jangle of these and a host of other influences, on average, the economic commonalities of a class will yield the predicted broad characteristics within the overall economic behavior of the class's members. Engels diverges from his class average, thus becoming Marx's friend and ally, but in doing so, he in no sense violates Marx's claims about that class's average properties.

Returning to my view of Marxism, I say Marxism is an array of concepts and claims about how to comprehend attributes of society and history in specific cases. I say Marxism's concepts have many virtues – but that they also have two overriding faults which make me feel that we must transcend this framework.

The first fault, potentially correctable even while one is a Marxist, is a relative overemphasis on class and its associated economic sphere of life with a concurrent underemphasis on race, gender, sexuality, and political position, and the associated kinship, cultural, and political spheres of social life. The claim is that groups of adherents to Marxist concepts will collectively highlight how economy affects the other spheres of life, but largely overlook how those other spheres affect the economy. The users will highlight how classes can be central agents of oppression and liberation, but will downplay how genders, sexual groups, races, religious and ethnic and other cultural groups, and political formations can be central agents of oppression and liberation.

Importantly, any individual Marxist will do better or worse on these matters depending not only on how he or she mechanically utilizes narrow economic and class concepts, but also on his or her familiarity with, and use of, other perspectives when thinking about relations and developing agendas. Despite that variation, given that the societies we live in tend to make us not only classist, but also racist, sexist, homophobic, and authoritarian, and given the exigencies of difficult daily practice and political struggle, and in particular given the pressures and benefits of collective unity, my claim is that on average, groups of Marxists working together will be relatively weak in their comprehension of, and commitment to addressing, the non-economic dimensions of social life, and that this weakness will be exacerbated whenever attending to broader matters seems to conflict with their shared insights about class and economy.

Please notice, I don't say Marxists are racist, sexist, authoritarian people. I say, instead, that there is a built-in conceptual bias, powerfully exacerbated by conditions, that is overwhelmingly likely to lead to harmful results, as historical evidence shows. In the clash and jangle of many factors, the shared economic concepts tend to swamp broader insights.

The solution, one might argue (as I have earlier), is for Marxists to append insights from other perspectives. And that's fine, as long as Marxists are prepared to permit it. But here is the wrinkle. For many Marxists, particularly in groups that work hard to attain and maintain a collective identity, such innovation violates a major tenet to do with the priority of class and economy; if it is undertaken at all, it tends to be jettisoned later.

I think a much better solution, therefore, is to adopt a new conceptual framework which keeps what continues to be valuable from Marxism but gives new gender, cultural, and political concepts the same priority as economic concepts.

Okay, that's one issue of proposed change, but as I have indicated above, it is not the biggest issue of dispute, because many Marxists and Marxist Leninists try to deal with it – and to a degree succeed – just as many feminists try to deal with overemphasizing kinship and gender at the expense of other critical factors, and to a degree succeed.

The most intractable difference I have with Marxism Leninism is, instead, my rejection of Marxism's conceptualization of the economy itself, and my rejection of Leninism's practical strategy and vision.

I think Marxist consciousness on average in real struggle leads to insufficient attention to the agendas and possibilities of what I call the coordinator class, up to and including championing an economy that elevates the coordinator class to ruling status. And I think that Leninist strategy on average in real struggle generates collective allegiances to both authoritarian and coordinatorist results.

Now when some Marxist or Leninist says, hold on, that isn't me, or says, I can name a Marxist who doesn't have the failing you mention, or says, I can name a

Leninist who doesn't have those failings, it has virtually no impact on the argument I am making, just as when some sociologist says hold on, Mr. Engels owned capital, or hold on, Mr. Moneybags just wrote a very humane book; those facts have no impact on Marxist assertions about the average implications of ownership of private property.

Probably due to a failing in my presentation, Marxists and Leninists never quite hear my criticism the way I intend. They instead seem to hear an easily dismissible claim that every single person who calls him or herself a Marxist or a Leninist thinks in one particular way. They do not hear a more subtle claim that the commonalities among people who call themselves Marxists, and particularly among people who operate in Marxist Leninist parties, tend to overwhelm the myriad of other attributes present, so that when the clash and jangle of diverse factors resolves itself into average outcomes, the result is overwhelmingly economism, authoritarianism, sectarianism, and, in particular, coordinator-serving strategy and vision.

What's my evidence for this claim?

Well, having described the concepts of Marxism and the strategic commitments of Leninism in a way that yields the above prediction, the evidence for its validity is that the prediction is borne out by the practice of every single Marxist Leninist party that has ever attained power or even attained any significant size and scope, and by every single serious Marxist Leninist model for a post-capitalist economy, as well.

I don't know how much more evidence one could possibly offer. Okay, some will dispute pieces of it. They will find no fault with East Germany circa 1980, or no fault with Russia under Stalin, or more likely only before that, or will find no fault with the Bolsheviks before they took power ... or with early Mao, but not middle or late Mao, or with late Trotsky but not his early incarnation, or some other permutation. But really, even ignoring how weak these assertions are, is all this anything other than special pleading?

And what would Marxists and Leninists need to do to rectify the situation? All that it would take to get well under way is to admit that the historical framework is insufficient and flawed. The next step would be to agree that other spheres of social life are as key as economics is, and most of all to realize that, yes, class refers to groups defined by their economic relations, including, but not confined to, property relations.

And here is where I annoy even Leninists who are my friends. It seems to me that the difficulty of taking these steps most often has more to do with a religious cast of mind and with issues of personal identity and group commitment than it has to do with anything rational or moral.

I find no other convincing way to explain why, when I and Marxist and also Leninist friends talk about politics and dissent, without using concepts that explicitly put the Marxist framework in question, and without criticizing historical actors from the Leninist heritage, things often go swimmingly, but the minute something comes up that explicitly implies a gap in the Marxist Leninist identity, guards go up and what seems like obtuse denial and aggressive defensiveness set in.

Contrary to how people often react to my suggestion that non-rational factors affect Marxist Leninist allegiances, putting the proposition forth isn't extreme or nasty. The truth is that we all behave this way sometimes. It is the essence of self-defense against loss of self-image or denial of group allegiance. Everyone has some matters or behaviors or linkages or viewpoints that, when challenged, spur a defensive reaction. The problem is that this reaction is particularly problematic when its presence defends beliefs that are not only wrong, but are also harmful to ourselves and to others, and especially when it occurs collectively, with each person not only abetting but also encouraging the steadfastness of others, and with the overall impact thereby made that much greater.

Anyhow, to all the Leninists who may hopefully read this chapter and whose practice and commitment and courage I admire, what can I say? We agree on a lot. I feel that if we direct the conversation carefully over dinner, or in a congenial online debate, or even in some struggle situations, we can have a delightful time together. Yet I also fear that if we vary just a few words, or make reference to certain historical epochs, all hell will break loose. And I suspect you have the same impression.

Is this a behavioral conundrum of little consequence? Or are these dynamics basic to some of the left's substantive and recurring difficulties? Hopefully, in the future we can comprehend, and perhaps even overcome, our remaining differences, including dealing better with the social and interpersonal dynamics of disagreement.

16 Anarchism

LIKE MOST SOCIAL MOVEMENTS, anarchism is diverse. Most broadly, an anarchist seeks out and identifies structures of authority, hierarchy, and domination throughout life, and tries to challenge them, as conditions and the pursuit of justice permit. Paraphrasing the famous and pivotal Russian anarchist Mikhail Bakunin, anarchists realize that wielding authority tends to make people unjust and arbitrary. Succumbing to authority tends to make people subservient and servile. Authority corrupts its holder and debases its victim.

Anarchists work to eliminate domination and subordination. They focus on political power, economic power, power relations among men and women, power between parents and children, power among cultural communities, and power over future generations through effects on the environment.

Anarchists challenge the state and the corporate rulers of the domestic and international economy, but they also challenge every other instance and manifestation of illegitimate authority. As geographer, humanist, and anarchist Peter Kropotkin puts it, capturing the anti-authoritarian sentiment but also, perhaps, foreshadowing complications to come: "We already foresee a state of society where the liberty of the individual will be limited by no laws, no bonds, by nothing else but his own social habits, and the necessity which everyone feels, of finding cooperation, support, and sympathy among his neighbors."

The two faces of anarchism

Why wouldn't everyone concerned that people ought to have appropriate control over their lives admire anarchism? Problems arise because, from being opponents of illegitimate authority, one can grow movements of incomparable majesty, on the one hand, and movements that are majestically unimpressive, on the other hand. If anarchism means mostly the former, good people will admire and gravitate toward anarchism. But if anarchism means mostly the latter, then good people will have reservations about it, or even be hostile.

So what's the not so admirable, or even counterproductive, version of anarchism that turns off potential advocates? And what is the admirable and worthy version of anarchism that is now increasing its support around the world? And do the admirable strands incorporate sufficient insight to be successful?

Counterproductive anarchism

Counterproductive anarchism is the brand that dismisses political forms per se, or institutions, or even plain old technology, or that dismisses fighting for reforms – as if all political structures, institutional arrangements, or even technological innovations intrinsically impose illegitimate authority, or as if relating to existing social structures to win immediate limited gains is an automatic sign of system-support or hypocrisy.

Anarchists holding these counterproductive views see that the contemporary state uses force to subjugate the many, but wrongly deduce that this is an out-growth of trying to adjudicate, or legislate, or implement shared aims, or even just of trying to cooperate on a large scale per se, rather than seeing that it is instead an outgrowth of doing these things in particular ways to serve narrow elites. Following from this thinking is the idea that we need to fulfill the functions more positively. We don't need no polity, as some anarchists claim, we need a good polity, an anarchist polity, which is by no means a contradiction in terms.

Similarly, anarchists with counterproductive views correctly see that many, and even most, of our institutions, while delivering to people food, transport, homes, services, etc., also restrict what people can do in ways that subvert human aspirations and dignity. These anarchists wrongly deduce that all institutions must be oppressive, so that instead of lasting institutions, we should favor only voluntary spontaneous interactions in which at all times all aspects are fluidly generated and dissolved. The contrary truth is, of course, that without stable and lasting institutions that have well-conceived and lasting norms and roles, advanced relations among disparate populations and even among individuals are quite impossible. While institutional roles that compel people to deny their humanity or the humanity of others are abominable, institutional roles that permit people to express their humanity more fully and freely are not abominable at all, but are part and parcel of a life-enhancing social order. We don't need no institutions, as some anarchists feel; we need instead good, liberating institutions, which is by no means a contradiction in terms.

The situation with technology is similar. The anarchist with counter-productive views looks at assembly lines, weapons, and energy use that despoil our world, and says there is something about pursuing technological mastery that intrinsically breeds these horrible outcomes so we'd be better off without technology. Of course, this misses the point that pencils are technology, clothes are technology, and indeed all human artifacts are technology, and that life would be short and brutish, at best, without technology. So, the issue isn't to decry and escape technology, but to create and retain only technologies that serve humane aims and potentials. We don't need no technology, we need good technology, humane technology, which is by no means a contradiction in terms.

And finally, regarding reforms, counterproductive anarchism rightly notices that with many reforms the gains we win are fleeting, and elites even manage to use our gains to reinforce their legitimacy and extend their domain of control by first granting, but then domesticating, and later even eliminating, the advances. But the missing additional observation is that these problems don't result from change or reform per se, but from change that is conceived, sought, and implemented in ways that presuppose rather than challenge system maintenance. What's needed isn't to have no reforms, which would simply capitulate the playing field to elites, but to fight for reforms that are non-reformist; that is, to fight for reforms that activists conceive, seek, and implement in ways that lead activists to seek still more gains, in a trajectory of change leading ultimately to new institutions.

It shouldn't be necessary even to discuss the "bad trajectory" of anarchism and its anti-political, anti-institutional, anti-technological, and anti-reform confusions. It is perfectly natural and understandable for folks, when first becoming sensitized to the ills of political structure, contemporary institutions, current technologies, or the problems of reform struggles, to go momentarily awry and blame each entire category for the ills that the worst instances embody. But if this confusion were thereafter to be addressed naturally, it would quickly become clear that without political structures, institutions, and technology, not to mention without progressive reforms, humanity would barely survive, much less prosper and fulfill its many capacities.

But this prediction of the easy transcendence of worthy views over counter-productive ones neglects the fact that media and elites repeatedly portray nega-tive aspects of anarchism as representing the whole of it, highlighting confused and unworthy ideas and ignoring more valuable ideas to discredit the whole undertaking. In this way, unsustainable and objectionable approaches gain far more visibility than would be warranted by their numbers, much less by their logic or values, and also a certain tenacity. Interest in anarchism as a whole is thereby reduced.

Desirable anarchism

What about the type of anarchism that is more positive yet less visible in the media? This is the widely awakening impetus to fight on the side of the oppressed in every domain of life, from family, culture, state, economy, and the now very visible international arena of "corporate globalization," and to do so in creative and courageous ways that win immediate improvements in people's lives, even while simultaneously leading toward new, future, institutions.

The good anarchism transcends narrow forms that have often characterized the approach in the past. Instead of arising from a conceptual orientation that is mostly politically anti-authoritarian but not as focused on other facets of life, nowadays anarchism implies having a gender, cultural, and an economic, as well as a politically or power-rooted orientation, with each aspect taken on a par with, and also informing, the rest.

This is in many respects new, at least in my experience of anarchism, and it is useful to recall that many anarchists as little as a decade back, and perhaps even more recently, would have said that anarchism addresses everything, yes, but primarily by means of an anti-authoritarian focus prioritizing power, rather than by simultaneously elevating concepts owing to other dimensions of life in their own right.

Such past anarchists thought, whether implicitly or explicitly, that analysis from an overwhelmingly anti-authoritarian angle rooted in understanding power could explain the nuclear family better than an analysis rooted as well in kinship concepts, and could explain race or religion better than an analysis rooted as well in cultural concepts, and could explain production, consumption, and allocation better than an analysis rooted as well in economic concepts. Those who succumbed to this narrowness, whether advocating it or just falling into it, were wrong, and it is a great advance that most modern anarchists know this and are broadening their intellectual approach so that anarchism now highlights not only the state and power in all its manifestations, but also gender relations in their specificity, the economy and also cultural relations and ecology, and indeed freedom in every form it can be sought. Most importantly, anarchism now highlights each of these, not solely, or even just primarily, through the prism of authority and power relations, but through the equal inclusion of richer and more diverse concepts rooted in other practices.

This desirable anarchism not only doesn't reject technology, it becomes familiar with, and employs, diverse types of technology as appropriate. It not only doesn't reject institutions, or political forms, it tries to devise new institutions and new political forms for activism and for a new society, including new ways of meeting, making decisions, implementing programs, and so on –

most recently revitalizing the idea of closely based and trusting affinity groups and the more original spokes structures by which they combine into larger assemblies.

And this good anarchism not only doesn't reject reforms, it struggles to define and win non-reformist reforms, attentive to people's immediate needs and bettering people's lives now, as well as moving toward further transformative gains.

So why doesn't the good anarchism visibly trump the not-so-good or counterproductive anarchism out of visibility, so to speak, leaving the way clear for most everyone on the left to gravitate toward anarchism's best side?

Part of the answer, already noted, is that elites and mainstream media highlight the not-so-good viewpoints, giving them far more weight and tenacity than they would otherwise amass, and thereby turning away people who might otherwise gravitate toward anarchism. But part of the answer is also that the good side of contemporary anarchism is in various respects too vague to rise above the rest. What's the problem? I think it's in considerable part that the good anarchism doesn't posit clear and compelling goals.

Anarchist vision?

Anarchism has historically focused on power, which is certainly evident in and an outgrowth of the political dimensions of life, including arriving at shared norms and decisions about shared activities, adjudicating disputes, etc. But even regarding political functions, the emerging anarchism of today's movements doesn't clarify what an anarchist polity could be; instead it often dismisses the idea of vision, much less of providing a new political vision, as irrelevant or worse. But given that societies need to fulfill adjudicative, legislative, and implementation functions and that societies need to do this through institutions made up of citizens, it is more than reasonable to wonder about what those institutions should be. Anarchists who say only that they don't want a government, or don't want a state, are not usefully answering this question.

If the counterproductive trend is to say that we favor no political institutions but only spontaneous face-to-face interaction of free individuals, each doing as they choose with no constraints on them, then what is the good trend's better viewpoint, that fulfills the same guiding aspirations of delivering freedom, but doesn't sacrifice collectivity and continuity?

What kind of structures, with what kinds of recurring social roles and norms, will accomplish political functions while also propelling freedom and participation that we support?

It is perhaps premature to expect the newly re-emerging anarchism to produce from within a compelling vision of future religion, ethnic identification, or cultural community, or a future vision of kinship, sexuality, procreation, or socialization relations, or even a future vision of production, consumption, or allocation relations. But it seems to me that anarchism ought to be where the visionary action is when it comes to attaining, implementing, and protecting against the abuse of shared political agendas, adjudicating disputes, and creating and enforcing norms of collective interaction.

Has there been any serious anarchist attempt to explain how legal disputes should be resolved? How legal adjudication should occur? How laws and political coordination should be attained? How violations and disruptions should be handled? How shared programs should be positively implemented?

In other words, what is the anarchist's full set of positive institutional alternatives to contemporary legislatures, courts, police, and diverse executive agencies? What institutions do anarchists seek that would advance solidarity, equity, justice, participatory self-management, diversity, and whatever other life-affirming values anarchists support, while also accomplishing needed political functions?

Up to the present, even the best of anarchism has often been only a rejection of oppression, and sometimes even only of a few dimensions of oppression, and not a vision of liberation. Alexander Berkman writes: "In all times and in all places, whatever be the name that the government takes, whatever has been its origin or its organization, its essential function is always that of oppressing and exploiting the masses, and of defending the exploiters and oppressors. Its principle characteristic and indispensable instruments are the policeman and the tax collector, the soldier and the prison". Okay, how then can one organize political functions in accord with anarchist values? What is the positive political agenda?

Errico Malatesta tells us more broadly that what anarchists want "is the complete destruction of the domination and exploitation of person by person; we want people united ... by a conscious and desired solidarity, all cooperating voluntarily for the well being of all; we want society to be constituted for the purpose of supplying everybody with the means for achieving the maximum well being, the maximum possible moral and spiritual development; we want bread, freedom, love, and science – for everybody". Yes, yes, but how?

Huge numbers of citizens of developed societies are not going to risk what they have, however little it may be in some cases, to pursue a goal about which they have no clarity. How often do people have to ask anarchists what they are for before anarchists give people some serious, sufficiently extensive, carefully thought through and compelling answers?

Offering a political vision that encompasses key structures for legislation, implementation, adjudication, and enforcement, and that shows how each would be effectively accomplished in a non-authoritarian way that promotes positive outcomes, would not only provide contemporary activism much-needed hope, it would also inform immediate responses to today's electoral, law-making, law enforcement, and court system, and thus help orient many strategic choices.

So shouldn't today's anarchist community be generating such political vision? I think it should – after all, where else should it come from to have hopes of dealing with issues of power desirably? Indeed, I suspect that until there is a widespread component of anarchism that puts forth positive political goals, the counterproductive tendency of anarchism that rejects all political structures and even all institutions will remain highly visible and will greatly reduce potential allegiance to anarchism.

Some will say in reply that anarchism has more than enough vision already, or that its commitment to people controlling their own lives not only in polity, but in economy and other dimensions too, is enough vision. Too much vision will constrain ingenuity and innovation, they say. I respond that this is the same type of mistake as dumping all political structures, or dumping all institutions, or dumping all technology, or dumping all reforms. The problem isn't vision in itself; it is vision that is held and owned only by elites and that serves only elites. Public, accessible descriptions of viable and worthy institutions which serve the whole populace, political and otherwise, are precisely what we need.

21st-century anarchism

So what about good anarchism's potentials? I guess I would say that if anarchism truly meets the need for culture-based, economy, gender, and polity-based concepts and practice, and if anarchism can support vision originating in other movements about non-governmental social dimensions while itself providing at least compelling political vision, and if the anarchist community can avoid strange confusions over technology, political structures, institutions, and seeking to win non-reformist reforms – then anarchism has a whole lot going for it. It could become a main 21st-century source of movement inspiration and wisdom in the effort to make our world a much better place, attracting not thousands or even millions but tens or hundreds of millions of activists.

As to parecon and anarchism, I think parecon is consistent with the impetus I describe above that characterizes the worthy and desirable anarchism, and that parecon even constitutes, with that usage of the label anarchist, an anarchist economic vision that minimizes class and other economy-related hierarchy and that would be consistent with, and even propel, other anarchist aspirations. Parecon is, in these senses, anarchist economics as well as solidarity economics, diversity economics, equitable economics, self-managed economics, and sustainable economics.

Addendum: Primitivism

Above I suggested that anarchism focuses on identifying structures of authority, hierarchy, and domination throughout life and challenging them as surrounding conditions and the pursuit of justice permit. Anarchism seeks to eliminate subordination based on political and economic power, power relations among men and women and between parents and children, power among cultural communities, power over future generations, and much else as well. I suggested that emerging from this were different strands of activism. One, I argued, went on to reject technology, institutions, and reforms outright. Without further evidence that this negative type of anarchism exists, some may wonder if I am fabricating an unreal position. I therefore offer the following comments to address such skepticism head on and, I admit, to critique more aggressively the counterproductive views that I think harm anarchism.

The most visible advocate and exemplar of what I call "not so desirable anarchism" has of late been John Zerzan. Of course many other folks are also in this camp, and the broad views percolate among grassroots anarchists who even dispute with or despise Zerzan, for that matter, but sticking to Zerzan's work should amply display the most touted arguments behind the positions I labeled counterproductive.

Zerzan starts out by reasonably rejecting all authoritarian constraints on human well-being and development. This is admirable, of course, but where does he wind up?

Zerzan rejects technology per se. He rejects all institutions that distinguish different tasks, which is all institutions. He contributes to rejecting reforms outright because in his view no institution is worthy of improvement, so no improvements are worthy of allegiance. Beyond these three themes, Zerzan also rejects language, math, and even the idea of counting things or registering the passage of time. I think all these rejections repeat the same error that other opponents of technology, institutions, and reforms make, though Zerzan does it most relentlessly.

Zerzan tells us "that technology has never been neutral, like some discreet tool detachable from its context. It always partakes of and expresses the basic values of the social system in which it is embedded. Technology is the language, the texture, the embodiment of the social arrangements it holds together".

This is unobjectionable as far as it goes, but it neglects another point that Zerzan never returns to. Yes, technologies bear the mark of the society they are born and used in. How could it be otherwise? However, technologies not only reflect their society's attributes, including sometimes their worst attributes, but also often meet real needs and expand real potentials. So you get electric chairs to kill people and assembly lines to constrain them, but you also get warm clothes for people to wear, and penicillin to enhance people's longevity.

Zerzan says technologies are contextual, and of course he's right that they are. They arise in some social setting. They don't spring spontaneously from nothing, with no lineage and imprint. Nor are technologies utilized in social vacuums. Zerzan is correct that each technology, whether a pencil or a shoelace, much less a guided missile or an assembly line, bears a social inscription carrying the imprints of the motives of its conception, production, and utilization – some of which generally reflect the defense of social elites, but others of which reflect the need to accomplish certain functions.

We should, therefore, expect technologies conceived, produced, and utilized in feudal times to be different than those in prehistoric times, or capitalist times. This is elementary, and true.

Zerzan moves on, however. He says, "The idea that [technology] is neutral, that it is separable from society, is one of the biggest lies available. It is obvious why those who defend the high-tech death trap want us to believe that technology is somehow neutral". This is disingenuous hand-waving, I think, or else evidences an immense confusion.

When someone says that technology per se is neutral, they mean that technology does not, by its internal logic, have to serve only dominating elites. Technology can serve any constituency, including broad populations. Technology can arise in any social setting and system, and can accomplish diverse tasks that can be beneficial or horrendous, humane or cruel, liberating or stultifying.

Technology isn't necessarily prehistoric, or feudal, or capitalist, or anything else, other than always a product of human design and labors. Having a human origin imposes on technology no particular social direction, no universal social stamp.

Zerzan rightly notices that our contemporary technologies encapsulate forces at play in our contemporary societies. He wrongly concludes, however, that all technology must forever and always be as our technology is now. It is therefore not true that if we don't like specific instances of our technology now, to get rid of them we must dispense with all technology forever.

The most obvious way to discern the unwarranted leap in Zerzan's claim is to note that without technology humans would have no clothes, no source of power outside their own muscles, and not even agriculture to renew their muscles. Life would be brutish, isolated, and short. Disease would be rampant. Communication, mobility, knowledge, music, art, play, and pretty much everything else would be harshly limited.

This alone ought to close the case, of course, by showing that eliminating technology per se is not the way to avoid the ills of harmful technologies. But since for many anarchists who take this line, this does not suffice as rebuttal, another way to see the problem rests on examining Zerzan's logic.

Suppose I were to say that all human thought, all human expression, emotion, and even locomotion, manifests an imprint of the society in which it occurs. This is certainly as true as saying that all technology bears such a societal imprint. Is it sensible that I next follow Zerzan to deduce that because all human thought, expression, emotion, and even locomotion – like technology – are socially imprinted, they must always embody oppressive attributes, and I must reject them all in the same way that Zerzan says we should reject technology? Or should I instead assert that in desirable social settings (and to a degree even in undesirable ones), human thought, expression, emotion, and even locomotion also have wonderful and essential attributes that we certainly don't want to reject, and that in good environments the defining features can become over-whelmingly positive, making the idea of rejecting them utterly ridiculous?

I prefer the latter logic, both for human attributes and for technologies. Zerzan prefers the former logic. Zerzan's mistake is rightly to notice various horrible technologies, but then wrongly to attribute the problems they pose, not to mutable social structures and institutions which impose the bad features on the technologies and the bad technologies on us, but to technology itself.

Consistent use of this leap – from disliking instances of some category to rejecting the whole category – would lead to rejecting pretty much everything that is social, or otherwise a product of human exchange and thought, but that frequently turns up with horrible aspects in contemporary societies. It would thus imply a desire for people to revert to a kind of pre-human state. Amazingly, Zerzan follows exactly that line of reasoning.

Thus, Zerzan offers that "my working hypothesis is that division of labor draws the line [between a desirable prehistory and everything since], with dire consequences that unfold in an accelerating or cumulative way. Specialization divides and narrows the individual, brings in hierarchy, creates dependency and works against autonomy". And he continues by deducing that "tools or roles that involve division of labor engender divided people and divided society".

Again, Zerzan drags partial truths to outrageous conclusions. Of course typical corporate divisions of labor diminish and even destroy individual and social potentials. Zerzan points out, for example, that "the first 'breakthrough' for me was in terms of the Industrial Revolution in England. Namely, it became clear that the factory system was introduced in large part as a means of social control. The dispersed craftsmen were deprived of their autonomy and brought together in factories to be de-skilled and disciplined. This shows that technology was not at all 'neutral'".

It may be that Zerzan first encountered the brilliant expression of such ideas a quarter century ago in the same places I first encountered such ideas, for example, in the wonderful essay by Stephen Marglin, "What do bosses do?", or in Harry Braverman's *Monthly Review* work. But if so, Zerzan missed the key insight that the imposed division of labor served specific social relations and elites, and that the problem posed for suffering humanity wasn't that different people were doing different tasks per se. It was the particular limited combinations of tasks that most of the people were compelled to do, as well as the pittance they received for it.

Zerzan is certainly right that (corporate, sexist, and racist) divisions of labor have buttressed hierarchy, imposed dependency, and impeded autonomy. And he is also right that many institutions incorporate these damaging divisions of labor and therefore deserve rejection. But beyond this, he fails to note that virtually all institutions involve roles that diversify people's tasks and responsibilities. To jump from the correct and familiar insight that some divisions of labor are so horrible that institutions embodying them are unworthy, to more comprehensively claiming that no division of labor at all can be abided and therefore all institutions are unworthy, says that each individual must, in essence, do everything for him or herself or, at any rate, without lasting institutional coordination with others. It rejects roles per se and leads to an anti-institutional, anti-social, and, I think, ultimately, even anti-human stance.

So rather than solely rejecting imposed divisions of labor that are contrary to our aspirations, which would be quite sensible, Zerzan slip-slides all the way to the extreme claim that all divisions of labor of any kind have to go.

Should we reject divisions of labor that relegate many people to obedience and to rote boredom, while privileging an elite few with empowering and engaging endeavors? Of course we should. About this Zerzan and I presumably agree. But the way to do this isn't to have everyone do everything, with no differentiation of different people's responsibilities. And the way to do this is not to ignore that people have diverse tastes and inclinations and that they wish to express these in their actions. And it is not to forego the worthy gains that can accrue from taking advantage of skills and training.

Why throw out the baby of productivity, individuality, and diversity with the bathwater of alienation and hierarchy? Why not divide tasks into jobs that are balanced for empowerment and quality of life implications (to eliminate hierarchy) and that are self-managed (to eliminate alienation and authoritarianism), even as they also respect each individual's personal tastes (to further diversity and benefit from creativity)?

Get rid of the hierarchy-inducing (bathwater) aspects, of course. But keep the fulfilling and beneficial attention to different people's preferences and the utilization of diversity to increase the breadth of our collective experiences, while also increasing output and diminishing required labor.

So why does Zerzan pose the problem as no division of labor versus a bad division of labor (and similarly as no technology versus bad technology), rather than as a bad division of labor versus a good division of labor (or as bad technology versus good technology)?

One possible line of thought leading someone to propose such limiting polarities would be to notice something that all divisions of labor (and all technologies) have in common, which is that they are human and social creations, and then to decide that this commonality somehow inevitably infects them with harmful aspects. I am not sure Zerzan believes this, nor sure if it matters much what he believes, because in any event, whether intended or not, this is the practical and intellectual implication of his stance.

Thus, Zerzan says, "it seems evident that industrialization and the factories could not be gotten rid of instantly, but equally clear that their liquidation must be pursued with all the vigor behind the rush of break-out. Such enslavement of people and nature must disappear forever, so that words like production and economy will have no meaning".

In other words, we not only have to eliminate bad economic activity that divides us into unequal classes, exploits us, despoils us, or degrades us, all of which I certainly agree with, but we have to eliminate economic activity completely. Human artifacts must go, it seems. As with technology and the division of labor, so with the economy as a whole: we must opt for all or nothing.

No more production for Zerzan. No more workplaces. And what do we put in their place? Foraging, it seems, because that bears no mark of specifically human invention. So Zerzan rejects tools and roles, technologies and institutions, and even production and economy. Amazingly, he doesn't stop there.

Zerzan takes this line of thought all the way to its ultimate destination, and in doing so reveals the illogic and other flaws of "counterproductive anarchism" most graphically, which is why I am spending so long on him.

Zerzan rejects even language. He tells us that "the process of transforming all direct experience into the supreme symbolic expression, language, monopolizes life. Like ideology, language conceals and justifies, compelling us to suspend our doubts about its claim to validity. It is at the root of civilization, the dynamic code of civilization's alienated nature. As the paradigm of ideology, language stands behind all of the massive legitimation necessary to hold civilization together. It remains for us to clarify what forms of nascent domination engendered this justification, made language necessary as a basic means of repression".

The problem is now civilization. Zerzan rejects humans entwined in social arrangements of their own creation, conceived to allow each to pursue their lives as they will without having to operate atomistically or in opposition to all others. Since words are a big part of the glue of such arrangements, says Zerzan, let's dispense with them too, rather than try to fulfill their potential.

"Words bespeak a sadness; they are used to soak up the emptiness of unbridled time. We have all had that desire to go further, deeper than words, the feeling of wanting only to be done with all the talk, knowing that being allowed to live coherently erases the need to formulate coherence," says Zerzan.

And of course Zerzan is correct that we don't want to live by words alone, or bread alone, or technology alone, or anything else alone. But what Zerzan misses, is that noticing that fact does not justify wanting to dispense entirely with each.

Of course we express sadness in words, but also in deeds and feelings. Should we reject not only words, but also deeds and feelings? Consciousness is surely often a bulwark of existing oppressions. Consciousness sometimes manifests sadness and is often used in authoritative ways. Should we lobotomize ourselves, too? For that matter, why not notice that sexual intercourse has very often been fraught with painful ramifications, outright violations, and, virtually universally to date, with asymmetries of power? Why not saltpeter? Shortly after Zerzan has his way there will be no more humans, and, Zerzan is correct, there will also be no more human suffering.

Terminating just short of this species suicide, Zerzan's agenda, or hope, seems to be that we should end divisions of labor, reject technology, discard institutions, silence language, eliminate numbers, reject time, and perhaps dispense with consciousness – though not reproduction – returning to prehistoric relations. And the mainstream media tells everyone that Zerzan is an exemplar of anarchism. And anarchism has trouble finding recruits.

If you think I exaggerate all this, judge for yourself. Zerzan says, "My tentative position is that only a rejection of symbolic culture [that is, language] provides a deep enough challenge to what stems from that culture". Thus: reject language. Or, "Only a politics that undoes language and time and is thus visionary to the point of voluptuousness has any meaning". Not just language, but time too.

Wordplay is all well and good for provocative or aesthetic exercises or for entertainment. But Zerzan claims to be challenging the realities that delimit people's lives. Being revolutionary on behalf of liberty carries a responsibility to attend to reality.

Zerzan rejects numbers too. To explain why, he tells us that "Euclid developed geometry – literally, 'land measuring' – to measure fields for purposes of ownership, taxation, and the assignment of slave labor". And: "When members of a large family sit down to dinner, they know immediately, without counting, whether someone is missing. Counting becomes necessary only when things become homogenized". Can this be serious? Apparently so. The thought pattern is by now familiar. I am writing about it, at brutal length, in hopes that such thinking will no longer distract good people from worthy issues.

Zerzan rightly notes that numbers can be used in harmful or alienating ways and to service authority and power. Anyone would conclude that in some pursuits we are better off without numbers. We shouldn't try to quantify love or dignity. Fair enough. But Zerzan wrongly extrapolates that we'd be best off without numbers at all. Goodbye to language, goodbye to numbers and time, goodbye to technology and institutions … why not goodbye to sex too? I guess Zerzan thinks that would be an unpopular stance. The fact that the rest is popular in some quarters is what is perhaps most astonishing.

In the early part of this chapter I commented on important confusions about technology, institutions, and reforms that I think are diminishing the effectiveness and worth of a particular strand of "counterproductive anarchism". I also discussed the more positive insights into breadth of focus, new vision, and non-reformist reforms that give another strand of anarchism the potential to become central to successful activism in years ahead.

Zerzan's thinking may or may not explain why some folks hold the counterproductive views they do about technology, institutions, and reforms. I have no way of knowing for sure. But the views are prevalent and Zerzan is most forthright in their defense. The Zerzan quotations I used are from various of his essays and interviews available on the internet. Hopefully his stance will disappear in time.

17 Aspirations

LEFTISTS THROUGHOUT THE WORLD, today and in all past times, have sought what are actually conceptually simple outcomes: each person should be as free as all others and able to enjoy the fruits of labor and the virtues of social engagement in an environment that optimally supports and furthers such pursuits for all.

Leftists have sought an end to illegitimate authority, illegitimate inequality, and illegitimate hierarchy of all kinds, as well as an end to the prejudices that were previously thought to justify such structures. These prejudices have included those about race and other cultural differences, gender differences, national differences, age differences, sexual differences, differences in ownership, and differences in occupation.

When people have battled against classism, exploitation, authoritarianism, patriarchy, sexism, heterosexism, ageism, racism, ethnocentrism, religious persecution, and inequality and hierarchy of all kinds, their best efforts have always been in the name of just or equitable outcomes, variety, mutual empathy, and enabling people to have control of their own lives.

Parecon arises from and respects these historical and contemporary aspirations. Rank and file activists and citizens who have risen over and over, very often in grassroots council organizations and movements, have always sought the broad economic results parecon seeks to embody. It is not only repressive obstacles and forces from without, but also our own confusions due to manipulations, ineffective methods, or overtly contrary class interests or other contradictory views nurtured within our projects, that have impeded our attaining real liberation.

I have tried to argue that while parecon doesn't itself answer visionary questions bearing on race, gender, polity, and other social concerns, it is at least compatible with and even, in some cases, perhaps necessary for, doing so. Hopefully, in the future, stronger and better conceived movements than we now have will prevail in all these domains. To conclude this discussion, however, a summary is in order.

Suppose beyond economics we want a new society to have a new set of political institutions to accomplish legislation, adjudication, and the implementation of shared and otherwise collectively mandated projects in a just and liberatory rather than in an authoritarian way.

Suppose too that we want a new society to have a new set of kinship institutions to accomplish procreation, nurturance, socialization, sexual relations, broader gender relations, and the daily functions of home life in a feminist and liberatory way rather than in a sexist, homophobic, and ageist way.

Suppose we additionally want a new society to have a new set of cultural institutions to accomplish community identification, communication, celebration, and exploration of moral and social group relations in a multicultural and liberatory way rather than in a racist, ethnocentric, bigoted, or otherwise mutually derogatory (or even genocidal) way.

Suppose also that we want a world of new societies to have a new set of global institutions to accomplish international exchange of resources, material products, cultural ideas, and even people and social relations, in a peaceful, mutually beneficial and liberatory way rather than an imperial, colonial, or even warring way.

Suppose we also want our new society to relate to nature mindful of resource depletion and of the effect our choices have on the environment and on us and other species, rather than in a polluting, self destructive, and even unsustainable way.

Suppose we want our society to explore the content of the cosmos and employ the ensuing insights in new technologies benefiting human well-being and development rather than subordinating people to narrow interests or prejudice.

Suppose we want our society to have the means to avoid illness and to treat disease and disorder when they arise, with each person having equal rights to these benefits and capacities, rather than having a society that systematically produces ill health and dispenses care unequally.

Suppose we want our society to have a minimum of theft, fraud, and violent negation of one or more parties by others, rather than an epidemic of all these anti-social phenomena, and to deal with the results in ways that are just and don't abrogate rights and priorities, rather than repressively and without dignity and hope.

Suppose we want our society to have a new set of educational institutions that enable all citizens to discover and fulfill their potentials, in accord with all others having room and opportunity to do likewise, rather than restraining and restricting most citizens to be subordinate, and elevating only a few citizens to be informed and confident.

Suppose we want our society to have a new set of media institutions to accomplish journalistic and entertaining communication in a truthful manner, sustaining both social awareness and dissidence, rather than in a manner designed to enforce and reproduce existing social biases and submerge dissent.

Suppose we want our society to have artistic, athletic, and all diverse creative and engaging human pursuits, carried out at an optimal level of accomplishment, but also in accord with social solidarity and self-management, rather than at a stunted commercialized biased level of accomplishment and in a manner dividing people into competitive opposition.

Parecon, I have claimed, is a vision of the economic structures of a new post-capitalist and post-coordinator economy that efficiently meets needs and fulfills potentials while furthering solidarity, diversity, equity, and self-management in a classless manner – and that would match well with and even facilitate all the above agendas.

Parecon is not a blueprint of a whole economy, much less of a whole society. It is an institutional proposal for how economies can exist in accord with our highest aspirations for economic life and also for other social spheres and practices revolutionized in their own ways.

Insofar as social movements seeking a better world need, among other visions, an economic one, parecon is a proposal to that effect. Our assessment of the theory of parecon will determine the extent to which we become intellectual advocates for it, or devote ourselves to refining it. And our judgement of pareconish proposals in action will determine whether or not we become practical activists to attain it. Alternatively, if we judge that parecon fails to meet our widest needs, we have to come up with a vision that does so more successfully.

18 Dissent

THERE IS NO END TO HISTORY. There is no end to dissent. A parecon has, I believe, highly desirable features. For a new economy to eliminate unjust income differentials, produce solidarity rather than anti-sociality, diversify rather than homogenize social outcomes, engender self-management rather than authoritarianism, and attain classlessness rather than class rule, will be major advances for humanity, but not the last advances humanity achieves.

Within a society with a parecon there will be frequent issues and situations which call forth dissent. Even more, there will sometimes be dissent directed not only at a specific policy or an enduring habit, but at underlying institutional features.

It is not that there will arise desires to return to capitalism. That would seem very unlikely. Like a character in Ursula Le Guin's novel *The Dispossessed,* we can expect that a citizen enjoying parecon who hears a description of capitalism would be horrified. It would "bore him past endurance". It would be "like listening to somebody interminably recounting a long and stupid dream". The parecon citizen, after years of involvement with parecon's logic, would not be able even to "force himself to understand how banks functioned and so forth, because all the operations of capitalism" would appear to him "as meaningless ... as the rites of a primitive religion, as barbaric, as elaborate, and as unnecessary". Such a future pareconish person would, if asked to consider a possible return to capitalism, wonder how anyone could ever have engaged "in the rites of the money-changers, where greed, laziness, and envy were assumed to move all men's acts" and where "even the terrible became banal".

So, while I think dissent in a parecon will be unlikely to look backward, I think that there could arise movements to make levels of fulfillment, pleasure, and dignity of all people equal even beyond parecon's making the material conditions and social relations that contribute to these desirable states equal. Or maybe a new aim will be removing the whole idea of measure regarding human traits or rewards, or even the whole idea of warranting rewards at all. Here is one of

LeGuin's characters, again: "Do not speak of what men deserve. For we each of us deserve everything, every luxury that was ever piled in the tombs of the dead Kings, and we each of us deserve nothing, not a mouthful of bread in hunger. Have we not eaten while another starved? Will you punish us for that? Will you reward us for the virtue of starving while others ate? No man earns punishment, no man earns reward. Free your mind of the idea of deserving, of earning, and you will begin to be able to think". Whether this viewpoint will make sense and rise to prominence beyond parecon's logic, or whether some other new set of aspirations will arise, we can't know. In any event, whatever types of dissent do arise, how should society react to them?

First, there is a place in human life for caution, perhaps more so than many radicals and revolutionaries would care to admit. Longstanding gains, hard won outcomes, and social habits and relations honed over decades, centuries, and even eons, can certainly have virtues that transcend first appearances, just as innovations can have debits that go unnoticed in moments of excited advocacy. For both reasons, it is often wise to be cautious in seeking major change. But, while a cautionary attitude has merit in that it helps us avoid carelessly losing hard won gains or imposing horrible flaws, an attitude that denies any justification for moving forward and that claims we should never be more than we are, goes too far.

We should always realize that there is no final resting place for progress. A degree of caution about rejecting past achievements makes sense, yes, but there will always be moments in history when innovation makes even more sense. In other words, simultaneous with our caution, it also behooves us to be always open to, and even to welcome, possibilities for change.

Even more, we know that changes come almost always on the heels of criticism. It is when some individual or some group makes a compelling case that inadequacies exist, and when other people begin to devise alternatives and agitate for innovations, that serious changes occur.

Criticism and seeking innovation are the lifeblood of major gains for humanity. Shouldn't humanity therefore welcome dissent and not repress it?

To use an economic analogy: think of an investment. We get some inkling of an idea that something could be beneficial. We think it through a bit and get excited about the prospects. We give time, energy, and insight to attaining it.

Of course, not every such effort pans out. Some investments tell us what doesn't work, but give us nothing new. Others barely even manage that much. Nonetheless, we don't say that we shouldn't support investments at all on the grounds that not all investments succeed. Instead we cautiously gamble because we know that enough investments work to make up for those that fail.

Similarly, consider the composer, writer, painter, or scientist. Each will often embark on a path in their discipline that seems promising but later fails. Are they being a bad composer, writer, painter, or scientist when they undertake a project which doesn't pan out as they hoped?

No, successes won't come without failures. We don't know outcomes before the fact. We can try to avoid frivolous boondoggles, though we should do it cautiously since it may be us, and not the composer, writer, painter, or scientist we reject as frivolous, who is ignorant, but for the most part, where there is a reasonable level of competency and reasonable seriousness, pursuing new ideas makes sense.

The same goes for dissent. Perhaps a good society should on occasion ignore, dismiss, or even obstruct what seems without doubt to be frivolous or ignorant dissent, though there should be a considerable burden of proof on doing so. But in serious, informed cases, society ought not just to abide dissent against its own structures, it should encourage such dissent.

Indeed, a case could even be made that we will only have a civilized society when it is able to welcome and even promote dissent against itself.

If this is a mark of a good society, how will a parecon fare? A parecon has diversity as a central value, and it is hopefully a natural extension from favoring diversity within a system to favoring diversity regarding the nature of the system.

Likewise, a parecon equips all its participants with confidence and knowledge in accord with their inclinations, laying a basis for critical thought.

Moreover, a parecon supports economic initiative and innovation whenever these show sensible promise of meeting needs and developing potentials – so why not support, with the same vigor, dissent that has the potential to produce institutional innovations that would benefit people?

There is no reason, one hopes, for any advocate of a parecon to feel an insecure fear about his or her economy that would lead him or her to defend pareconish values or institutions from critique to the point of reflexively rejecting prospects for innovation.

Why should even a sensibly cautious pareconist oppose exploring the possibility of structural alterations that would further benefit humanity?

In a parecon, economic costs and benefits are equitably distributed. Any proposal for innovation that violates the fairness of the system by giving advantages to some people at the expense of others will presumably meet stiff resistance, at the very least from those who would be disadvantaged. But why would any proposal that makes a compelling case to benefit everyone meet reflexive dismissal or opposition? People might doubt an idea is realizable, of course. But the answer is not to reject the idea a priori, but to test it and explore its potential.

A parecon should, by its logic and values, accommodate to and even propel the idea of society continually subsidizing experiments in its own renovation and redefinition. A society that includes a parecon and a compatible and comparably worthy political, kinship, cultural, and environmental orientation will be, on this score too, a civilized rather than a pre-civilized system.

What about now? What about before we win a new economy and a new world? What about dissent from the parecon vision while it is barely even born?

For the economy, I want workers and consumers to have control over their own economic lives.

I want everyone to have fair conditions that fully utilize their talents and potentials.

I want incomes that correspond to the duration, intensity, and onerousnesss of the work people do.

I want what is produced, by whom, under what conditions, and with who consuming the product, all geared toward enhancing human well-being and development and decided by the people involved.

I want an end to hierarchies of power and wealth and an end to class division where most people are subordinated to an elite few.

To accomplish all these economic ends I favor the institutions of participatory economics – worker and consumer councils, remuneration for effort and sacrifice, balanced job complexes, and participatory planning.

I believe, after years of evaluation and considerable experimental implementation, that these choices are worthy and viable, so I advocate them. But if someone should argue that parecon's institutions would somehow fail to accomplish necessary economic functions or would have social or personal by-products that would outweigh their benefits, I and other advocates must listen to those claims, hear and comprehend them, and address them. We should hope that we could refine the parecon vision and improve its qualities.

And if someone should find flaws that resist correction and preclude improvement of the vision, I and other advocates should return to the drawing board. We should never give up on developing a viable vision, but should always be open to improving or even replacing any vision we advocate.

Exploitation, alienation, poverty, disempowerment, fragmented and debilitating labor, production to profit a few – much less homelessness, starvation, and degradation – are not like gravity. These ills arise from institutional relations established by human beings. New institutions, also established by human beings, can generate vastly superior outcomes that liberate our talents and spirits, entwine our desires and cares, multiply our options, equilibrate our costs and benefits, and deliver the kind of worthy freedom that extends to all.

Defining and working to attain those new institutions ought to be our economic agenda. Defining and working to win a new world ought to be our social agenda.

References

Page

vii John Maynard Keynes, "National Self-Sufficiency", *The Yale Review*, Vol. 22, no. 4, June 1933, pp. 755–69.

2 John Stuart Mill, *Principles of Political Economy*, W. J. Ashley, ed., Longmans, Green, and Co., London, 1926, p. 748.

2 Eduardo Galeano, *Upside Down*, Picador USA/Henry Holt, 2000.

7, 171 Peter Kropotkin, "Kropotkin's Revolutionary Pamphlets", *Anarchist Communism: Its Basis And Principles*, Roger N. Baldwin, ed., Vanguard Press, Inc., 1927.

12 Adam Smith, "On The Need For Choice And Competition In Education", in *An Inquiry Into the Nature and Causes of the Wealth of Nations,* Edwin Cannan ed., fifth edition, London: Methuen and Co., Ltd., 1904.

14 Charles Kettering Reference: Juliet B. Schor, *The Overworked American: The Unexpected Decline of Leisure*, Basic Books, 1991, pp. 119–20.

20 Stephen Shalom, *Parpolity*, ZNet, http://www.zmag.org/shalompol.htm

20 Pierre J. Proudhon, *General Idea of the Revolution in the 19th Century* (first published 1851), trans. J.B. Robinson. London: Freedom Press, 1923.

29 Milton Friedman, *Capitalism and Freedom*, Chicago: University of Chicago Press, 1962, Chapter 1, "The Relation Between Economic Freedom and Political Freedom," pp. 7–17.

35 Nancy Chodorow, *The Reproduction of Mothering*, University of California Press, 1978.

40 Batya Weinbaum, *Curious Courtship of Women's Liberation and Socialism*, South End Press, 1978.

45 Arundhati Roy, "Democracy, Who's She When She Is At Home", *Outlook India Magazine*, 6 May 2002.

46 W.E.B. Dubois, *The Souls of Black Folks*, Bantam Classics (original publication 1903).

48 Milton Friedman, *Free to Choose*, Harcourt, 1st edition, 1 January 1980.

69 Andrew Bard Schmookler, *Illusion of Choice: How the Market Economy Shapes Our Destiny*, SUNY Press, 1993; see also *Fool's Gold: The Fate of Values in a World of Goods*, Harper Collins, 1993.

78 *Amicus Curiae Brief of 72 Nobel Laureates, 17 State Academies of Science, and 7 other scientific organizations, in support of Appellees Robert A. Klayman, Walter B. Slocombe[*], Jeffrey S. Lehman, Beth Shapiro Kaufman*, Caplin & Drysdale, Chartered, One Thomas Circle, N.W., Washington, D.C. 20005, (202) 862-5000, Attorneys For Amici Curiae.

78 Richard P. Feynman, *Surely You're Joking, Mr. Feynman!: Adventures of a Curious Character*, W.W. Norton, 1985.

80 George Monbiot, "The corporate stooges who nobble serious science", *The*

Guardian, 24 February 2004, available from
http://www.guardian.co.uk/comment/story/0,3604,1154585,00.html (accessed
May 2004).

81   Tuskagee Orr, "The Corruption and Redemption of Science",
      http://www.zmag.org/Content/showarticle.cfm?ItemID=5934

84   David Noble, "David Noble's Battle to Defend the 'Sacred Space' of the
      Classroom", from *The Chronicle of Higher Education*, 31 March 2000.

89   Andrew Bard Schmookler, *Illusion of Choice: How the Market Economy Shapes Our
      Destiny*, SUNY Press, 1993; see also *Fool's Gold: The Fate of Values in a World of
      Goods* (Harper Collins, 1993).

89   Yves Engler, "Hospital Health", ZNet Commentary, Aug. 2004,
      http://www.zmag.org/Sustainers/Content/2004-08/25engler.cfm.

90   Stephen Bezruchka, "Health Olympics", ZNet Commentary, Sept. 2004,
      http://www.zmag.org/sustainers/content/2004-09/02bezruchka.cfm.

93   Paulo Freire, *Pedagogy Of The Oppressed*, New York: Continuum Books, 1993.
      First published 1970.

95   H.L. Mencken, *Notes on Democracy*, New York: Alfred A. Knopf, 1926.

109   Edward S. Herman, "The Propaganda Model: A Retrospective, Against All
      Reason", December 9, 2003. http://www.chomsky.info/onchomsky/
      20031209.htm; and Noam Chomsky and Edward S. Herman, *Manufacturing
      Consent*, Pantheon Books, 1988.

110   Danny Schechter, *The More You Watch the Less You Know*, Seven Stories Press,
      1997.

110   Noam Chomsky, *The Pentagon System*, Z Magazine, February 1993.

123   Manning Marable, "Race-ing Justice: The Prison Industrial Complex",
      http://www.zmag.org/ZSustainers/ZDaily/1999-09/30marable.htm

124   Roger Doyle, "By the Numbers", *Scientific American*, Aug. 1999.

138   Robin Hahnel, *Economic Justice and Democracy: From Competition to Cooperation
      [Pathways Through the Twenty-First Century]*, Routledge, 2005.

145   Frederick Engels, *Speech at the Grave of Karl Marx*, 1883.

163   Trotsky and Lenin quoted in *What Is To Be Undone*, Porter Sargent Press – out of
      print – available online at http://www.zmag.org/WITBU/witbuTOC.html.

176   Alexander Berkman, *What is Communist Anarchism?* New York: Dover
      Publications Inc., 1972. Errico Malatesta, "Anarchism and Anarchy",
      http://www.zabalaza.net/texts/txt_anok&anok_em.htm.

178   John Zerzan, "Future Primitive," http://www.primitivism.com/future-
      primitive.htm and Collected Works at http://melior.univ-montp3.fr/
      ra_forum/en/people/zerzan_john.

181   Stephen Marglin, "What Do Bosses Do? The Origins and Functions of
      Hierarchy in Capitalist Production", in Anthony Giddens and David Held, eds.,
      Classes, Power, and Conflict: Classical and Contemporary Debates, Berkeley: University
      of California Press, 1982.

181   Harry Braverman, *Labor and Monopoly Capital: The Degradation of Work in the
      Twentieth Century*, New York: Monthly Review Press, 1998 (first published 1974).

188   Ursula K. LeGuin, *The Dispossessed*, Millenium, 1974.

Index